A

COVERT

AGENDA

A COVERT AGENDA

THE BRITISH GOVERNMENT'S UFO TOP SECRETS EXPOSED

NICK REDFERN

PARAVIEW
Special Editions

New York

ISBN: 1-931044-70-8
Library of Congress Catalog Number: 2003115840

for my parents

CONTENTS

ACKNOWLEDGEMENTS

I AM DEEPLY INDEBTED TO THE FOLLOWING FOR THEIR
CONTRIBUTIONS TO THIS BOOK:

Leslie Banks; Graham and Mark Birdsall and all at *UFO Magazine*,
without whose fine investigations the story of DI55 could not be told;
Captain John E. Boyle (USAF); the British UFO Research Association
and BUFORA Director of Publications Mike Wootten, for securing
me permission to cite several important cases from BUFORA files; the
Central Intelligence Agency; the Civil Aviation Authority; Robert Dean;
the Defence Intelligence Agency; Jonathon Dillon of UFO Watch; Robert
Durant, for the extract from one of his many research papers; the Federal
Bureau of Investigation; Martin Fletcher, Lisa Shakespeare, Jacquie Clare,
Gillian Holmes, Glen Saville and all at Simon & Schuster for their fine
work; *Flying Saucer Review*; the editors of *Fortean Times*, Paul Sieveking
and Bob Rickard; Nigel Foster; Chris Fowler; premier researcher of the
Roswell UFO crash of 1947, Stanton T. Friedman; Margaret Fry, for
data on the 1974 UFO incident at Bala; Paul Fuller, for the use of his
interview with Flight Lieutenant W. Wright (RAF); Timothy Good, for
a wealth of advice and for taking the time to read the original manuscript
of *A Covert Agenda*; the Government Communications Headquarters;
Paul Greensill; Chester Grusinski; Her Majesty's Stationery Office; the

Heywood Advertiser, Victor Kean; John Lear; my agent, Andrew Lownie, for believing in the project and for working so diligently to sell the book; Philip Mantle; Steve Mills; the Ministry of Defence; the Mutual UFO Network; the National Security Agency; the *News of the World*, Ralph Noyes; Mrs J.D. Oliver, for the use of her late husband's account; Kerry Philpott; Nick Pope of the Ministry of Defence, for answering my many questions on official policy regarding the UFO subject and for supplying me with several photographs; the Provost and Security Services (RAF); the Public Record Office, for kindly granting me permission to cite a number of important documents from their archives; Jenny Randles, for allowing me to reference a variety of UFO reports from her magazine, *Northern UFO News*, my father, Frank Redfern, for showing me that the UFO subject was one worthy of study; the Royal Air Force; Ernie Sears; John Smith; the Staffordshire UFO Group, particularly the group's president, Irene Bott, and vice president Graham Allen, Mark Haywood and Carl Nevin; the *Sunday Express*, Jonathon Turner; Air Commodore J.L. Uprichard (RAF); The US Departments of the Air Force, Navy, and State; Matthew Williams, for permitting me to use his aerial photographs of RAF Rudloe Manor; and Frederick Wimbledon.

I would also like to acknowledge the late Leonard Stringfield, a true pioneer in the UFO field, who, several months before his untimely death in 1994, very kindly allowed me to make use of material contained within his crucially important papers on 'crashed UFO' incidents.

Nicholas Redfern
1997

NICK POPE

OVER A SERIES OF NIGHTS IN DECEMBER 1980, UFOS WERE SEEN BY numerous military personnel at the twin United States Air Force bases of RAF Woodbridge and RAF Bentwaters. Strange indentations were found on the ground in nearby Rendlesham Forest, at a location where a guard patrol had witnessed a small metallic craft. Radiation readings were taken from these indentations, and the Defence Radiological Protection Service calculated that the radiation was ten times higher than was normal for the area. The Ministry of Defence says that these events are of no defence significance.

On 5 November 1990, a squadron of RAF Tornado fast jet aircraft flying over the North Sea was casually overtaken by a UFO. The pilots made an official report. The Ministry of Defence view is that this encounter was of no defence significance.

On 31 March 1993, a UFO flew directly over two military bases; it was seen by a guard patrol at RAF Cosford and by the Meteorological Officer at RAF Shawbury, who described it as being a triangular-shaped craft only marginally smaller than a Boeing 747. It flew over the base at a height of about 200 feet, was making a low humming sound, and was seen to fire a beam of light at the ground. It was moving very slowly, but suddenly shot off at several times the speed of a fast jet. Nothing was detected on radar. That this event took place is not disputed, and indeed it has been confirmed to the House of Commons by the Minister of State for the Armed Forces, in response to a Written Parliamentary Question. Again, incredibly, the official view of the Ministry of Defence is that the event was of no defence significance.

What on earth is going on? Officially confirmed events such as these illustrate beyond a shadow of a doubt that our sophisticated air defences are being breached by structured craft of unknown origin. The intruding technology is clearly more advanced than the defending technology. This is self-evidently a serious defence issue, so what lies behind the Ministry's official stance? Is it simply that the ignorance and prejudice of a few individuals makes them blind to the evidence, causing them to close the file on incidents such as those mentioned above without carrying out proper investigations, and without passing the information up the chain of command? Or is there something more sinister behind the denials? Are certain people within the world of officialdom covering up a shocking truth about UFOs? These are some of the questions addressed in this book.

UFO sightings are always controversial and provoke a range of responses that vary from credulous acceptance to aggressive scepticism. Those who dismiss the phenomenon as a combination of misidentifications and hoaxes are quick to criticize the sloppy and unscientific investigation carried out by some of those who research UFOs. They point out – not without some justification – that many UFO sightings are supported by nothing more than the testimony of the witnesses. They ask, not unreasonably, that evidence be put forward to support the extraordinary claims being made. *A Covert Agenda* might be seen as a response to this challenge. The book does not concern itself with stories about lights in the sky seen by people out walking their dogs; it concentrates on those UFO sightings that are supported by hard evidence, and focuses on cases that involve the Royal Air Force and the Ministry of Defence.

I should declare an interest. For much of the early Nineties I worked in a Ministry of Defence division called Secretariat (Air Staff) 2a, where my duties included researching the UFO phenomenon, and investigating those sightings that were reported to the Department. I started out as a sceptic, but at the end of my tour of duty I was convinced that while most UFOs had conventional explanations, a small percentage of them

were almost certainly extraterrestrial in origin. This official evaluation –
which was a view shared by more people within the Ministry of Defence
than might be supposed – was made on the basis that some UFO sightings
did seem to involve structured craft which exceeded the capabilities of
the best of our own technology (including stealth aircraft and various
prototype craft), both in terms of speed and manoeuvrability.

It was while working in Sec (AS) 2a that I first encountered Nick
Redfern. He was one of a number of regular correspondents, but what
set him aside from most of the others was the interest that he showed in
the official Government UFO files held at the Public Record Office. It is
from these records (which might be called the real *X-Files*) that Nick has
pieced together the extraordinary history that you are about to read. The
strength of *A Covert Agenda* is that it is a case for an extraterrestrial reality
constructed largely on the basis of official documentation which Nick has
obtained through skilfully and aggressively exploiting the provisions of the
Public Record Acts.

It will become clear to readers that there are areas on which my
views and Nick's differ. He believes that elements within the world of
officialdom know all about UFOs, but are withholding the information
from the public. I disagree, seeing bureaucracy, rather than conspiracy, as
being what lies behind some of the admittedly suspicious-looking goings
on highlighted in this book. On this point, readers will have to make up
their own minds.

Notwithstanding the divergence of views on the possibility of an official
cover-up, there is much common ground between us. We certainly agree
that the Ministry's view of UFOs as being of 'no defence significance' is
at odds with a whole mass of evidence – much of which is contained in
this meticulously researched and comprehensively referenced book.

UFOs used to be regarded by many people as a joke. Those who showed
an interest were portrayed as quirky and if the topic was mentioned in the
media, it was usually in a light-hearted way. Recently, this has begun to
change. Defence correspondents on national newspapers are beginning to
take an interest, as are Members of Parliament; there have been over thirty
formal Parliamentary Questions tabled on the UFO phenomenon in the
past year, dealing with both official policy on UFOs, and with a number
of specific cases. *A Covert Agenda* is therefore a most timely book, because

the serious way in which it deals with the UFO phenomenon ties in well with the new-found respectability that this subject is enjoying.

Nick Redfern has written a splendid account of the way in which the British Government and the military have been involved in the UFO phenomenon over the last fifty years. Like a good intelligence analyst, he is always careful to differentiate between what he thinks and what he knows. He highlights the most convincing evidence available, which includes visual sightings backed up by radar, and sightings by trained observers such as police officers and pilots. *A Covert Agenda* also contains official accounts of how Royal Air Force jets have been scrambled in attempts to intercept UFOs, and how UFOs have often been observed in the vicinity of military bases, or taking a close interest in military exercises. And perhaps most disturbingly, the book details some near collisions between UFOs and aircraft – incidents which are officially confirmed by the Civil Aviation Authority.

Overall, whatever one's views on whether information on UFOs is being covered up by the Government, it is clear that this book makes a significant contribution to the debate about UFOs. Nick Redfern drives a coach and horses through any mistaken notion that UFOs are of no defence significance; he highlights the serious defence and national security issues raised by the UFO phenomenon, and proves that contrary to the official line, UFOs are of *extreme* defence significance.

Nick Pope works for the Ministry of Defence and for much of the early nineties he was responsible for carrying out official research and investigation into the UFO phenomenon. His controversial conclusions were that some UFOs were extra-terrestrial in origin. Concerned by the defence and national security implications of these unauthorised intrusions into British airspace, Nick wrote *Open Skies, Closed Minds* in an attempt to bring this information to the public's attention. It was an instant bestseller, staying in the *Sunday Times* top ten for over ten weeks. His second book *The Uninvited*, an exposé of the alien abduction phenomenon, was also a bestseller.

PROLOGUE

FOR ALMOST HALF A CENTURY, YOU HAVE BEEN DENIED ACCESS to the facts which lie behind two discoveries of monumental proportions: Planet Earth has extra-terrestrial visitors and unidentified flying objects exist. I do not make such claims lightly, nor do I expect the reader to accept those same claims on faith alone.

Through the use of both official documentation and witness testimony, it is my hope that what you are about to read will conclusively prove that, since the late 1940s, British Governments have been acutely aware that our planet has been 'targeted' for visitation by creatures from elsewhere.

As represented by the Ministry of Defence, the current stance of officialdom is that the bulk of its research into reported UFO sightings is undertaken by a small body of staff operating out of Whitehall. As a result of an intense investigation, however, I am now in a position to reveal that a whole host of governmental departments – on a worldwide scale, no less – are intimately involved in the study of this most perplexing phenomenon.

While conducting research for this book I was given the opportunity to study more than a thousand pages of once-classified papers directly pertaining to UFOs, and many of those same papers are reproduced here for the first time. I was also able to secure interviews with a variety of both retired and serving MOD civil servants, Royal Air Force pilots, and military personnel, who have left me in no doubt that the UFO issue is one of the most important of our time – to ignore it may prove costly to our species, in more ways than one.

Since 1947 there have been an untold number of incidents recorded where RAF crews have engaged in aerial 'dogfights' with UFOs, the details of which have been covered up with the utmost secrecy. Forty or fifty years on, they are no longer held by the constraints of their security oaths. Some of those involved have been willing to go on record and speak out. Their testimony is both shocking and illuminating.

Far more shocking is the possibility that British authorities have in their possession the wreckage of several extra-terrestrial spacecraft which have come to grief on British soil. Once again, I do not make such claims lightly, and would urge the reader to examine each case on its own merit. If only one of the accounts in hand proves to have a firm basis in fact, then I submit that this will firmly lay to rest the misconception that UFOs are a perceptual, rather than a physical, mystery.

I will also show that at a variety of military facilities around the British Isles, specialist staff are on constant readiness to monitor the movements of any potentially hostile 'unknowns' in Britain's airspace. And, if that hostility is confirmed, to respond in kind.

Having conducted an in-depth study of the UFO subject, I am firmly convinced that the British Government is in possession of irrefutable proof which confirms that an extra-terrestrial species, covert in nature, is currently operating on our planet. I am equally convinced that our elected leaders do not know how to break this news to us in a non-alarming and non-sensationalist manner.

In view of this it could be argued that, by writing this book and revealing much of the information which the MOD, amongst others, has acquired, the potential is there to upset what could be a vital national security issue. I concede that this may be so. However, if Earth is being intruded upon by creatures from elsewhere, do we not, as citizens of this planet, have the right to know the truth? I believe that we do. Indeed, I have held this belief since 1978 when, as a fourteen year old, I was told a remarkable story by a source I know to be entirely honest and trustworthy – my own father, Frank William Redfern.

*   *   *

Almost twenty years have now passed since I first became truly aware that UFOs were something more than a mere fantasy, and yet when I think about it, it seems like only yesterday that my exposure to this bizarre subject began in earnest.

It was 10.30 p.m. on a dark Wednesday evening as I walked with my father through a deserted Walsall street. A biting wind sliced through the air, and I buried my hands deep in my coat pockets in a vain attempt to keep warm. We headed towards the multi-storey car-park.

'Well, what did you think?' asked my father.

'I thought it was great,' I responded, continuing, 'Do you think it could really happen?'

My father looked at me out of the corner of his eye; a knowing smile crossed his face: 'Maybe it already has,' he replied, his voice dropping ever so slightly.

The subject of this cryptic conversation? Steven Spielberg's classic film *Close Encounters of the Third Kind*, which told the story of mankind's first face-to-face meeting with an alien species, and which we had just seen at the now-demolished Walsall ABC cinema.

We climbed the stairs of the car-park and headed for my father's Ford Capri, and I thought about his curious comment.

'What did you mean, "Maybe it already has"?'

'Hang on,' he replied. 'Let's get out of the car-park and I'll tell you.' And as we drove home on that autumn evening, the shocking facts surrounding my father's involvement in the UFO subject came tumbling out.

Like the majority of young men in the early 1950s, my father was required to serve a three-year term in the military under National Service regulations. Because of his keen interest in aviation he chose the Royal Air Force. During his time with the RAF he served at a variety of camps, but by far the most memorable experience occurred at RAF Neatishead, Norfolk. It was September 1952 and he was serving as a radar mechanic.

'So, what happened?' I asked, as we drove out of Walsall town centre.

'Well, I remember that we were taking part in an exercise, Mainbrace it was called, and I was on duty,' he replied. 'It was early in the morning – four or five o'clock – maybe a bit later. Things were pretty normal until the radar picked up something weird on the scopes.'

'What was it?' I butted in.

'At first we thought it might have been an aircraft, but we knew soon enough that it was something else,' he told me. 'We had this object, this UFO, whatever you want to call it, on the scopes at fifty thousand feet and flying over the North Sea and parallel to the English coast. The speed of it meant there was no way this was a plane.

'The report went up the chain, and aircraft were scrambled from Coltishall, which was a base nearby. Coltishall sent up Venoms and Meteors to try and get a look at the object. We were watching all this on the screens thinking that it would turn out to be something ordinary, but when the planes closed in, the UFO suddenly streaked away and headed towards Norway. The pilots didn't have a chance.

'The next day,' he continued, 'something strange happened. A bunch of people came, a photographic team from Coltishall, and they had some really good gear which they set up to record the radar's Plan Position Indicator tube in case the UFO came back.

'Well, the day following this, it did come back. We tracked it; the planes went up, but this time we had it all on film.'

'What happened then?' I eagerly asked.

'We never knew. The guys from Coltishall removed everything: the radar tapes, the records, all of it. They never told us what the result was, and the UFO never came back, but I won't forget it.'

I sat back in the car seat, amazed at what I had just heard. UFOs, so often the subject of ridicule, really existed. And, more significantly, Britain's military knew it. The remainder of the journey home was made in silence; me trying to take in these remarkable facts, and my father recalling his long-gone RAF days.

Today, two decades after relating his experience to me, my father still recalls the events of September 1952 and is convinced that no normal phenomenon could account for what took place. I agree and were it not for my father I would not have set out on the journey which ultimately led to the writing of this book. Thanks, Dad.

Come with me now as we enter the bizarre world which is home to the most secretive official operations: the Provost and Security Services, the

Defence Intelligence Staff, Airborne Early Warning, Ground Environment and Sec(AS)2a. And home, of course, to those elusive UFOs.

C H A P T E R   1
_____

IN THE BEGINNING

THE 'FLYING SAUCER' ENTERED OUR CONSCIOUSNESS, AND OUR
vocabulary, in 1947. At approximately 3.00 p.m. on the afternoon of June
24, Kenneth Arnold, an American pilot, viewed nine unidentified aerial
objects flying in a wedge-shaped formation over the Cascade Mountains,
Washington State, USA. Describing the UFOs as 'crescent-shaped',
Arnold likened their movements to those that a saucer would make if
it were skimmed across a pool of water.

In a statement made available to me by the US Federal Bureau of
Investigation, Arnold said at the time: 'I never asked nor wanted any
notoriety for just accidentally being in the right spot at the right time
to observe what I did. I reported something that I know any pilot would
have reported. I don't think that in any way my observation was due to
any sensitivity of eyesight or judgement than what is considered normal
for any pilot.'

To fully recognize the importance of Arnold's encounter, let us look
at his own account:

On June 24th, Tuesday, 1947, I had finished work . . . at
Chehalis, Washington, and at about two o'clock I took off
from [Chehalis Airport] with the intention of going to Yakima,
Wash. My trip was delayed for an hour to search for a large

marine transport that supposedly went down near or around the south-west side of Mt. Rainier in the state of Washington and to date has never been found.

I flew directly toward Mt. Rainier after reaching an altitude of about 9,500 feet . . . I had made one sweep of this high plateau to the westward, searching all of the various ridges for this marine ship and flew to the west down and near the ridge side of the canyon where Ashford, Washington is located.

Unable to see anything that looked like the lost ship, I made a 360 degree turn to the right and above the city of Mineral, starting again toward Mt. Rainier.

I hadn't flown more than two or three minutes on my course when a bright flash reflected on my airplane. It startled me as I thought I was too close to some other aircraft. I looked every place in the sky and couldn't find where the reflection had come from until I looked to the left and the north of Mt. Rainier where I observed a chain of nine peculiar looking aircraft flying from north to south at approximately 9,500 feet elevation and going, seemingly, in a definite direction of about 170 degrees.

They were approaching Mt. Rainier very rapidly, and I merely assumed they were jet planes. Anyhow, I discovered that this was where the reflection had come from, as two or three of them every few seconds would dip or change their course slightly, just enough for the sun to strike them at an angle that reflected brightly on my plane. These objects being quite far away, I was unable for a few seconds to make out their shape or their formation. Very shortly they approached Mt. Rainier, and I observed their outline against the snow quite plainly. I thought it was very peculiar that I couldn't find their tails but assumed they were some type of jet plane. I was determined to clock their speed, as I had two definite points I could clock them by; the air was so clear that it was very easy to see objects and determine their approximate shape and size at almost fifty miles that day.

I remember distinctly that my sweep second-hand on my eight-day clock, which is located on my instrument panel, read one minute to 3.00 p.m. as the first object of this formation passed the southern edge of Mt. Rainier. I watched these objects with great interest as I had never before observed airplanes flying so close to the mountain tops, flying directly south to south-east down the hog's back of a mountain range.

They flew like many times I have observed geese to fly in a rather diagonal chain-like line as if they were linked together . . . What kept bothering me as I watched them flip and flash in the sun right along their path was the fact that I couldn't make out any tail on them, and I am sure that any pilot would justify more than a second look at such a plane.

The more I observed these objects, the more upset I became, as I am accustomed and familiar with most all objects flying whether I am close to the ground or at higher altitudes. As I was flying in the direction of this particular ridge, I measured it and found it to be approximately five miles so I could safely assume that the chain of these saucer-like objects [was] at least five miles long. As the last unit of this formation passed the southern-most high snow-covered crest of Mt Adams, I looked at my sweep second-hand and it showed that they had traveled the distance in one minute and forty-two seconds. Even at the time this timing did not upset me as I felt confident after I would land there would be some explanation of what I saw.

History has shown, of course, that no explanation for Arnold's sighting ever did surface, and the mystery has raged for nearly half a century. Even the FBI felt moved to comment: 'It is difficult to believe that a man of [Arnold's] character and apparent integrity would state that he saw objects and write up a report to the extent that he did if he did not see them.'

Arnold went on to make a statement which, I am quite sure, anyone who has ever seen a UFO can identify with: 'I would have given almost anything that day to have had a movie camera with a telephoto lens and from now on I will never be without one.'

Perhaps inevitably, Arnold's sighting quickly caught the imagination of both the public and the media, as Arnold recalled: '. . . the news that I had observed these spread very rapidly and before night was over I was receiving telephone calls from all parts of the world; and, to date, I have not received one telephone call or one letter of scoffing or disbelief . . . I look at this whole ordeal as not something funny as some people have made it out to be. To me it is mighty serious . . . I have received lots of requests from people who told me to make a lot of wild guesses. I have based what I have written here on positive facts and as far as guessing what it was I observed, it is just as much a mystery to me as it is to the rest of the world.'[1]

Following the Mt. Rainier sighting, more and more strange vehicles were observed in the skies of North America – something demonstrated by a report of July 29, that same year. Still partly censored by the US Government, it reveals:

> [Witness] stated in substance that he was a First Lt. in the Reserve and that on the 29th of July 1947 shortly after 12 noon he had just landed from a routine training flight when [censored] called his attention to an unidentified flying object that was following a P-80 aircraft at a terrific rate of speed . . . A moment later a second object appeared and flew a course described as something similar to a fighter aircraft maneuvers . . . [Witness] could not estimate the size of the objects nor actual altitude, though he did not believe them to be beyond six thousand feet. [Witness] described the objects as being milky white in color, and unlike any conventional type aircraft he had ever seen.[2]

On August 4, 1947, the crew of a Pan American Constellation aircraft en route to La Guardia Field, New York, viewed an unusual aerial device at approximately 4.00 p.m. while nearing the Bedford radio beacon close to the city of Boston. According to the co-pilot, the UFO was cylindrical in shape, 'bright orange' in colour, and flying at a speed of 150 miles per hour. An official report into the incident was drawn up by the Air Defense Command HQ at Mitchell Field, New York, and details were forwarded to several Government agencies, including the FBI, whose copy of the report I have cited.[3]

As the events of 1947 began to unfold, it became apparent to the

American Government that the UFO mystery was a global problem, rather than one solely confined to the USA. This is perfectly demonstrated by a one-page report extracted from the US Air Transport Command's Weekly Intelligence Summary of August, 1947:

> FLYING OBJECTS IN GUAM: Unidentified flying objects have been observed by three enlisted men of the 147th Airways and Air Communications Service Squadron at Harmon Field, Guam. The men report that at 1040 hours on 14 August 1947 the two objects, which they describe as small, crescent shaped and traveling at a speed twice that of a fighter plane, passed over them on a zig-zag course in a westerly direction at an approximate altitude of twelve hundred feet. The objects disappeared into clouds and a few seconds later a similar object, possibly one of those previously observed, emerged from the clouds and proceeded west. No further details have been reported.[4]

As a result of the literally hundreds of UFO sightings reported throughout the United States in the summer of 1947, US authorities were galvanized into action. As well as the FBI's inquiries, investigations were launched by Naval Intelligence, and the then-combined Army Air Force. It really did appear that the North American continent was playing host to unearthly visitors. A document which originated with the US Air Intelligence Requirements Division demonstrates the line of thinking that was being pursued within Government circles at the time. More importantly, it shows that UFOs were not only perceived to be intelligently controlled craft – the possibility that they were 'interplanetary' in origin was something discussed by the US military nearly half a century ago:

> An alleged 'Flying Saucer' type aircraft or object in flight, approximately the shape of a disc, has been reported by many observers from widely scattered places, such as the United States, Alaska, Canada, Hungary, the Island of Guam, and Japan. This object has been reported by many competent observers, including USAF rated officers. Sightings have been made from the ground as well as from the air.

This strange object . . . may be considered, in view of certain observations, as long-range aircraft capable of a high rate of climb, high cruising speed and highly maneuverable and capable of being flown in very tight formation. For the purpose of analysis and evaluation of these so-called 'flying saucers', the object sighted is being assumed to be a manned craft of unknown origin . . . it is the considered opinion of some elements that the object may in fact represent an interplanetary craft of some kind.[5]

Since June 24, 1947, the American Government has continued to play a key role in the UFO mystery. Under the terms of the US Freedom of Information Act (FOIA), literally tens of thousands of pages of previously classified papers have been released by a veritable host of Government agencies – including the Central Intelligence Agency, the Defense Intelligence Agency, the National Security Agency, Air Force Intelligence, the Department of State, the Federal Bureau of Investigation, and the Atomic Energy Commission.

All of these agencies continue to participate in monitoring UFO activity to this day, and official documentation continues to enter the public domain periodically, indicating that the human race may not be the only species to have ventured into space.

More interestingly, as they themselves concede, every one of the aforementioned bodies is continuing to sit tight on a wealth of official papers, directly relating to UFOs, which they refuse to release to the general public.

Almost fifty years have now passed since Kenneth Arnold's sighting. If, during that time, inquiries into the UFO subject on the part of the American Government have confirmed that our planet is being intruded upon by creatures from elsewhere, then we can only hope that those in the know have had the situation under some form of control. Back then, as US authorities were taking their first faltering steps into the strange realm of unidentified flying objects, on the other side of the Atlantic their British cousins were also stumbling confused . . .

CHAPTER   2
_____

THE EARLY YEARS

IT IS SOMEWHAT SURPRISING THAT THE EARLIEST ACCOUNT OF A UFO
incident involving the British Royal Air Force actually pre-dates Kenneth
Arnold's sighting by some five months. And it is ironic that details of the
case only surfaced when the relevant records were released into the public
domain by the American Government. How did this come about?

On July 30, 1947, the FBI issued a statement agreeing to lend assistance
to the US Army Air Force's study of UFO reports. As a result of this,
details of numerous UFO encounters were forwarded to the Bureau by
the USAAF, including the following which originated with the British
Air Ministry:

> During normal night flying practice at 2230 on 16th January,
> 1947, one of our Mosquitos was vectored on to an unidentified
> aircraft at 22,000 feet. A long chase ensued commencing over
> the North Sea about 50 miles from the Dutch coast and ended
> at 2300 hours over Norfolk. Two brief contacts were made but
> faded quickly. The unidentified aircraft appeared to take efficient
> controlled evasive action. No explanation of this incident has been
> forthcoming nor has it been repeated.

It could be argued that this case involved nothing more unusual than a foreign aircraft of terrestrial origin. However, it should be remembered that the FBI's only concern at the time was with 'flying saucers' and 'flying discs'. If the USAAF suspected that this particular incident simply involved a Russian bomber, for example, then it would have been pointless for them to have contacted the FBI. The investigation of Soviet aircraft sightings over the United Kingdom has never rested with the Bureau. Therefore the USAAF must have been of the opinion that something far stranger than a mere aeroplane was seen on the night in question.

Although 'pre-Arnold' UFO incidents in the UK are indeed scarce, the North Sea encounter was not a singular event. For example, during that same month an astonishing incident occurred at Baginton Aerodrome, near Coventry. The precise date remains elusive, but this in no way diminishes the importance of what took place.

While driving along a road adjacent to the aerodrome, a bus driver and conductor were amazed to see a brightly lit object suddenly 'dive-bomb' the perimeter of the base in a somewhat aggressive manner. As one of the witnesses would later recall, during the nerve-racking few moments that the UFO was in view, it appeared tangible enough to violently shake the chain-link fence which surrounded the aerodrome. Whatever the nature of the phenomenon, it quickly soared away into the winter sky, never to return.

Obviously amazed by what they had seen, the witnesses duly filed a report with their supervisor, who in turn contacted the Air Ministry. I have made a cursory study of the available Ministry papers at the Public Record Office which might possibly refer to this event, but so far have been unable to shed further light on the encounter. However, Steve Mills, a Coventry-based researcher who related details to me in a January 8, 1996, interview, has spoken with one of the witnesses and is impressed by his sincerity, not to mention his desire for anonymity.

There is good reason to believe that at some point in 1947, a discussion of sorts took place between the Governments of Britain and USA on the UFO mystery. On August 5, 1948, a Top Secret 'Estimate of the Situation' was prepared by the US Air Force's Air Technical Intelligence Center (ATIC), which concluded that UFOs were indeed interplanetary spacecraft. This caused widespread dismay amongst the highter echelons of the Government, and the conclusions of the report were rejected, largely on the orders of Chief of Staff, General Hoyt Vandenberg, who argued that the 'Estimate' was bereft of any firm evidence to support such beliefs.

In 1956 Captain Edward J. Ruppelt of the USAF stated that contained within ATIC's Top Secret report were references to 'the English "ghost airplanes" that had been picked up on radar early in 1947'.[1] There is little doubt in my mind that the encounter of January 16, 1947, over the North Sea was one of those reports which Ruppelt was talking about. But the reference to 'ghost airplanes', in the plural, suggests that there were other reports in existence which so far remain closed to the general public. In view of the fact that the British reports of early 1947 were ultimately published in a US Air Force report with Top Secret status, I submit that this is indicative of an early high-level UK–USA collaboration on the UFO subject.

Ronald Anstee of Canada has divulged some interesting details concerning an incident which occurred at RAF Bentwaters, Suffolk, in mid-1947. Anstee's source, a relative tangentially involved, revealed that on a particular afternoon a circular UFO, fifty feet in diameter, was seen by numerous on-base personnel.[2] As a result, senior officials were flown in and extensive meetings were convened to deal with the matter. According to Anstee's relative, the encounter was somehow connected with a new type of radar which was being utilized in the area.

It will become apparent that RAF Bentwaters has been implicated in a number of other UFO incidents since 1947, including a notorious encounter in December 1980. And there was still more to come in the summer of 1947.

It may be relevant to note that the Air Ministry had been working on various radar-related projects as far back as the 1930s. On January 28, 1935, the Tizard Committee, established under the directorship of Sir Henry Tizard, convened its first meeting, which ultimately led to the development of a workable radar system of the type employed in the Second World War.[3] Most pertinent of all, much of that research was conducted at Bawdsey Manor on the Deben Estuary, just north of Felixstowe and a mere stone's throw from RAF Bentwaters.

Secondly, on January 1, 1994, the British Government declassified two files of papers concerning its inquiries into the UFO mystery in the early 1960s. Contained within one of the files are three long letters written by Ronald Anstee to the Air Ministry. In those letters, Anstee made mention of a number of UFO incidents which had been brought to the attention of the British Government in the 1950s, including a report which had been filed by Flight Lieutenant James Salandin in 1954, and a UFO sighting at Wardle, Lancashire, in 1957.

A study of Anstee's correspondence and the Air Ministry's subsequent reply (which came from a department known as Secretariat 6) shows that the Government was not keen to discuss the UFO issue with him in any way whatsoever. In fact, the only response that Anstee received was a one-sentence note acknowledging receipt of his letters. I suspect that the reason for the Air Ministry's reluctance to enter into debate with Anstee was because (as I shall explain shortly) the incident at Wardle was one which caused the Government a great deal of concern, to the extent that the use of the Official Secrets Act was sanctioned to silence those involved. I also find it particularly notable that Anstee's letters were kept on file with the British Government for more than thirty years prior to being finally made available for scrutiny at the Public Record Office.[4]

A now-retired service source has informed renowned investigator Graham Birdsall of an important encounter, involving the tracking of a UFO on radar, which occurred over London during the same time-frame as the incident recalled by Ronald Anstee. According to the information imparted to Birdsall, the UFO was 'larger than any ordinary aircraft', and was tracked moving at a speed of around 2,000 mph. 'I remember just standing there, watching the blip race along – not in disbelief . . . but in astonishment,' Birdsall was told.[5]

The Ministry of Defence currently maintain that statistical figures for the number of UFO reports filed with the Air Ministry in 1947 are not known. The earliest available figures date from 1959, so they inform me.[6] Fortunately, reports such as those cited are slowly beginning to surface showing that, as in the USA, 1947 was a pivotal year for the British Government.

In 1992 I interviewed a retired British Army source who informed me that he was involved in a UFO incident at Seremban, Malaysia, in July 1948. While taking part in early morning manoeuvres both he and a platoon of troops viewed a globe-shaped UFO hovering over a densely forested area. The UFO was small, perhaps eight to ten feet in diameter, and emitted a slight hum. Curiously, during the time that it was in sight all electrical apparatus belonging to the platoon was rendered useless. Those involved were later questioned at length and a bulky case file was forwarded to the War Office in London for additional study. The results of that study remain unknown.

Details of the following incident, shrouded in secrecy for more than forty years, were forwarded to me in 1991 by author and investigator, Timothy Good. Although the official records pertaining to the case are absent from the Public Record Office, one of the prime witnesses, Mr J.R. Oliver, formerly a radar operator at RAF Sandwich, recalls what took place:

> . . . In August 1949, in order to test the updated air defences of England against attack, Operation Bulldog was launched. Operation Bulldog's attacking forces consisted of aircraft of the Benelux countries supported by US air squadrons based on the continent. Flying from various airfields in Holland, France, Belgium and Germany, their objective was to attack London and other prime targets in southern and midland England, without being officially 'downed' by fighter aircraft brought into action by the defensive network of Fighter Command.
>
> The radar defence chain extended from Land's End, along the south coast and up to the north of Scotland, overlapping at all heights from sea level to about 100,000 feet. Even so long ago, it was almost impossible to fly a glider across the Channel without it being plotted. The exercise ran for fifteen days and was structured in such a way that the technical resources and personnel of the defensive screen were stretched to the limit.
>
> I was, at the time, a radar operator AC1, stationed at RAF

Sandwich in Kent, a Ground Control Interception station, used to verbally direct fighter aircraft onto target aircraft by means of radar guidance and radio transmission. In conjunction with neighbouring radar stations, our function, especially during Bulldog, was a busy one. As can be appreciated, air and sea traffic in the vicinity of the Channel tended to be heavier than in other areas of the UK and this reflected in the general high performance of radar stations in that area.

All personnel at RAF Sandwich were fully skilled and right on top of their job. Two watches were kept, A and B, on alternate twelve-hour shifts for the duration of Bulldog.

About a week into the exercise, after a few hours of being busy, we were stood down, about midnight. Things had gone slack and 'Group' had advised us that we could take a break. This was in the normal run of things during the exercise and except for one radar operator to keep general watch and one other to man the PBX, there was a general move into the small canteen across the corridor.

Within about fifteen minutes, the PBX operator came in, approached the Duty Controller and advised him that Beachy Head radar was passing a plot to us on a large flying object and would we track it? At that time I was the Controller's 'dog', working on the same screen as him and directly with him. We were the first to see the contact and my plot was the first to go on the plot board. As other operators took their positions, more plots were called out concerning position of the object and its height . . . The object was flying roughly parallel with the south coast, from west to east.

Reaching a position out to sea off the 'heel' of Kent, it abruptly turned north and as it approached the Thames estuary we passed it on to Martlesham radar, with whom we had been in contact via the PBX link, and whose radar area impinged on our own. Shortly after, we lost contact with it, due to the limit of our radar range.

It was a simple matter to assess the speed of the object from the times and distances between plots and its height was directly read from our Type 13 radar, designed specifically to read the height of any aircraft within its range. Flying at close to 50,000 feet, the air speed of the object we had observed and plotted in accordance with RAF standard procedures was assessed at very nearly 3,000 miles per hour.

The general concensus regarding its size, among the very experienced radar personnel engaged in the operations, was that the object offered an echo similar to that of a large passenger or freighter surface vessel, something in the region of 15,000 or 20,000 tons. Word filtered down . . . that on approaching Bempton radar in Yorkshire, the object suddenly increased speed and headed directly upwards, vanished off-screen at about 100,000 feet.

Naturally, there was quite a bit of buzz about this, especially as at that time speeds in excess of the speed of sound were just not on. Neither were aircraft the size of liners.

The airspeed record at that time stood at 606.36 mph and the largest aircraft in general use was probably the USAAF Superfortress, which lumbered along at about 350 mph.

At our usual relief time, 'B' Watch stood down and went to breakfast and bed at the domestic site at Stonar House. We were awakened from our watch slumbers by Sergeant Platt and assembled in front of Stonar House, with our Sergeant Belcher, Sergeant Hatter, and various minor NCOs in attendance, for an address by Squadron Leader Mundy. He reminded us of our duties as serving members of the RAF and the requirements of the OSA and to forget especially the odd occurrences of the past night and not to mention same to anyone not connected to the RAF.

Going on watch that evening we found that the Duty Watch Book, normally only replaced when completely full, which recorded every air engagement, every PBX message, every official order by the watch-keeping officer, made during every official part of previous watches, including the previous night's activities, as an official Watch Book is required to do . . . had gone. Replaced by a brand new shining Duty Watch Book. I wonder why? Removing a half empty Watch Book was unheard of, during exercises such as Bulldog especially.

The rest of the exercise took its natural course and about a month later my service with the RAF ended. Whether there were any further developments regarding this incident I do not know but it seems likely that evidence of its happening must be on file somewhere.

This incident was observed by such a large and highly trained audience, its progress so well documented and meticulously recorded and, no doubt, the technical aspects so well scrutinized by top-ranking experts that the official documentation of its occurrence would settle the UFO controversy permanently.

All aspects of Operation Bulldog were due to be analysed in great depth in order to bring our defence against possible nuclear attack to the highest level. There is no doubt that the incident I have described, totally beyond the expectations of the organizing authorities as it must have been, would receive the closest scrutiny and that many opinions must have been placed on record.

In addition to the personnel directly involved in the tracking of the object, it is highly likely that a good many people must have gained knowledge of this occurrence and therefore proof of it happening may not be too far in finding.[7]

Despite Mr Oliver's optimism that the records pertaining to the case should now be available for public viewing, no paperwork, either official or unofficial, has surfaced in respect of this incident. Does it, even after nearly half a century, remain classified, buried deep within the vaults of the Ministry of Defence?

Sadly, Mr Oliver passed away in 1993, but his historic record will stand as a testament to his courage in speaking out on that most challenging issue of our time – the UFO.

An intriguing UFO sighting in Kent was filed with the Air Ministry in 1950, according to official documentation. It occurred at 7.30 p.m. on the night of December 10. One of the three witnesses was a Group

Captain Cartmel, an Equipment Officer with more than 1,400 hours' flying experience in no fewer than eighty-one different types of aircraft. According to Cartmel, the object was seen near to the Wildernesse Country Club, approximately one and a half miles north-east of Sevenoaks, Kent. Described as a 'bright light' moving in the sky, the object was estimated to have been flying at a height of 3,000 feet and at a speed of 150 mph – a speed identical to that reported by the Pan-American crew near Boston, USA in 1947. 'The matter which really drew my attention to it was the complete absence of sound,' said Cartmel, commenting on the unusual object.

Following the sighting a report was filed by Cartmel and forwarded to the Air Ministry for examination. For its part the Ministry seemed none too impressed, and suggested that the Group Captain had simply observed the moon, partially covered by cloud. Not an impossible scenario, but one would have expected an officer of Cartmel's experience to have recognized the moon when he saw it.

Regardless of the outcome of the Air Ministry investigation, this particular case is of significant historical importance because it is one of the earliest on record which is supported by a now-declassified official file which can be examined at the Public Record Office.[8]

In August 1952 the Air Ministry announced that a 'full intelligence study' had determined that all reported UFO sightings could be attributed to hoaxes, optical illusions, mistaken identities, and known astronomical phenomena. This study was apparently undertaken in 1951 (although no record of its existence can be found amongst the available papers at the Public Record Office) and the Ministry's statement was made following an enquiry on the part of the prime minister, Winston Churchill.[9] The subject had been brought to Churchill's attention following the now-famous wave of UFO encounters which occurred in the USA in 1952, and which reached its peak on July 19–20 of that year when there was a proliferation of sightings over Washington D.C.[10]

One person known to have been involved in the 1951 study was R.G. Woodman who, after the end of the Second World War, became Deputy Superintendent of Test Flying at Boscombe Down. Following a 'request from the government', Woodman conducted the special study and was given access to a variety of UFO reports filed by air crews from both the Royal Air Force and the Royal Navy. He concluded that the cases he examined were merely the result of misperception and natural phenomena. Woodman also had the opportunity to discuss the subject of unidentified flying objects with qualified American test pilots, who were 'astonished and amused that the British should take an interest in such a matter which they treated as rubbish'.[11]

Whilst I see no reason to doubt Woodman's recollections they seem, as with many facets of the UFO puzzle, to cloud further an already murky issue. For example, according to the Air Ministry's minute of August 9, 1952, the 'full intelligence study' had provided satisfactory explanations for every single UFO sighting submitted for analysis.

One can only wonder what satisfactory explanations existed to resolve the numerous incidents reported throughout 1947 and that involving J.R. Oliver in 1949. In the latter case, for example, independent radar tracks of the movements of the UFO were reported – wholly independent of each other – by staff at four separate Royal Air Force stations in the United Kingdom – Beachy Head, Sandwich, Martlesham and Bempton.

Moreover, on *no* other occasion has the British Government ever issued a proclamation stating that it has successfully explained *every* UFO report brought to its attention. Even today the Ministry of Defence concede that there is a small residue of UFO encounters which appear to defy explanation.[12]

Finally there is the matter of the American test pilots. It may certainly be the case that those personnel who talked to Woodman did view the UFO subject with some scepticism; however, this was far from being the overall consensus of the US administration. Recall that as far back as 1947 the US Air Force had admitted that it was the considered opinion of 'some elements' that UFOs represented 'interplanetary craft of some kind'. Even more significant, during the same time-frame in which Woodman's study was conducted, a sizeable number of UFO reports were filed with the American military by highly qualified observers, as is demonstrated by the following report of February 10, 1951:

Unidentified object seen at 0055 10 Feb at 49 degrees 50 min north, 50 degrees 03 min west by crew of Navy 6501, VR1, Potuxent River, Maryland. Originally seen as heavy light in distance on the surface as lights of city. The yellowish light, like a fire in color, approached rapidly and grew very bright and very large with a semi-circular shape. It was on a true course of about 125 degrees, plane on a true course of 225 degrees, as it approached the plane it suddenly turned almost 180 degrees and disappeared rapidly over the horizon as a small ball. Speed 'was terrific'. Seen from an angle of about 45 degrees looking down from the plane. Crew all experienced North Atlantic fliers . . . all saw object over a period of from seven to eight minutes. Plane flying at 10,000 [feet] altitude.[13]

A further encounter dating from 1951 has strong correlations with the 1949 episode at RAF Sandwich, Kent:

. . . [O]n Sept. 10, fifty-one, an AN/MPG DASH ONE Radar set picked up a fast moving low flying target, exact altitude undetermined at approximately 11.10 a.m., south-east of Fort Monmouth at a range of about twelve thousand yards. The target appeared to approximately follow the coast line, changing its range only so slightly but changing its azimuth rapidly . . . target also presented an unusually strong return for aircraft being comparable in strength to that usually received from a coastal ship. The operator . . . realized that it could not be a ship after he observed its extreme speed.[14]

As these two reports show, certain elements within the American Government were aware that an extraordinary phenomenon existed, even if word had not filtered down to personnel such as those referred to by Woodman.

It is possible, however, that the Woodman study was not given access to reports of incidents such as those recalled by Ronald Anstee and J.R. Oliver, in which the presence of a solid, intelligently controlled vehicle was apparently confirmed. Certainly, disclosures enabled by the American

Freedom of Information Act show that in the late 1940s and early 1950s, many agencies in the US administration were involved in the investigation of UFO sightings – the CIA, the FBI, the National Security Agency, the Air Force and both Army and Naval Intelligence. Is it not reasonable to assume that a similar situation may have existed in the British Isles, with the Air Ministry, the Admiralty and the War Office all vying for a place in the investigation of the UFO phenomenon? My opinion is yes, most definitely. Therefore it may be the case that more exotic UFO reports were handled by an entirely separate division.

It is unfortunate that none of the very few disclosed Air Ministry records which refer to the 1951 study give details of its classification level. But, according to information obtained by researchers Andy Roberts and David Clarke, the study undertaken by Woodman was 'unofficial' in nature, which suggests to me that its classification level was, most probably, relatively low.[15] Moreover, there is every indication that the UFO encounters at RAF Bentwaters in 1947 and at RAF Sandwich in 1949 were immediately classified. I consider it most unlikely that staff assigned to an unofficial study of UFO sightings would have been made aware of cases where the preservation of secrecy was of paramount importance.

What of the possibility that other departments within the British Government – such as the War Office and the Admiralty – may have had a hand in the investigation of UFO reports in the 1950s? Gordon Creighton, a retired diplomat, has an interesting story to tell: '. . . I think [the account] should now be placed on record, as it agrees so closely with some of those tales and rumours that were heard in Whitehall during the 1950's.'

The source of Creighton's information was a relative who confided in him some extraordinary facts gleaned during his Navy years. Specifically, Creighton's relation learned from a British naval officer, who had worked in the Admiralty in the post-World War Two era, that on one particular occasion at headquarters, he happened to visit the room of a very senior officer and chanced to see 'what he ought not to have seen': files on the UFO question, and photographs of strange, disc-shaped objects on the surface of the sea.[16]

Where are those files and photographs now? Most definitely they are not at the Public Record Office, nor are they open for inspection at any other military archive or museum. Whatever their status, they only serve to reinforce my conviction that, somewhere, there is a massive body of UFO evidence to which we are being denied access.

It should also be noted that Creighton has an impeccable background. A fellow of the Royal Astronomical Society, and a graduate of Cambridge University, he spent many years in diplomatic posts in China, Belgium, USA and Brazil, and subsequently served for seven years as an intelligence officer in Whitehall.[17]

So what of the statements made to Winston Churchill that the UFO mystery comprised nothing more than optical illusions, hoaxes and mistaken identities of known astronomical phenomena? The evidence cited appears to negate the Air Ministry's hypothesis, suggesting the shocking possibility that Churchill was purposefully kept in the dark. Is this likely? At present, I am willing to suspend judgement on the matter until such a time that further information surfaces. But there can be no doubt that, for whatever reason, Prime Minister Churchill remained ignorant of the full facts of at least two contemporary UFO sightings.

A series of events took place barely a month later which radically altered the British Government's attitude towards the subject of UFOs, and which left little doubt in the minds of those in authority that they were a force to be reckoned with.

MAINBRACE

IN SEPTEMBER 1952 THE NORTH ATLANTIC TREATY ORGANISATION (NATO) co-ordinated a huge military exercise in the North Sea and North Atlantic. Dubbed 'Mainbrace', the exercise utilized the armed forces of Britain, USA, Canada, Norway, Denmark, France, Netherlands and Belgium.[1] Approximately 85,000 personnel took part. Its purpose was to demonstrate to the Soviet Union that NATO was fully prepared to withstand, and counter, any possible Soviet attack on Western Europe.

Barely one day into the exercise at least two reports of UFO encounters were filed with authorities by naval personnel on board ships in the Atlantic between Ireland and Iceland. The first such encounter involved a 'blue/green triangle' which was observed flying over the sea at a speed of 1,500 mph. Later that same day, three unidentified objects, travelling at around the same speed, were seen flying in a triangular formation. All three craft reportedly emitted a 'white light exhaust'.[2]

As part of the Royal Air Force's involvement in Mainbrace, 269 Squadron, which was based at RAF Ballykelly, Ireland, was posted to RAF Topcliffe in Yorkshire.[3] It was at Topcliffe, on September 19, 1952, that one of the most historically important UFO sightings was reported – by a serving member of the Royal Air Force. A document written and signed by Flight Lieutenant Dolphin of RAF Topcliffe, to Headquarters, No. 18 Group, and dated September 20, 1952, states: 'In accordance with your instructions, herewith a report on the unidentified object which was seen over the station earlier today.'4 The report was prepared by one of those who witnessed the UFO, Flight Lieutenant John Kilburn:

Sir,

I have the honour to report the following incident which I witnessed on Friday, 19th September, 1952. I was standing [illegible] with four other aircrew personnel of No. 269 Squadron watching a Meteor fighter gradually descending. The Meteor was at approximately 5000 feet and approaching from the east. Paris suddenly noticed a white object in the sky at a height between ten and twenty thousand feet some five miles astern of the Meteor. The object was silver in colour and circular in shape, it appeared to be travelling at a much slower speed than the Meteor but was on a similar course.

It maintained the slow forward speed for a few seconds before commencing to descend, swinging in a pendular motion during descent similar to a falling sycamore leaf. This was at first thought to be a parachute or engine cowling. The Meteor, meanwhile, turned toward Dishforth and the object, while continuing its descent, appeared to follow suit. After a few seconds, the object stopped its pendulous motion and its descent, and began to rotate about its own axis. Suddenly it accelerated at an incredible speed towards the west turning onto a south-easterly heading before disappearing. All this occurred in a matter of fifteen to twenty seconds. The movements of the object were not identifiable with anything I have seen in the air and the rate of acceleration was unbelievable.

Flying Officer R.N. Paris, Flight Lieutenant M. Cybulski, Master Sergeant Thompson, Sergeant Dewis and Leading Air-craftsman Grimes, all of No. 269 Squadron, who were with me at the time and witnessed the phenomenon, concur with this report. The weather conditions at the time were clear skies, sunshine and unlimited visibility.

I have the honour to be, Sir, Your obedient Servant J. Kilburn, Flight Lieutenant, No. 269 Squadron.[5]

As well as Kilburn's sighting, a number of reports made by civilians were forwarded to RAF Topcliffe. A document formerly classified at 'Confidential' level, dated September 25, 1952, and signed by J.A.C. Stratton, Group Captain, Officer Commanding, RAF Topcliffe, mentioned that other people in the York area had seen a similar object on the day in question.[6]

The Air Ministry was sufficiently concerned by the Topcliffe incident to forward a one-page report on the case to the Commander-in-Chief, Air/East Atlantic, a NATO subdivision:

Following unusual incident observed RAF Topcliffe by number officers and airmen aircrew 191053 local time. Meteor aircraft observed at approx. 500 feet and descending. White object was seen 5 miles astern at approx. 15000 feet and moving at comparatively slow speed on similar course. [Object was] swinging in pendular motion like a sycamore leaf. Thought by observers to be parachute or cowling from Meteor aircraft. Aircraft had turned towards Dishforth and object. Whilst still descending, appeared to follow suit. Pendulous motion and descent ceased. [Object] suddenly accelerated at an incredible speed in a westerly direction but turning to a S.E. course. Observers stated that the movements were not identifiable with anything they had seen in the air and acceleration was in excess of that of a shooting star. Duration of incident 15/20 seconds.[7]

Copies of this report were also forwarded to a number of Government offices, namely the Chief and Assistant Chief of the Air Staff, the Secretary of State, and the Air Ministry's Directorate of Scientific Intelligence.[8]

Also stationed at RAF Ballykelly was Leslie Banks, who at the time was Commander of 240 Squadron. For the duration of Mainbrace, his squadron was detached to Stavanger, Norway. Following the successful completion of the exercise, both Kilburn and Banks returned to Ballykelly at approximately the same time. Banks distinctly recalls discussing the case with Kilburn and well remembers how impressed and shaken the Flight Lieutenant and his men were by their sighting.[9]

The major American presence in Mainbrace was the 45,000-tonne aircraft carrier, the USS *Franklin D. Roosevelt*, which was under the overall command of Vice Admiral Felix B. Stump. On September 20, 1952 (one day after the incident at RAF Topcliffe), an American press photographer, Wallace Litwin, was on board the *Roosevelt* to take photographs of aircraft launching from the carrier. He sighted a circular, silver-coloured object which was manoeuvring above the American fleet. Litwin was shooting with colour film and was able to secure three photographs of the object with the *Roosevelt* in shot. This gave the pictures depth of field and assisted in determining the size of the UFO, which was, according to Litwin's report, considerable. Extensive checks were made to see if the UFO was some form of military vehicle. The answer was negative.[10]

I received copies of Litwin's photographs in 1993 from Mr Chester Grusinski, who was stationed aboard the *Roosevelt* between 1958 and 1960.[11] Whilst the photographs are not of exceptional quality, they do indeed show a circular object positioned high above the Roosevelt, fully demonstrating the reality of the encounter.

Twenty-four hours after Litwin's experience, a similar object was reported seen over the North Sea. Again, the UFO was silver in colour and circular in shape.[12] On that occasion an interception was attempted by a number of RAF fighter aircraft engaged in the exercise. The UFO easily outdistanced itself from the planes.

Additional confirmation of the Mainbrace events may exist within the files of the US Central Intelligence Agency. Amongst the many pages of UFO-related documents released to the general public by the CIA in the late 1970s are a large number of foreign newspaper reports.[13] One report in particular may have a bearing on the Mainbrace incidents.

As part of their routine monitoring of foreign press agencies, the CIA obtained a copy of a Norwegian newspaper clipping concerning an incident of September 1952. The CIA stated that the report was published in a four-times-a-week newspaper in Harstad, Norway. A translation of the article gives us the following information:

> On 18 September, at 1400 hours, three forestry workers who were working right outside Kirkenes, noticed a flat, round object hovering motionless at about 500 meters altitude. The object appeared to have a diameter of 15–20 meters. After the workers had observed the object for a while, it suddenly flew away at great speed in a northwesterly direction. It appears that only these workers saw the object; they swear, however, that their report is true.[14]

On the face of it, this would appear to be a fairly typical UFO report. However, there are three points worth considering. One, the incident occurred on September 18, one day before the Topcliffe and Mainbrace encounters. Two, the characteristics displayed by the object are very similar to those reported during Mainbrace. Three, the fact that this incident occurred over Kirkenes may be of significance, given the account of my father, who recalled that the UFO tracked at RAF Neatishead was lost as it was on a heading for Norway.

Furthermore, the pronounced lack of official British reports found within the CIA's released UFO files suggests to me that some sort of prior arrangement for secrecy was made between the two countries' authorities. This is not as unlikely as it may sound. For example, although the CIA have conceded that they do monitor the UFO subject, and have to date released approximately 1,000 pages of once-classified papers on UFO activity, it has been suggested that this represents the tip of the iceberg. Many more pages, possibly in the order of 15,000, are currently being withheld by the Agency.[15]

It will be recalled that one of the countries which took part in Mainbrace was Denmark. It is intriguing to note that on September 20, 1952, the same day that Wallace Litwin took his historic photographs, a shining, disc-like aircraft was sighted over Karup, one of the most strategically important airfields in Denmark. The object was observed at 7.30 p.m. by three officers of the Danish Air Force.[16]

Adding further mystery to this particular encounter is a paper, titled 'OPERATION MAINBRACE: REPORTS ON POSSIBLE REPER-CUSSIONS IN DENMARK', which is kept at the Public Record Office. Unfortunately, this file is closed to the public for fifty years. This in itself is puzzling, since many other records pertaining to Mainbrace, including those which detail the Soviet response to the exercise, are openly available for inspection.[17] It would appear that there are many more papers concerning the Mainbrace sightings which the Government has deemed unreleasable. For instance, on December 7, 1952, a report was published in the *Sunday Dispatch* newspaper to the effect that each of the six witnesses to the Topcliffe encounter had been interviewed separately by officers from RAF Intelligence. None of the documentation which must surely have been generated following these interviews has surfaced under the terms of the British Government's 'thirty-year ruling'.[18] Moreover, in his book *The Report on Unidentified Flying Objects*, Edward J. Ruppelt – former head of the US Air Force's 'Project Blue Book' (one of a number of projects established by the American administration to examine UFO encounters) – admitted that an RAF Intelligence officer, on an exchange visit to the Pentagon, had stated that it was the sightings reported during Mainbrace which had caused the British Government to officially recognize the UFO. Curiously, Ruppelt also stated that prior to the commencement of the exercise, it had been suggested by someone in the Pentagon that Naval Intelligence should 'keep an eye open for UFOs' during Mainbrace.[19]

Mention has already been made of the Air Ministry's Directorate of Scientific Intelligence (DSI). Certainly DSI was provided with a copy of the official report on Topcliffe. But is there any evidence to suggest deeper involvement on the part of DSI? This is a difficult question to answer with certainty but it is worth examining the available evidence. Initially, in 1990, I approached Mr Bruno Pappalardo of the Public Record Office's Search Department, who replied:

The records of the Defence Ministry's Scientific Intelligence

Branch, Public Record Office class reference DEFE 21 are under arrangement and so [are] not available for general access as yet. It is possible that some documents contained in this class may become available for inspection in 1991. Please note that because of the nature of these files many will be under extended closure and so closed for 50, 75 or 100 years.[20]

I pursued this issue further, specifically with regard to the DSI and its possible involvement in the investigation of UFO sightings by military personnel. This brought forth the following response from the Public Record Office:

The records currently under arrangement at MOD are of (a) the Scientific and Technical Branch (STIB) and (b) the Directorate of Scientific Intelligence (DSI). The activities of the former would not have embraced UFOs and whilst the latter may have, their records are concerned with DSI's relationship with STIB and matters which do not extend to UFOs. Whether material touching on the subject of your enquiry survives amongst the records of DSI and, if so, whether it would be made available, is not within my knowledge, and I have therefore passed a copy of this letter and the related correspondence to the MOD Departmental Record Officer for consideration.[21]

In their reply of January 8, 1991, the Ministry of Defence stated:

The Public Record Office Inspecting Officer advised you, in his letter . . . that your enquiry regarding a particular piece within Class DEFE 21 was being passed to the MOD Departmental Record Officer (DRO) for consideration. I can now advise you that an examination of the pieces listed under DEFE 21 revealed that the earliest anything might be released is in 1993. In the meantime, I am afraid that I am unable to comment on the content of the material due to be released. I am sorry to have to give you such a disappointing reply.[22]

Why would DSI be involved in the investigation of UFO reports? First, it is known that DSI obtained extensive files on Soviet rocket research which the Soviet Union had obtained from German scientists captured at the end of the Second World War. Second, the Topcliffe, Neatishead and Mainbrace incidents seem to confirm that *unknown* aerial vehicles were operating in and around British airspace during highly significant military manoeuvres. It is therefore my opinion that DSI was interested in investigating any scientific advances that could be made from studying UFO reports. Unfortunately, since we are not allowed access to the relevant files, we can only speculate as to the extent of the DSI's involvement.[23]

Meanwhile, I have been encouraged to see that a number of DSI files, unrelated to the UFO enigma, have now been declassified and can be examined at the Public Record Office. These cover the period 1939–1954 and include the following reports: 'German pilotless aircraft'; 'Examination of German secret weapon in Sweden'; 'German long range rocket programme'; and 'USSR: Notes on aircraft design and production'.[24] One hopes that this positive move will lead to the release of further papers from the files of DSI and that some of our questions pertaining to UFOs will eventually be answered. For now, at least we have food for thought.

In the 1953 book, *Flying Saucers Have Landed,* co-author Desmond Leslie related details of a spectacular UFO encounter which was recorded by the Royal Air Force in 1952. Leslie's informant was an RAF officer and the son of a famous London editor and theatre critic. The officer related to Leslie that, whilst on duty in November 1952, he personally tracked the movements of a vast object flying in cloud, from the River Humber in Yorkshire to the Thames Estuary. The object reportedly covered the 200-mile distance in two and a quarter minutes![25]

CHAPTER 4

UNUSUAL AERIAL PHENOMENA

THE AIR MINISTRY WAS STILL UNABLE TO EXPLAIN THE UFO sighting at Topcliffe eleven weeks after the event: '... the special branch dealing with this is keeping an open mind on the subject and all reports received are still being studied,' said a Government spokesperson.

On January 13, 1953, a little more than a month after that announcement, Fighter Command Headquarters issued a new document outlining the procedures to be followed in the event that 'unusual targets' were detected on radar. Was this as a result of the radar-confirmed UFO encounters reported by my father at RAF Neatishead? Given the great lengths to which the Air Ministry went to ensure that evidence relating to those particular sightings was preserved for analysis, this possibility must rank highly.[1]

Also in 1953, Flight Lieutenant Cyril Townsend-Withers was informed that the Air Ministry had established a project to examine UFO reports with the extra-terrestrial hypothesis in mind.[2] In public, the Ministry never admitted to the existence of such a project. However, in light of the many now-documented UFO encounters reported by the British military in September 1952, Townsend-Withers' testimony carries weight. And it adds credence to the suspicion that, more than forty years ago, the British Government was seriously considering the possibility that we were being visited by an alien species which appeared to be our technological superior.

As if in response to the Ministry's new regulations, in 1953 UFO activity reached an all-time high. Sightings were recorded across the globe by the RAF. They were directly involved in a 'UFO chase' which occurred near a British military base in Hong Kong.

Michael Forrest, a retired lecturer in engineering design at Loughborough University, remembers all too well what took place: 'I was part of an armed flight section scrambled to intercept an object detected by the ground control radar. But, when we were within the usual sighting distance of five miles, we could not see anything.' Despite this, ground radar showed a distinct 'blip' which indicated that whatever the object was, it recognized the presence of the RAF interceptors.

'All we could hear was the panic of the ground controller who was convinced we were on a collision course,' said Forrest, who later learned that the controller had actually seen the two radar blips merge on the screen. 'So whatever it was, we were flying alongside it and then with it, without ever seeing it,' he concluded.[3] Was the object somehow capable of rendering itself invisible to the human eye? As bizarre as such a theory may sound, similar incidents occurred throughout the 1950s which appear to supply further evidence for it.

Clive Thomas, who joined the RAF in 1947, has disclosed his knowledge of a UFO seen near RAF Heaby, Southern Rhodesia (now Zimbabwe), in 1953: 'The saucer was dull grey in colour, and had a central dome on top. We all saw it quite clearly, including a blackened window of some sort. Its size was roughly 30 feet in diameter. None of us thought to sound an alert, or reach for a telephone; we were literally mesmerized by the thing.'

Back in England, in October of that year, there were numerous independent sightings, covering several hours, of a UFO traversing the evening sky over East Anglia. One witness, Mr John Smith of Kessingland, Suffolk, was a member of the Royal Observer Corps (ROC). At approximately 6.45 p.m. on the 6th, Mr Smith was travelling by motorcycle from Wrentham to Kessingland along the old A12 road across Latimer's Dam. Although he was wearing a crash-helmet Mr Smith became acutely aware of a form of 'atmospheric vibration' which he described as similar to a low-frequency hum. Looking skywards and out towards the coast, he saw what appeared to be four large rays of orange light moving inland.

Being a member of the ROC, and naturally curious, Mr Smith immediately pulled up in order to obtain a better view of the phenomenon. As he did so the lights travelled overhead and disappeared in the vicinity of the nearby Foxborrow Wood. As it passed close Mr Smith was able to get a view of the object from which the light beams emanated. Flying at a height of about 200 feet was a circular craft with a diameter of roughly fifty feet. Mr Smith was then able to see that the light beams seemed to be projected from a raised dome which sat atop the main body of the UFO. Although the entire incident was over in a short space of time, it left a deep impression on Mr Smith, who related the details to me in 1994.[4]

At 7.15 p.m., what appears to have been the same UFO was sighted over the city of Norwich by Mr F.W. Potter, a member of the Norwich Astronomical Society. Whilst scanning the night sky with a 3.5-inch refractor telescope, Mr Potter noticed a 'very bright object' travelling from the south-west:

> I focused upon it and found the light given from the object was not reflected sunlight, as I first believed, but an internal light being sent out from a fixed apparatus situated around a dome. The rays or beams of light could be seen distinctly from the dome and attached directly beneath it was a much larger and flattened dome with a protruding band running in a circumference around its edge. This was clearly seen in the telescope by the rays of light thrown out from the apertures in the top dome. The underneath of the large flattened bottom dome was hollow and appeared to be glowing red, but there were no vapour trails or gases to be seen.
>
> It did not rotate but kept the same portion of the dome towards the telescope until it changed its angular course. Then it gave me a chance to visualise another of the apertures that previously had been hidden from view. It was then travelling to the north-east and disappearing from view.[5]

Apparently, the UFO soon returned. Mr F. Dewing, also of Norwich, saw the same object approximately one hour later when it was travelling in the opposite direction to that described by Mr Potter.[6]

Following a report on the case which was published in the *Eastern Evening News*, two further witnesses, J.H. Gosling and the son of one W. Mace, came forward and testified that they too had seen the UFO in the Norwich skies on the same evening, at 8.15 p.m. and 9.45 p.m. respectively.[7]

It is fortunate that this particular UFO was witnessed by at least three highly credible observers; namely two gentlemen from the Norwich Astronomical Society and a member of the Royal Observer Corps. The fact that the UFO was seen continually throughout the skies of East Anglia on that evening, suggests to me that it was following some form of pre-determined agenda. Taking into consideration the many military bases which existed in the area at the time, a reconnaissance mission would be a logical explanation for the UFO's behaviour.

Three days after the incidents at Norwich and Kessingland, at least four UFOs were tracked on ground radar, approaching the British coastline in the area of Harwich, Essex, at 1.00 p.m. They were first sighted by radar operators attached to the nearby RAF Bawdsey. Believing that the UFOs were potentially hostile, Fighter Command Headquarters at RAF Bentley Priory, Middlesex, ordered the scrambling of aircraft from No. 63 Squadron based at RAF Waterbeach.

Although the aircrews were unable to locate the UFOs, a supervisor at RAF Bawdsey recorded a visual sighting at 1.02 p.m. Numerous enquiries were made at military facilities throughout the country and on the continent but the origin of the UFOs could not be ascertained.

All relevant documentation was then forwarded to the Air Ministry at Whitehall and the incident was classified 'Secret' in its entirety. The final report on the case, dated December 22, 1953, and prepared by Group Captain R.N. Bateson, confirms that the incident remained on file as being unresolved.[8]

As that investigation was taking place, yet another UFO report was filed by an RAF crew, this time based at West Malling, Kent. At 10.00 a.m. on November 3, 1953, Flying Officers Geoffrey Smythe and Terry Johnson were airborne at a height of approximately 20,000 feet in a two-seater Vampire jet fighter. Their attention was suddenly drawn towards a very bright, stationary light which appeared to be at an altitude somewhat higher than theirs. After Smythe and Johnson had observed the object for about thirty seconds, and had been able to determine its circular shape, it suddenly accelerated out of the area at an exceptional rate.

Upon returning to West Malling, they filed a report with their Station Commander, Group Captain P.H. Hamley (who was himself involved in a UFO experience during World War Two), and the HQ at Bentley Priory was informed of the details. Both men were later questioned by Air Ministry officials for two hours in a confidential interview, the details of which have never been made public.

After having been pressed by questioners in the House of Commons, the then Parliamentary Secretary to the Air Ministry informed the House that the object had merely been a meteorological balloon. Indeed, the 'balloon' theory was one that would serve the Air Ministry well in future UFO incidents.[9]

Four and a half hours after the West Malling encounter, an unusual object was tracked by personnel testing a new radar set in the Anti-Aircraft Command Centre at Lee Green, Kent. For around half an hour the UFO was continuously monitored on the radar scope, something confirmed by several witnesses: A.J. Jeffrey, technical storeman, D. Fuller, fitter mechanic, S. Russell, anti-aircraft group workshop, and Sergeant H. Waller. Interestingly, Sergeant Waller stated that this was not the first time that he had seen UFOs on the radar scopes. The Ministry again trotted out its by-then-reliable 'balloon' theory, thus discounting the testimony of four qualified observers, all of whom were adamant that the object had not been a balloon.

In early 1996 both Terry Johnson and Geoffrey Smythe spoke out publicly with respect to the West Malling case, and Johnson disclosed an interesting, little-known fact: 'We were called up to the Air Ministry to give a full report of the incident to the Duke of Edinburgh's equerry. We were told that Prince Philip was interested in flying saucers.'[10]

The Air Ministry's official line was that the majority of UFO sightings were simply the result of misperception. But, thanks to the provisions of the British Government's 'Thirty Year Ruling', we can now see that those public statements contrasted sharply with discussions that were taking place behind the closed doors of Whitehall. This is borne out by a document titled 'Reports on Aerial Phenomena', dated December 16, 1953, which was widely circulated within the RAF to ensure that all UFO reports filed by service sources reached the Air Ministry under cover of the utmost secrecy. I quote from the document in question, prepared by Flight Lieutenant C.P.B. Russell of No. 11 Group:

1. It has been decided that sightings of aerial phenomena by Royal Air Force personnel are in future to be reported in writing by Officers Commanding Units immediately and direct to Air Ministry, (D.D.I. (Tech.)) [*Author's note*: 'Deputy Directorate of Intelligence, Technical Branch'.] with copies to Group and Command Headquarters. In addition, any reports from civilians received by units should be acknowledged formally in writing and copies of the reports themselves forwarded direct to Air Ministry, (D.D.I. (Tech.)).

2. It will be appreciated that the public attach more credence to reports by Royal Air Force personnel than to those by members of the public. It is essential that the information should be examined at Air Ministry and that its release should be controlled officially. All reports are, therefore, to be classified 'Restricted' and personnel are to be warned that they are not to communicate to anyone other than official persons any information about phenomena they have observed, unless officially authorised to do so.

3. This procedure does not apply to the radar detection of unusual targets which is to be reported through the normal channels as required by Fighter Command Headquarters letter FC/S.45485/Signals, dated 13th January, 1953.[11]

This is obviously a radical departure from the statements made to Winston Churchill in the previous year. It is interesting to note that personnel were warned to report UFO sightings only to certain authorities. Clearly there was a desire to ensure that nothing of significance leaked outside of official channels.

We have already seen that following the UFO sighting at RAF Topcliffe in September 1952, a copy of the official report on the case was forwarded to the Scientific Branch of the Air Ministry. Yet the 'Reports on Aerial Phenomena' document seems to suggest that by late 1953 the task of investigating UFO reports rested exclusively with the Ministry's Technical Branch, DDI (Tech). Evidently, a change of policy had occurred within the Ministry regarding the co-ordination of research into UFO encounters.

It is intiguing that this tallies with the testimony of Cyril Townsend-Withers that the Air Ministry had established a project in early 1953 to examine UFO reports with the extra-terrestrial hypothesis in mind. This being so, the 'Reports on Aerial Phenomena' paper may be one of the very few documents currently available to the general public which originated with that particular project. Since there has been a blanket denial on the part of the British Government that any such project ever existed, we should perhaps consider it fortunate that this document has surfaced at all.

A potentially important case which has been overlooked for more than forty years took place at Templeogue, near Dublin, in the summer of 1954. The only known witness was Mr P.D. McCormack, a resident of Templeogue. He reported seeing a 'strange blueish-white' object in the night sky moving at a speed estimated to be no less than 1,000 mph. 'I saw this object travelling in a straight line over the Dublin mountains,' he recalled. 'Trails of flaming pieces seemed to fall away at each side . . . I would not take note of this if it were not something the like of which I had never seen before.'[12]

One might be forgiven for thinking that the witness had simply misperceived a conventional astronomical event, such as a meteor entering the earth's atmosphere. Mr McCormack, however, was no ordinary witness: a member of the British Interplanetary Society, he was employed as a research worker in the School of Cosmic Physics attached to the

Dublin Institute of Advanced Studies. Would he have been fooled by a perfectly routine phenomenon? I think it most unlikely.

In any case, it appears that the UFO investigators at the Air Ministry were busy enough in 1954.

Midway through a parliamentary question-and-answer session on May 15, 1957, it was revealed by the Secretary of State for Air, George Ward, that in 1954 the Ministry had examined six UFO reports for which it was unable to provide any explanation.

Although Ward did not give specific details of the incidents, the probability is that one related to the experience of Flight Lieutenant James Salandin, who viewed three UFOs whilst flying over Essex in a Gloster Meteor on October 14, 1954. I have not included a detailed account here since the case has been referred to widely in UFO literature, and a definitive account can be read in Timothy Good's *Above Top Secret*. Good, having interviewed Salandin in 1985, is of the opinion that the case is 'one of the most important [UFO] sightings to have been reported by an RAF pilot'.[13]

Furthermore, I am reliably informed that one of the reports in question concerned the sighting of a massive, diamond-shaped UFO by personnel stationed at RAF West Freugh, Wigtownshire (a station which features heavily in a similar 1957 incident for which I have located a copy of the original report filed with the Air Ministry at the time).

Another series of unexplained incidents, involving both the Air Ministry and the War Office, occurred shortly after Salandin's UFO encounter over Essex. As with the 1949 incident at RAF Sandwich, no visual sightings of the UFOs were recorded (that we know of). But according to Major Donald E. Keyhoe, formerly of the United States Marine Corps, between forty and fifty UFOs were simultaneously tracked over Britain in the latter part of 1954 by 'a score of War Office and Air Ministry radar stations'.[14] Keyhoe also discovered that in the course of conducting enquiries into the case, the Government ordered British intelligence agents on the continent to look into the matter.

Since the task of gathering intelligence data from overseas has almost always been the responsibility of MI6, this may be an early confirmation of Secret Intelligence Service involvement in UFO investigations. If this particular event was considered to be of such importance that it required a joint investigation by the Air Ministry, the War Office, and the Secret Intelligence Service, then one would imagine that a substantial file would have been built up on the case. Yet, as with so many other reported incidents, no trace of any such file can be found at the Public Record Office.

During that parliamentary session of May 15, 1957, Ward also stated that of all the UFO reports examined by the Air Ministry in 1955, none remained unidentified.[15] Perhaps, but 1955 was far from being a quiet year for the Air Ministry.

On the night of March 24, 1955, a brightly lit object was seen in the British skies by numerous people, including a number of RAF pilots. The Air Ministry's explanation that the object had been a meteor was severely tested the following year by researcher David Wightman (as we shall see in the next chapter). Moreover, it was reported at the time that some of the RAF pilots who attempted to pursue the 'meteor' said that not only did it change course, it also accelerated in speed.[16]

Two months later a cigar-shaped UFO, with a colour which resembled polished aluminium, was sighted by the pilot and co-pilot of a Portuguese 'Skymaster' aircraft flying between Dusfold and Epsom. 'It flashed past under the nose of our aircraft at a terrific speed,' said Radio Officer J.O. Almeida.[17]

Nine weeks after that, a 'boomerang-shaped' UFO, some forty feet in width, was seen at Lasham, Hampshire – apparently observing the National Gliding Championships which were taking place there! Mrs Yvonne Bonham, Secretary of the British Gliding Association, estimated that the UFO was at a height of 3,000 feet, and for a while appeared to actually hover over the glider of the British champion, Philip Wills, before disappearing at a high speed.[18]

Oddly enough, in August 1954 members of the Royal Air Force Gliding school at St Athan airfield, along with staff at Rhoose Airport, also witnessed a UFO at close quarters: 'The form I observed was that of a large double-convex lens viewed in vertical profile,' recalled one flying officer who attempted to pursue the UFO in his glider.[19]

*   *   *

This period is notable for one other reason: it saw the publication of the Air Ministry's 'Secret Intelligence Summary' which sought to provide appropriately down-to-earth answers to the UFO mystery. Although I have yet to ascertain exactly when the summary was written, it can have been no earlier than July 1, 1954, and no later than March 13, 1955.

I base this belief on the following: the four-page summary references a well-known and much-reported UFO sighting which took place over Canada on June 30, 1954.[20] Hence, the paper could not have been written prior to the beginning of July of that year. In addition, a copy of the summary was forwarded to Duncan Sandys MP on March 14, 1955, so it had to have been written at some point before that date.[21]

When I learned of the existence of this particular paper, and subsequently obtained a copy via the Public Record Office, I anticipated that it would be of extreme significance. After all, it had been written at a time when the UFO incidents reported throughout Exercise Mainbrace, and at RAF Bawdsey, West Malling and Lea Green were relatively recent occurrences. Yet, reading the Air Ministry's paper, one would be forgiven for thinking that they were of no more concern to the Government than sightings of Santa Claus atop his sleigh!

The paper reads very much like a standard reply that today's Ministry of Defence routinely forwards to enquiring members of the public. It gives much prominence to 'conventional' explanations for UFO sightings, including the misidentification of aircraft, balloons, car headlights reflected on clouds, birds, and astronomical phenomena such as planets and meteors. Not only that, the author of the report makes a statement which is unquestionably, and quite demonstrably, misleading: 'The investigation of reports of flying saucers presents very apparent difficulties, the major one of which is that, ninety-nine times out of a hundred, the scent is completely cold. It is only fair to point out that in every other case, i.e. when reports are telephoned and promptly checked on the spot, the sighted object has been identified as a balloon or a conventional aircraft.'[22]

While I have always been of the opinion that the overwhelming majority of all UFO reports can be explained in quite rational terms, for the Government to say that 'in every other case . . . the sighted object has been identified as a balloon or conventional aircraft' is totally incorrect.

The cases to which I have already referred underline that assertion at a stroke. One would be hard pressed to find a balloon or conventional aircraft that could satisfactorily explain the sightings at Bentwaters in 1947, Topcliffe in 1952, and RAF Heaby in 1953. By making absolutely no mention of this and by being highly selective with the cited data, the author of the Air Ministry's summary has left us with a deeply flawed paper. In view of this, can the Ministry's actions be accounted for?

At the time that it was written, the four-page report was classified at 'Restricted' level, which was in accordance with Government regulations introduced on December 16, 1953. However, it was ultimately published in an Air Ministry Intelligence paper which had 'Secret' status. Therefore the author of the paper must have had a security clearance equal to that level of classification and, in keeping with this line of thought, was surely able to access the Air Ministry's unexplained UFO reports. So why fail to make any mention of them in the 1955 summary?

One person well-qualified to answer this question is Mark Birdsall, a long-time student of UFOs and one of the first people to obtain a copy of the Air Ministry summary: 'I believe this report is both controversial . . . and clearly outdated. Without doubt it was prepared to calm the increasing awareness of politicians and authorities who were becoming concerned. A debunking exercise is perhaps the appropriate terminology . . .'

Whilst conducting research into the Air Ministry paper, Birdsall learned that the MOD was still using it as late as 1988 as a basis for issuing public statements on the UFO subject.[23] Since then I have been advised by the MOD that its policy on UFOs remains unchanged, which leads me to believe that this forty-two-year-old document is still being utilized. I concur with Birdsall that the paper was created essentially to debunk the UFO subject, and believe that this was largely as a result of the flood of UFO reports which the Air Ministry received in the 1952–1954 time period. With both the media and Parliament asking questions, 'damage control' was the order of the day.

A recently surfaced source who has filled in some of the blanks relating to hitherto unknown UFO incidents recorded by the Royal Air Force in the mid-1950s is Paul Stokes. According to Stokes, during the course of his service, which began in 1952, a number of encounters were recorded by the military: the sighting of a brightly lit UFO by a number of pilots based at RAF Horsham St Faith; a 1955 encounter involving nine oval-shaped objects seen by personnel at RAF Tangmere; and later encounters at RAF Stradishall, and at an RAF facility at Akrotiri on the island of Cyprus.[24] Given Stokes' testimony, it seems safe to assume that whatever the Air Ministry learned about UFOs in the mid-1950s, much remains unresolved.

C H A P T E R   5

'WE BELIEVE THESE THINGS EXIST'

IN APRIL 1956 DAVID WIGHTMAN, EDITOR OF *URANUS* MAGAZINE, wrote to the Air Ministry requesting an interview with a Government official conversant with the issue of unidentified flying objects. Shortly afterwards the request was granted and he travelled down to London full of expectation. For the purpose of the interview Wightman had arranged to meet a colleague, John Pitt, on the Air Ministry steps. This done, both proceeded into the building and were duly escorted up several floors to 'the office'.

Both men were greeted cordially, but learned little of substance. During the course of the two-hour interview Wightman and Pitt raised a number of issues, including the 1954 UFO sighting of RAF pilot James Salandin. Amazingly, the Air Ministry official professed to have no knowledge of the incident. Wightman and his colleague were also informed that the Air Ministry did not liaise with other countries on the 'saucer problem'. This is in direct contrast to the recollections of Edward J. Ruppelt, former head of the US Air Force's 'Project Blue Book'.

The interview was not without its moments, however, as Wightman recalled in the June 1956 issue of *Uranus*: 'We tried two more sightings and the pattern changed somewhat. Answers we got . . . but we were told we mustn't repeat them let alone print the information we had been given. This was because the answers contained secret material. The quotation regarding the Official Secrets Act was duly recited and there the matter ended.'[1]

Six months later Wightman decided to reveal further details gleaned during the interview. The Air Ministry had apparently solved at least two of the incidents brought to its attention in 1955, the first of which concerned the strange object seen over Britain on March 24. In that particular instance, Wightman and Pitt were informed, the Air Ministry was satisfied that the object had simply been a meteor. How had that conclusion been reached? Greenwich Observatory had said so. Less than satisfied with the Air Ministry's explanation, Wightman made his own enquiries with Greenwich, and received the following response which seems to contradict the Air Ministry's assertion: 'We had some enquiries at the time concerning an apparition in March of last year, but we were not able to comment or confirm as no observations of the object were made here.'

The second incident was the so-called 'Skymaster' encounter. 'Oh yes, we did investigate this incident; we are quite satisfied it was a long toy balloon,' a stunned Wightman and Pitt were advised. What conclusion did the two researchers come to following the interview? '. . . little or no satisfaction was gained from a discussion which lasted over two hours – "long toy balloons" and "meteors" were the order of the day. The report, which did appear in this magazine was purposely "mild": a much more critical write-up would have been a truer representation of both John Pitt's and your editor's reactions.'[2]

On the evening of August 13, 1956, an extraordinary series of events began which forever changed the Government's policy on UFO reports and led to a sudden upgrading in the secrecy level surrounding those reports. Not surprisingly, the relevant paperwork generated by British authorities has never surfaced. Fortunately, one such report which is pertinent to the case has been found among the declassified UFO papers of the US Air Force. Related below is the report filed by the Watch Supervisor on duty in the Radar Air Traffic Control Centre at the joint RAF/USAF base at Lakenheath, Suffolk:

It was the 5.00 p.m. to midnight shift. I had either four or five other controllers on my shift. I was sitting at the Supervisor's Coordinating desk and received a call on the direct line (actually I'm not sure which line it was). Anyway, it was Sculthorpe GCA Unit calling and the radar operator asked me if we had any targets on our scopes traveling at 4,000 mph. They said they had watched a target on their scopes proceed from a point 30 or 40 miles east of Sculthorpe to a point 40 miles west of Sculthorpe. The target passed directly over Sculthorpe, England, RAF Station (also a USAF Station). He said the tower reported seeing it go by and just appeared to be a blurry light. A C-47 flying over the base at 5,000 feet altitude also reported seeing it as a blurred light that passed under his aircraft. I immediately had all the controllers start scanning the radar scopes. I had each scope set on a different range – from 10 miles to 200 miles radius of Lakenheath. At this time I did not contact anyone by telephone as I was rather skeptical of this report. We were using [deleted] on our radar, which eliminated entirely all ground returns and stationary targets. There was very little or not [sic] traffic or targets on the scopes, as I recall. However, one controller noticed a stationary target on the scopes about 20 to 25 miles southwest. This was unusual as a stationary target should have been eliminated unless it was moving at a speed of at least 40 to 45 knots. And yet we could detect no movement at all. We watched this target on all the different scopes for several minutes and I called the GCA Unit at Lakenheath to see if they had this target on their scopes also. They confirmed the target was on their scope in the same geographical location. As we watched, the stationary target started moving at a speed of 400 to 600 mph in a north/northeast direction until it reached a point about 20 miles north/northwest of Lakenheath. There was no slow start or build-up to this speed – it was constant from the second it started to move until it stopped.

I called and reported all the facts to this point, including Sculthorpe GCA's initial report, to the 7th Air Division Command Post at London. They in turn notified 3rd Air Force Command Post and hooked into the line. I also hooked in my local AFB Commanding Officer and my Unit (AFCS,

Communications Squadron) Commander on my switchboard. And there could have been others hooked in also that I was not aware of. I repeated all the facts known to this point and continued to give a detailed report on the target's movements and location. The target made several changes in location, always in a straight line, always at about 600 mph and always from a standing or stationary point to his next stop at constant speed – no build up in speed, no set pattern at any time. Time spent stationary between movements also varied from 3 or 4 minutes to 5 or 6 minutes (possibly even longer as I was busy answering questions – listening to theories, guesses, etc., that the conference line people were saying). This continued for some time. After I imagine about 30 to 45 minutes, it was decided to scramble two RAF interceptors to investigate. This was done I believe by 3rd Air Force calling the RAF and, after hearing what the score was, they scrambled one aircraft. (The second got off after as I will mention later.)

The interceptor aircraft took off from an RAF station near London and approached Lakenheath from the southwest. Radio and radar contact was established with the RAF interceptor aircraft at a point about 30 to 35 miles southwest of Lakenheath, inbound to Lakenheath. On initial contact we gave the interceptor pilot all the background information on the UFO, his (the interceptor) present distance and bearing from Lakenheath, the UFO's (which was stationary at the time) distance and bearing from Lakenheath. We explained we did not know the altitude of the UFO but we could assume his altitude was above 1,500 feet and below 20,000 feet, due to the operational characteristics of the radar (CPS-5 type radar, I believe). Also, we mentioned the report from the C-47 over Sculthorpe that relayed the story about the light which passed below him. His altitude was 5,000 feet.

We immediately issued heading to the interceptor to guide him to the UFO. The UFO remained stationary throughout. This vectoring of the intercept aircraft continued. We continually gave the intercept aircraft his heading to the UFO and his distance from the UFO at approximately 1-to-2-mile intervals.

Shortly after we told the intercept aircraft he was one-half mile from the UFO and it was 12 o'clock from his position, he said, 'Roger, Lakenheath, I've got my guns locked on him.' Then he paused and said, 'Where did he go? Do you still have him?' We replied, 'Roger, it appeared he got behind you and he's still there.' There were now two targets, one behind the other, same speed, very close, but two separate distinct targets.

The first movement by the UFO was so swift (circling behind the interceptor) I missed it entirely, but it was seen by the other controllers. However, the fact that this had occurred was confirmed by the pilot of the interceptor. The pilot of the interceptor told me he would try to shake the UFO and would try it again. He tried everything – he climbed, dived, circled, etc., but the UFO acted like it was glued right behind him, always the same distance, very close, but we always had two distinct targets. (Note: Target resolution on our radar at the range they were from the antenna [about 10 to 30 miles, all in the southerly sectors from Lakenheath] would be between 200 and 600 feet probably. Closer than that we would have got one target from both aircraft and UFO. Most specifications say 500 feet is the minimum, but I believe it varied and 200 to 600 feet is closer to the truth and, in addition the tuning of the equipment, atmospheric conditions, etc., also help determine this figure.)

The interceptor pilot continued to try and shake the UFO for about ten minutes (approximate – it seemed longer to both him and us). He continued to comment occasionally and we could tell from the tonal quality he was getting worried, excited and also pretty scared.

He finally said, 'I'm returning to station, Lakenheath. Let me know if he follows me. I'm getting low on petrol.' The target (UFO) followed him only a short distance, as he headed south/southwest, and the UFO stopped and remained stationary. We advised the interceptor that the UFO target had stopped following and was now stationary about 10 miles south of Lakenheath. He rogered this message and almost immediately the second interceptor called us on the same frequency. We replied and told him we would advise him when we had a radar target, so we could establish radar contact with his aircraft. (He was not on radar at this time, probably had just taken off and was too low for us to pick him up, or too far away – we had most of the scopes on short range, so we could watch the UFO closely on the smaller range.) The number-two interceptor called the number one interceptor by name (Tom, Frank – whatever his name was) and asked him, 'Did you see anything?' Number one replied, 'I saw something, but I'll be damned if I know what it was.' Number two said, 'What happened?' Number one then switched frequencies to his home-base frequency. We gave number two the location of the UFO and advised him that we still didn't have him on radar, but probably would have shortly. He delayed answering for some seconds and then finally said, 'Lakenheath – (identification, aircraft call sign) – can't remember what call sign those aircraft were using. Returning home, my engine is malfunctioning.' He then left our frequency.

Throughout this we kept all the agencies, 7th Air Division, 3rd Air Force, etc., advised on every aspect, every word that was said, everything.

We then inquired what action they wanted to take. They had no more suggestions, then finally they told us to just keep watching the target and let them know if anything else happened. The target made a couple more short moves, then left our radar coverage in a northerly direction – speed still about 600 mph. We lost target outbound to the north at about 50 to 60 miles, which is normal if aircraft or target is at an altitude below 5,000 feet (because of the radiation loss of that type radar). We notified 7th Air Division Command Post and they said they'd tell everybody for us.

I made out a written report on all this, in detail for the officer in charge of my facility, and was told that unless I was contacted later for any further information, he would take care of it . . . I heard no more about it . . .[3]

What are we to make of the Watch Supervisor's report? Any balanced and reasonable assessment can only conclude that on the evening of August 13, 1956, an unidentified flying object, displaying flight characteristics which suggested that it was under intelligent control, manifested itself in British airspace; and despite valiant attempts at interception by those involved, it was easily able to outmanoeuvre and outperform experienced RAF pilots. One wonders what the outcome would have been had the intelligences behind the UFO displayed hostile intent . . .

There is another twist to this story which demands explanation. It has now been established that the interceptor aircraft were scrambled from RAF Waterbeach, in response to orders received from RAF Neatishead in Norfolk (which, as the reader will recall, had itself been the site of a similar UFO encounter in 1952).

The Flight Controller on duty at Neatishead on the night of August 13 was Frederick Wimbledon, who has confirmed to me that he gave instructions for the aircraft to scramble. Afterwards, he told me, a senior officer from the Air Ministry arrived at Neatishead for the express purpose of interrogating both him and his colleagues. Interviewed together, all five (a fighter controller of officer rank, a corporal, a tracker, a height reader and Wimbledon himself) were asked to describe what had occurred on the night and how the interception was carried out.

Wimbledon recalls: 'Either the log book was taken away or extracts [were] taken. I think the actual log book was taken away, which is more logical.' He also confirms that a high degree of secrecy was afforded the case by British authorities: 'Any of us who were involved in these things were sworn to secrecy under the thirty year rule and even then could still be "incurring the displeasure of Air Ministry" with subsequent threat of prosecution under the Official Secrets Act.'

Since both the British and American authorities had intimate knowledge of the bizarre encounters of August 13, 1956, one could sensibly expect that a joint investigation would have been set up to resolve the issue.

Frederick Wimbledon told me that attempts by American officials to prise information out of British authorities were met with professed ignorance. 'We have no knowledge of this event' was the message given to the Americans. 'This was back in the '70s,' Wimbledon explained, 'so much may have happened since then but I am not in a position to know.'

Wimbledon has also advised me that he was never entrusted with the results of the Air Ministry's investigation of the incident, nor was he informed which department within the Ministry was responsible for handling the matter. He does, however, have a firm opinion as to what was seen on the night in question: 'Some extraterrestrial, controlled machine, with a superlative performance quite outside the capability of earthborne existing aircraft. But from where?'[4]

A secondary source of evidence for this encounter is one Ralph Noyes, who retired from the Ministry of Defence in 1977 in the position of Under-Secretary of State. He revealed in an interview with Timothy Good that one of the pilots involved in the UFO chase had succeeded in shooting gun-camera footage of the UFO and that he, Noyes, had occasion to view this, and other similar footage, at Whitehall.[5]

The films were shown at a briefing which had been arranged by the head of S4, a department of the Ministry known to have been involved in the investigation of UFO sightings in the 1950s. Also in attendance were a representative from the Meteorological Office, the Director of Air Defence, and various personnel from the Air Staff.

Towards the end of 1993, the Ministry of Defence was asked (by myself and a number of other researchers including Timothy Good) about the status of the gun-camera footage and undertook a search. (I have made enquiries with staff at the Public Record Office and the film is not amongst their holdings.) This task fell to Secretariat (Air Staff) 2a, or Sec(AS)2a, in official-speak.

In an interview conducted in 1994, Nick Pope of Sec (AS) 2a advised me of his attempts to locate the film:

> I liaised with our archivist people, who are the sort of middlemen between ourselves and the Public Record Office. They made a number of checks and basically . . . a check was made of any place where this material might have ended. Now, that includes the PRO, it also includes anything that might have got lodged in a halfway house of archiving. They checked the Imperial War Museum and, I think, the RAF Museum.

No one is disputing that Ralph Noyes saw this footage and that it existed. That's not in dispute as far as I'm concerned. I think it's unfortunate, but I suspect that one of two things happened. Either it got lost or destroyed somewhere because it wasn't seen as being of public interest at the time; or old film footage deteriorates; it becomes unstable and you have to destroy it before it becomes a health and safety hazard. But, I think Ralph himself said that the footage wasn't that spectacular. We did have a thorough look for it and unfortunately it didn't turn up. Given that we've now had a proper look, I think it's unlikely it will turn up. All I can say is, we gave it our best shot.[6]

While I have absolutely no doubt that Pope was being entirely honest and sincere in his statements, I find it astonishing that such footage would have been routinely destroyed. It would have been a relatively simple task to make duplicate copies of the film, thus ensuring its survival for future reference. This becomes even more logical when one takes into consideration the defence aspects of the case. Here was an object, an apparent UFO, which flew through British airspace, was tracked on both airborne and ground radar, executed astonishing manoeuvres, far in advance of known capabilities, and made good its escape from two Royal Air Force interceptors! Would the Air Ministry, and its successor, the Ministry of Defence, really have allowed evidence pertaining to such an event simply to disappear?

If the footage has not been destroyed, and has not been lost, there is a third scenario: that it may still be classified by the Ministry of Defence. There is a small but growing body of evidence suggesting that highly covert investigations of UFO phenomena are undertaken by the MOD's Defence Intelligence Staff on a worldwide basis. Since the work of the DIS is tightly defined, I consider it most unlikely that Sec (AS) 2a – which largely handles UFO reports submitted to the MOD by members of the public – would be notified of any UFO incidents with a bearing on national security. Therefore, it is possible that, following the establishment of the DIS in 1964, the gun-camera footage may have been transferred to a division within the DIS specifically tasked with handling records relating to UFOs. It will became clear that DIS involvement in UFO activity runs deep.

Certainly, the very existence of the footage was considered a matter of some sensitivity by the Air Ministry, and steps were taken to ensure that knowledge of it did not leak outside of Whitehall. By way of illustration, Frederick Wimbledon told me that, despite his involvement in the incident, he was not aware that one of the intercepting pilots had succeeded in filming the UFO until he read Timothy Good's *Above Top Secret.* Moreover, Wimbledon never had the opportunity to speak with the aircrews after the event since they were interviewed separately at RAF Waterbeach.[7]

Although this particular encounter took place more than four decades ago, information continues to surface. During a 1996 interview with respected investigator Jenny Randles, she told me that she had tracked down one of the pilots and two of the navigators involved in the 'UFO chase' at Lakenheath. Yet their testimony confuses matters further, as Jenny informed me: 'Frankly, their stories downplay the case, if anything, and none claim to have seen the object [visually]. I know we have the correct crew as they have kept their log books with dates and times.'

Jenny has also advised me that the three crew members insisted that, since they did not view the UFO directly, they were unable to secure the gun-camera footage which Ralph Noyes recalls seeing at Whitehall. Is it conceivable that there were other aircrews involved in the encounter who have yet to come forward? If there are, this would certainly go some way towards resolving this puzzling aspect of the encounter. Remember that the Watch Supervisor on duty in the Radar Air Traffic Control Centre was very specific in his official report about the fact that a visual sighting of the UFO had been recorded by one of the pilots. 'I saw something, but I'll be damned if I know what it was,' was the wording one of the crew apparently used.

Despite these discrepancies, it is perhaps fitting that the final word should go to the interrogating officer from the Air Ministry, whose words Frederick Wimbledon recalls to this day: 'Do not imagine that you have imagined this; we believe these things exist.'[8]

*   *   *

As specialist staff at the Air Ministry continued to pore over the evidence relating to the encounter at Lakenheath, a similar occurrence took place off the south coast of Britain. The prime witness, W. Wright, was a Flight Lieutenant with 46 Squadron, whose account is one of the most credible I have come across.[9]

The date was August 30, 1956. Flying a Javelin aircraft, Wright was preparing to take part in a routine 'practice interception' mission with a second Javelin. Both planes carried a navigator. All seemed normal as the aircraft climbed above cloud-level to a height of 45,000 feet on what was described as being a 'bright, clear day ... with unlimited sun and visibility'. Both jets were flying on a westerly heading some miles south of the Isle of Wight, ready to commence their pre-planned interception. With one aircraft acting as the 'target' the planes separated and the exercise began.

Heading north-west Wright suddenly observed a strange disc-shaped object to his right. Checks with the navigator revealed that he had obtained a clear radar return of the UFO, estimated to be at a distance of nineteen miles. Fully aware that this was no ordinary aircraft, Wright attempted to correlate the size of the UFO against that of his little finger held against the cockpit glass. Subsequent calculations for the official report suggested that the UFO was at least 600 feet in diameter, and probably more!

Wright quickly radioed to ground control requesting that he be given permission to intercept and investigate the UFO. Permission granted, he turned north. As he did so the UFO seemed to slow its forward speed, maintaining station with the Javelin. Meanwhile, the second Javelin arrived on the scene and confirmed the presence of the UFO. Both aircraft then banked steeply northward, keeping the UFO in sight at all times. Without warning, the UFO then moved to a dead-ahead position and came to an ominous halt.

Intent on a face-to-face confrontation, both pilots pressed on. At a distance of approximately ten miles, the huge UFO was seen to be 'discus-shaped' and metallic-grey in colour. Suddenly, at a radar-established distance of eight miles, the UFO rapidly accelerated skywards. Its movement was so fast that in an instant it completely disappeared from the radar scopes of the astonished navigators. Later estimations showed that it had vanished at the inconceivable speed of 18,000 mph!

Upon returning to base, all four officers were ordered to submit a full report, which was then forwarded to the Air Ministry. It was later discovered that a ground radar station at Sopley, near Bournemouth, had also tracked the UFO.

It was disclosed in the *Daily Herald* of September 23, 1956, that the Lincolnshire town of Cleethorpes had been 'rocked' by a mysterious explosion on September 15. Approximately one week later, a strange flying object was sighted in the same vicinity. One witness likened it to 'a glass globe with something white inside'.

The UFO was also sighted by staff of the Meteorological Office at the nearby Manby RAF Station. 'I don't know what it is. It certainly is not a balloon from here,' commented a spokesperson from the base, who had been able to study the UFO with a pair of binoculars.[10]

Following the incidents at Lakenheath and the Isle of Wight, it became apparent to an increasingly concerned Air Ministry that the UFO riddle was not going to disappear, much as that might have been the wish of the Government. Quite the contrary. It appeared that in both the 1956 cases the UFOs had been 'toying' with the aircrews, goading them into what was inevitably futile action. Was someone 'out there' testing the air defences of the British Isles? Were these merely random penetrations of British airspace, or were they the forerunners of an invasion force? The Air Ministry was taking no chances, and on December 6, 1956, new orders were issued to RAF stations in the event that any similar UFO encounters were reported.

The Ministry's previous instructions, 'Reports on Aerial Phenomena', had been circulated and classified at 'Restricted' level. Now, that was suddenly upgraded to 'Secret' level and, once again, personnel were warned not to discuss matters relative to UFOs outside of official channels. The updated version of the document contains a number of interesting amendments concerning the detection of UFOs by radar:

Radar detection of unusual targets is to be reported by stations through the normal channels. They should make a special report of any unusual response, i.e. any responses moving at a ground speed exceeding 700 knots, at any height and at any speed above 60,000 feet. When an unusual response is seen, the supervisor or NCO [in charge of the] watch should be informed and he should then check that the echo is not spurious, and arrange for the necessary records to be made to provide the information listed . . . below.

Reports on such phenomena should contain a personal assessment of, and where applicable a copy of, the following:

(a) Appearance of the echo.
(b) The signal strength of the echo (strong, medium and weak) throughout the time of observation, including pick-up and fade points.
(c) Range and bearing of initial plot and fade points.
(d) Ground speed.
(e) Whether painting of echo is continuous or intermittent.
(f) A copy of the record sheets, together with a track tracing.[11]

This highly important document, prepared by Squadron Leader G. D. Edwards of HQ No. 11 Group, again received a wide distribution. There is some evidence to suggest that the Lakenheath and Isle of Wight encounters were not the only ones that caused the Ministry concern in 1956. Nine months after Lakenheath, Conservative MP Major Patrick Wall learned that the Government had the details of six UFO sightings on file from 1956, none of which could be readily explained in conventional terms.[12]

As 1956 drew to a close, the Air Ministry continued to sift uneasily through the myriad reports, radar tapes, and film footage it had amassed concerning UFOs. It became clear that someone, or something, was taking an unhealthy amount of interest in the military capabilities of the British Government. And it wasn't about to go away.

CHAPTER 6

CLOSE ENCOUNTERS

WARDLE, LANCASHIRE, WAS THE FOCAL POINT FOR UFO ACTIVITY IN early 1957. On February 15, an unidentified aerial craft was sighted by a number of people in the area and the resulting publicity caused questions to be raised in the House of Commons. Obliged to answer, Mr Charles Orr-Ewing, Under-Secretary of State for Air, advised the House that those who had reported seeing the UFO had been mistaken. So what had been seen? Two hydrogen-filled toy balloons, illuminated by a torch bulb, which had been released into the air by a laundry mechanic from Rochdale![1] Incredibly, Orr-Ewing's explanation seemed to satisfy the House, and there the matter was laid to rest.

A full thirty-two years later, intriguing new information surfaced which cast doubt on the official explanation. Following a well-publicized UFO sighting at Heywood, Lancashire, on May 19, 1989, the editor of the *Heywood Advertiser* recalled his involvement in the Wardle mystery:

> Many years ago, as a young reporter, it fell to our lot to report on a strange sighting of an unusual object over Wardle . . . We went into it very thoroughly indeed and no matter what the discreditors threw at us, we proved them to be wrong . . . we continued to report the pros and cons of the debate for several weeks. That all came to an end when the very top man from the Ministry of

Defence called at our office personally, took us into a private back room and read the Official Secrets Act to us with the warning to discontinue reporting further on that strange occurrence.[2]

Responding to the 'toy balloon' explanation, the editor elaborated: 'How well I remember that laundry man! I asked him how he had filled the balloons with hydrogen and he was unable to explain, although he admitted it was not possible with the equipment he had. His story was untrue – and so were other hoax claims investigated at that time. It was after exploding these myths that I was silenced by the Official Secrets Act.'[3]

That the Government of the time would go so far as to invoke the use of the Official Secrets Act to silence the staff of a local newspaper implies that there was much more to the Wardle sighting than officialdom cared to admit. Perhaps we should not be too surprised that the Air Ministry's file on Wardle has failed to materialize.

Throughout 1957 there was an alarming rise in the number of UFO sightings reported around military stations. As far as I have been able to ascertain, the first such intrusions took place in March. Formerly classified at 'Secret' level is a one-page report outlining what took place:

(a) A report was received from Royal Air Force Church Lawford on 26th March, 1957 of a sighting of an unusual nature. The object moved at a speed timed as exceeding 1400 mph. This in itself was unusual as the object had accelerated to this speed from a stationary position. No explanation has yet been found for this sighting but a supplementary report, including a copy of the radar plot, was requested and has been received from Church Lawford this afternoon.

(b) Signals from Royal Air Force Stations Bempton and Laken-heath on 19th March reported unusual responses which did not resemble those from conventional aircraft. Aircraft sent to find the object made no contact with anything in the area of response. The Meteorological Office are at present trying to find whether any unusual phenomena were observed by their stations in that area.[4]

It is obvious that any object which has the capability to accelerate to 1,400 mph from a stationary position cannot remotely be classed as conventional. Such manoeuvres are far beyond the capabilities of even the most advanced aircraft flying today. Such seemingly impossible aerial feats are not uncommon in UFO reports. For example, according to a document found in the files of the US National Security Agency, two UFOs were seen over a radar installation at Flamenco Island, Fort Amador, on the Panama Canal, on March 10, 1958. The US Air Force Intelligence report on the case states: 'An attempt was made by members of the Radar Site, Flamenco Island, to observe the objects by searchlights. When the light touched the objects they traveled from an altitude of 2000 feet to 10,000 feet in five to ten seconds.'[5]

There can be no doubt that the reports filed by Church Lawford, Bempton and Lakenheath both puzzled and alarmed the Air Ministry, particularly since Lakenheath had witnessed a similar visit only months before.

Approximately two weeks after the sighting at Church Lawford, a further penetration of British airspace occurred, this time at RAF West Freugh, Wigtownshire. The official Air Ministry report on the case, classified for thirty years, has now been released:

1. On the morning of April 4th radar operators at West Freugh detected unidentified objects on the screens of their radars. A summary of this incident is given below:

2. The object was first observed as a stationary return on the screen of a radar at Balscalloch. Although its range remained appreciably constant for about 10 minutes its height appeared to alter from about 50,000 to 70,000 feet. A second radar was switched on and detected the 'object' at the same range and height.

3. The radar sets used were capable of following objects auto-matically besides being manually operated. The information is obtained in the form of polar co-ordinates. This information can be fed into a plotting board which displays the position of the object by means of an electronically operated pen, while the height is shown on a meter.

4. The unidentified object was tracked on the plotting table, each radar being switched on to the table in turn to check for discrepancies. After remaining at one spot for about 10 minutes the pen moved slowly in a NE direction, and gradually increased speed. A speed check was taken which showed a ground speed of 70 mph, the height was then 54,000 feet.

5. At this time another radar station 20 miles away, equipped with the same type of radars, was asked to search for the 'object'. [An] echo was picked up at the range and bearing given and the radar was 'locked on'.

6. After the 'object' had travelled about 20 miles it made a very sharp turn and proceeded to move SE at the same increasing speed. Here the reports of the two radar stations differ in details. The two at Balscalloch tracked an 'object' at about 50,000 feet at a speed of about 240 mph while the other followed an 'object' or 'objects' at 14,000 feet. As the 'objects' travelled towards the second radar site the operator detected four 'objects' moving in line astern about 4,000 yards from each other. This observation was confirmed later by the other radars, for when the object they were plotting passed out of range they were able to detect four other smaller objects before they too passed out of range.

7. It was noted by the radar operators that the sizes of the echoes were considerably larger than would be expected from normal aircraft. In fact they considered that the size was nearer that of a ship's echo.

8. It is deduced from these reports that altogether five objects were detected by the three radars. At least one of these rose to

an altitude of 70,000 feet while remaining appreciably stationary in azimuth and range. All of these objects appear to be capable of speeds of about 240 mph. Nothing can be said of physical construction except that they must have been either of considerable size or else constructed to be especially good reflectors.

9. There were not known to be any aircraft in the vicinity nor were there any meteorological balloons. Even if balloons had been in the area these would not account for the sudden change of direction and the movement at high speed against the prevailing wind.

10. Another point which has been considered is that the type of radar used is capable of looking onto heavily charged clouds. Cloud of this nature could extend up to the heights in question and cause abnormally large echoes on the radar screens. It is not thought however that this incident was due to such phenomena.

11. It is concluded that the incident was due to the presence of five reflecting objects of unidentified type and origin. It is considered unlikely that they were conventional aircraft, meteorological balloons or charged clouds.[6]

That the West Freugh sightings remained unidentified was something which caused the Air Ministry a considerable amount of unease – even more so when it became apparent that the media had latched on to the story. Witness the following 'Secret' report prepared by DDI (Tech):

It is unfortunate that the Wigtownshire radar incident fell into the hands of the press. The two other radar incidents have not been made public and reached us by means of official secret channels. We suggest that S. of S. [Secretary of State] does not specifically refer to these incidents as radar sightings. We suggest that . . . S. of S. might reply: 'Of the fifteen incidents reported this year, ten have been identified as conventional objects, two contain insufficient information for identification and three are under investigation.'[7]

On April 17, 1957, Stan Awbery, Labour MP for Bristol, raised the UFO issue with Secretary of State for Air, George Ward. '. . . what recent investigations have been made into unidentified flying objects; what photographs have been taken; and what reports have been made on this subject?' asked Awbery. In his response, Ward stated that: 'Reports are continually being received, and we investigate them wherever the details are sufficient. Most of the objects turn out to be balloons or meteors. One photograph recently received some publicity but was faked.'[8]

Why Ward did not inform the House of the recent incidents at Wardle, West Freugh, Bempton, Church Lawford and Lakenheath is something of a mystery. That is unless one takes the view, as I do, that the UFO subject was deemed so sensitive by the Air Ministry that the non-disclosure of information to Members of Parliament was thought justified.

Ward's assurances would not stand unchallenged for long. At 10.22 a.m. on April 29, two pairs of Hunter aircraft took off from RAF Odiham to engage in a mid-air exercise. At 45,000 feet one of the pilots found himself confronted by an unidentified aerial craft. I quote from the Air Ministry report generated in response to the pilot's encounter:

> . . . when over Hayling Island Mission 28 No. 2 saw a large white object at 10 o'clock slightly above. The object was circular with a white slightly curving tail hanging below. The time was approx 1110. Formation Leader was informed and both pairs turned east onto a northerly heading to look for the object. At first the object was thought to be a parachute but later it was realized that the object must have been larger and at a greater distance because of the slow passing speed.[9]

At 8.38 that evening the pilot of a Javelin aircraft, also based at RAF Odiham, was vectored onto a UFO reportedly seen some twelve miles from his position. No visual contact was made by the pilot and he eventually returned to base.[10] This encounter received coverage in a number of newspapers, and on May 1 an Air Ministry spokesperson made a brief statement to a journalist from the *Western Mail*: 'All we can say is that we are investigating the matter. Until inquiries are completed we have nothing further to add.'[11]

Following the Media coverage of the Odiham sightings, questions were once again asked in the House of Commons. '. . . what was the nature of the aircraft or other object sighted on the radar air defence screens on Monday night and which occasioned the dispatch of aircraft of Fighter Command?' asked Labour MP, Frank Beswick.

'They were two of the large number of Hunters of Fighter Command which were engaged in a training exercise on the night in question,' replied George Ward. 'Their movements as observed by radar were somewhat unusual, and aroused the suspicions of the radar defences. As a precaution, Javelins on patrol were ordered to intercept but the interception was abandoned when it became clear that the incident was a false alarm.'[12]

Since the once-secret file on Odiham has now been declassified, it can be seen that Ward's statement did not exactly sit well with the facts – especially his version of how the interception was abandoned. The official records do not say that 'it became clear that the incident was a false alarm?' Rather, they maintain that the pilot, having been sent to the location of the UFO sighting, simply failed to find anything – the distinction may be slight, but failure to locate something does not rule out its existence. Even more curiously, Ward made absolutely no mention of the large, white object seen earlier that day.

On the same day as the Odiham affair, a similar occurrence took place at RAF Ventnor on the Isle of Wight. According to the Air Ministry's own records, a civilian, Mr L. Humfreys, telephoned RAF Ventnor to report that he could see two metallic-like objects to the south-east of Shanklin, at a height of approximately 30,000 feet. 'The object appeared as a steady, metallic, very bright pinpoint of light, with a suggestion of [a] smaller round object immediately behind,' stated Mr Humfreys, whose account received support from three additional witnesses.

At 8.10 p.m., staff at the radar station at Beachy Head reported to Ventnor that they were tracking two unidentified responses flying at a height of 25,000 feet. Almost one hour later, Beachy Head contacted Ventnor again to report that RAF St Margarets was also plotting two fast-moving targets, but was unable to ascertain their height. One object was reported to be travelling in a south-westerly direction at a speed of between 750 and 800 knots.

Since all attempts to identify the objects failed, a detailed report was prepared by Pilot Officer R.F. Coles of RAF Ventnor, and all the relevant data (which included radar tapes) was forwarded to DDI (Tech) at Whitehall. Fortunately, the six-page report on the Isle of Wight encounters is now available for inspection in the archives of the Public Record Office.[13]

There is every indication that there are more events of 1957 waiting to be fully investigated. In 1992 Timothy Good and Dr John Mason, then President of the British Astronomical Association, took part in a radio interview on BBC Radio 5. During the course of the debate, a listener telephoned the studio to report the details of an incident in April 1957.

The caller related that at the time he was stationed at RAF Tangmere as part of his national service. During the course of one particular evening, he was on duty with an officer when an unknown target was picked up on the base radar scopes.

> We scrambled two jets from Tangmere; they went up and they said, 'What the hell are we chasing?' We said, 'We don't know; that's your job.' That's how the conversation went. As far as they were concerned they were chasing a green light. When they accelerated this thing moved away from them. We chased this thing for the best part of almost 300 miles and the jets had to come down because they were running out of fuel.
>
> A few days later the officer and I were called into a meeting with a lot of very senior officers, who said we'd been chasing a meteor . . . When [the officer] and I went back to look at the [radar] tapes, because everything we did was recorded, the tapes had been removed, and we were told the incident was closed.

A remarkable aerial encounter, which almost resulted in a mid-air collision between a UFO and a Meteor jet, occurred over RAF Gaydon, Warwickshire, on the evening of 21 October, 1957. As I have been unable to locate the Air Ministry's own assessment of the event, I quote from a report which was published on October 27 in the *Sunday Express*:

> The Air Ministry is investigating the sighting last week of an unidentified flying object over the airfield at Gaydon, Warwickshire, one of the RAF's top V-bomber stations. It was seen by a night fighter pilot and picked up by ground radar. Could the object have been a Russian spy plane? Last night there was no official explanation. The Air Ministry is awaiting the report of a senior intelligence officer who has visited Gaydon and other stations concerned. This is the first time that an unidentified flying object – as the Air Ministry calls them – has been detected both from the air and the ground.
>
> These are the facts confirmed by the Air Ministry. At 9.18 p.m. last Monday, Flying Officer D.W. Sweeney, a pilot of considerable experience, was flying a Meteor on a training exercise from RAF Station North Luffenham. At 28,000 feet, flying west, he almost collided with an object which, he said, was moving slowly and showing six lights. He calculated he was directly over Gaydon where atom-bomber crews train in Valiants.
>
> After taking violent avoiding action Flying Officer Sweeney approached the object from the starboard side. As he got near, the lights went out and the object vanished. On landing he reported the incident. He said the object was not very large and its outline was blurred.
>
> Senior officers at once connected Flying Officer Sweeney's report with a radar sighting reported a few minutes earlier from RAF Station Langtoff. This report confirmed that the object was at about 28,000 feet over Gaydon. A check on military and civil aircraft movements showed that the Meteor was the only aircraft in the area at the time.[14]

On the night of December 2, 1957, an unusual aerial device was sighted over Toppler's Hill, near Biggleswade in Bedfordshire. One of those who saw the object, which was later described as resembling a 'flying sun', was an RAF officer, Flight Lieutenant Jack Hunter, who was attending a course on guided missiles at Henlow. Thinking that no-one would believe his account, Hunter stayed silent for five months. When contacted by the press in May 1958, he stated, 'I was a complete sceptic about flying saucers.'[15]

Although reports of face-to-face encounters with extra-terrestrials are somewhat rare in the British Isles, one such incident, involving two members of the Territorial Army, took place in Scotland in November 1958.

As part of their training, an Aberdeen-based unit of the TA had been dispatched to an area near Balmoral to take part in weekend manoeuvres. During the exercise two of the group were deployed to guard a small hilltop and, fully equipped, set about digging themselves a trench for cover.

In the early hours of the morning, just as dawn was breaking, both heard what they described as a strange 'gurgling' sound which seemed to emanate from behind a group of trees, several hundred yards from their position. Somewhat curious, they set out to investigate, when two huge figures emerged from the shadows and proceeded towards them. Both witnesses were horrified to see that the creatures were more than seven feet in height. Naturally overcome with terror, the Territorials hastily retreated. As they ran they heard a 'swishing noise', and glancing over their shoulders saw a gigantic, disc-shaped object in the sky which appeared to be following them. Reportedly 'pulsating', the object swooped low over their heads and disappeared trailing a shower of sparks.

I have been unable to determine whether or not the incident was reported officially, but Charles Bowen, a former editor of *Flying Saucer Review*, was sufficiently impressed by the case to make mention of it in *The Humanoids*, one of the first books to document reports of so-called 'close encounters of the third kind' – incidents where non-human beings have been seen in close proximity to UFOs.[16]

Between 7.25 p.m. and 7.45 p.m. on the evening of February 25, 1959, an unidentified flying object was sighted hovering over London (now Heathrow) Airport by four separate witnesses. One of those fortunate enough to have seen the UFO was an Air Traffic Control Officer at the airport, who studied the craft for several minutes through binoculars before checking with operators to see if any unexplained air traffic had been monitored.

Although nothing untoward was picked up on radar, one of the witnesses stated that the UFO resembled 'the reflection of a searchlight on the clouds'. He was keen to stress, however, that the sky had been entirely devoid of cloud cover at the time of the encounter.

As a result of the sighting, officials at the airport asked RAF Fighter Command at Stanmore to conduct an investigation. They in turn authorized the release of the following statement concerning the UFO: 'Bright yellow light varying in intensity some 200 feet from the ground. It stayed in one position for about twenty minutes, then climbed away at high speed.'

Although the possibility was raised that the UFO had been a weather balloon, this was disproved when an official at London Airport informed the media that no balloons had been in the area at the time. Pressed for an answer, the Air Ministry found itself directly embroiled in the controversy and conceded that the sighting would be logged as 'an unidentified flying object because there was no immediate explanation for it'.

It would not be long before the Air Ministry maintained that the case had been resolved. According to a spokesperson at the airport, the stationary light viewed for approximately twenty minutes had been merely the planet Venus. What of the light that 'climbed away at high speed'? The nose cone of a civilian aircraft, said the Air Ministry.[17]

Frank Edwards, author of a number of books about UFOs, wrily questioned the Ministry's explanation:

> The Air Ministry announced that the glowing disc had been nothing more remarkable than 'the nose cone of a civilian plane'. How it had hovered in one spot for twenty minutes was not explained, of course.
>
> London Airport, unaware that planes can allegedly hover while their nose cones glow in the dark, issued a statement on that same morning of March 6. The Airport claimed that the hovering object had been 'the planet Venus, seen through a layer of clouds.'

[*Author's note*: We already have the testimony of one witness that
the sky was entirely cloud-free.] The Airport failed to mention the
alleged plane's nose cone . . . nor did they explain how Venus got
down to two hundred feet altitude . . .[18]

It was revealed on July 27, 1959, that for almost a year an unusual
phenomenon had been perplexing radar specialists at the Marconi Research
Station at Great Baddow, near Chelmsford, Essex. The mystery began
early one morning in mid-1958, when a number of scientists at the station
noticed the appearance of a strange point of light on their radar screens.
It appeared to spread out into a ring, then faded and vanished. This was
repeated several times, and the effect was likened to the spreading ripples
of water on a pond. The rings lasted for 2½ to 6 minutes. An identical
event occurred several days later, but this time the phenomenon had moved
from its original position to a different location.

The puzzled scientists began to investigate the strange 'ring angels', as
they later dubbed them, and over the following twelve months recorded
'ring angel' activity at more than seventy sites throughout the south-east of
England. Despite this, there were no corresponding visual sightings. The
rings began to appear all over the south and east of the country: reports
surfaced from Ipswich, Reading, Canterbury and Tunbridge Wells. Nor
were the 'ring angels' hindered by changing weather patterns, as evidenced
by the fact that a number of positive radar trackings were made in areas
engulfed by fog.

Was it possible that flocks of birds were the culprits? This theory
was examined by Dr E. Eastwood, Director of Research at the station, and it was found that several of the rings had been reported
in areas which were regular roosting sites for starlings. This speculation was weakened when it was noticed that some of the speeds
of movement displayed by the 'ring angels' were greater than those
expected of birds. Dr Eastwood elaborated: 'Another problem is that
if these are bird roosts, the birds don't use them every night. Our
once-a-week observations don't show the same centres each time by
any means.'

Another theory put forward was that they originated as a result of
changing patterns in the air itself. 'This makes it a very attractive theory,'

said Dr Eastwood, 'except that no-one has satisfactorily explained why the air should produce a radar echo.'[19]

Despite the lack of a conclusive answer, the rings presented no long-term interference to the practical use of the radar sets, nor to the mystified operators.

A brightly lit UFO was viewed by thousands of people in London and the south-east of England on the evening of September 5, 1959. The UFO was initially seen between 8.32 and 8.40 p.m. by the pilots of at least six different airliners flying a variety of routes throughout Europe. According to a pilot who had just taken off from Jersey, the object was 'giving off pink and blue sparks'. The crew of an Amsterdam-bound airliner reported seeing 'three green lights'. This was something supported by Captain Herbert Bailey, the pilot of a British European Airways flight en route to London from Paris:

> I first saw the object when I was about twelve thousand feet over Abbeville, in northern France. It was in the form of a vivid green line followed by an equally brilliant red flash, which cut horizontally right across the sky. It was not moving very fast and at one time seemed to fill a third of my cockpit window.
>
> I couldn't tell how far away it was, but from my own height I should say it was about twenty thousand feet from the ground. After a few moments the trail of light gradually broke up and sections set off at a tangent. The remaining largest pieces of light – that's all I can call it – circled down towards the earth and faded from my view.

As press interest in the case reached fever pitch, a senior London Airport official went on record with the following statement: 'We have no idea what this thing could have been, but we are treating the reports seriously since they are all from responsible sources.'

A control supervisor at the airport later logged the reports in his duty book, stating: 'It is not our responsibility to refer this kind of information to the [UFO] Department at the Air Ministry; that is up to the military.'

Shortly after Captain Bailey's aerial encounter, Dick Thomason, a farmer, of Bowers Gifford near Basildon, Essex, said that in company with his wife, he had seen the object as it headed towards the ground: '. . . we saw this thing coming in pretty low, looking like a miniature flying bomb with a blue flame behind it. It seemed to be coming down, but vanished as it got down to about tree-top height.'

As a result of the Thomasons' sighting, and other reports received at both Pitsea and Billericay police stations, five police cars were dispatched to Bowers Gifford to search for the object, which was presumed crashed. With the assistance of local villagers, an intensive search was conducted. No sign of the object was ever found.[20]

Ernest Sears served with the Royal Air Force during the Second World War and was de-mobbed in 1947. In 1960 he was witness to an encounter much like that which occurred on August 13, 1956, when two RAF fighter planes were ordered to intercept a UFO which had intruded upon British airspace.

Of particular interest is the setting: the Air Surface Weapons Establishment near Portsmouth. While walking through the nearby town of Gosport, Sears noticed a 'glowing cigar' in the sky which seemed to be hovering over the complex. 'I thought, well, it must be an aircraft struggling against the wind, and the sun is shining off it making it glow,' said Sears. Thirty minutes later he realized that his initial assumption had been very wrong. Without prior warning the sky was suddenly filled with the rumble of jet engines.

I ran to a vantage point where I could see where these aircraft were coming from. They were two Meteor jets, very low over the rooftops [and] very noisy. They were climbing up towards where, half an hour later, to my amazement, there was this 'cigar' still hanging in the sky. I immediately knew that it wasn't an aircraft. It hadn't moved an inch; it was just hanging there. These two jets climbed up towards it, and as they got near it, it turned on end and it was like somebody switching a light bulb out; it disappeared.

I ran to a phone box and I found the number of Thorney Island aerodrome. I got the control tower and said, 'Can you just tell me what that object was over Portsdown Hill that those two Meteor jets were chasing?' He said, 'You didn't see any object, neither did you see any jets.'

Somewhat bewildered by this, Sears remonstrated with the man and assured him of the veracity of his report. The Thorney Island official could not be budged: 'I repeat, you did not see any object; you did not see any jets.' Sensing that this was not getting him anywhere, Sears simply thanked the man and hung up.

'The odd thing was,' said Sears, 'my brother-in-law at the time used to work at [the Air Surface Weapons Establishment] on Portsdown Hill; he was an electrical draughtsman. He happened to come over the next night just for a social visit. He walked in and my wife went out into the kitchen to make him a cup of tea, and I just said to him, "You had some excitement over your place yesterday morning didn't you?" He looked at me, and his face went grey, then it went white and his mouth set in a grim line. I said, "OK, don't worry; forget I said it."'[21]

Having heard Sears' account I am completely satisfied that something truly extraordinary did occur on that day back in 1960. Perhaps in time the full story will surface – or does the fact that the encounter took place over a sensitive military establishment preclude our learning the truth?

On the night of September 9, 1960, an unidentified flying object, described as a 'triangular formation of lights with a red light in the centre' was viewed by various people in the Consett, South Shields, Fawdon and Fenham areas of Newcastle. Mr J. Leslie Otley said that his wife and two neighbours saw the UFO circling over Fenham between 9.15 p.m. and 9.40 p.m. 'A friend of mine, Mr A. Miller, telephoned to say he saw them too, over Consett at 8.30 p.m.,' added Mr Otley, who later telephoned RAF Acklington to report the sighting.

After having been pressed by the *Newcastle Evening Chronicle* for comment, a spokesperson at Acklington admitted that he had received two independent reports of the UFO, and that these were being forwarded to the Air Ministry for examination. He also added, somewhat cryptically,

'I have no further information about this, and even if I had, we are not allowed to release information.'[22]

Another intriguing incident occurred during the small hours of a Sunday morning in 1960. A Mr C.F. Coventry of Tilehurst, Reading, awoke from his sleep and, upon entering his bathroom, viewed through the open window a football-sized object, black in colour and surrounded by six very radiant lights. Since the object appeared to be almost stationary in the eastern sky, Mr Coventry returned to his bedroom which, like the bathroom, faced north-east.

'I pulled the curtains back wide and got back into bed and watched the strange object,' stated Mr Coventry. He proceeded to measure out some twelve to fifteen inches of the window pane which, he said, it took the object approximately fifteen minutes to cross. As he watched the UFO it appeared to change shape and its six lights gave way to nine. Mr Coventry continued to watch the UFO until 4.45 a.m. when, in complete silence, it disappeared in a northerly direction.

Mr Coventry was employed at the Headquarters of the RA Flying Training Command, Shifnal Park, in the Air Ministry Works Department. One would imagine that he was experienced in aircraft recognition. This object was, without doubt, something out of the ordinary and no conventional explanation is possible.

CHAPTER 7

OFFICIAL INVESTIGATIONS: 1961–1966

IN RESPONSE TO ENQUIRIES FROM THE GENERAL PUBLIC, THE Ministry of Defence, until recently, had always steadfastly asserted that the earliest UFO files held in its own archives and at the Public Record Office date from 1962; all reports prior to that time had been routinely destroyed. This was plainly astonishing, particularly when one considers the many UFO reports filed by military sources in the 1940s and 1950s. However, there is now an admission on the Ministry's part that a number of papers dating from earlier years – such as those detailing the sightings at West Freugh, Topliffe, Bempton, and the Isle of Wight – appear to have slipped through the net and can be examined at the Public Record Office at Kew.[1]

If, as the MOD admit, UFO files dating from 1962 were marked for permanent retention, one would imagine that in keeping with the Government's 'thirty-year ruling' these particular papers would have been routinely declassified at the end of 1992. This has not proven to be the case, as Nick Pope of the MOD explained to me in 1993:

> In my letter to you . . . I suggested that some pre-1967 material may have survived. I have recently looked into this, and confirm that this is the case; the reason for this is that although prior to 1967 it was not felt that UFO material was sufficiently important

to be kept, all files would have been kept for around five years anyway, prior to destruction. I believe that some material from as early as 1962 has survived. The reason why these reports have not yet been released is that they are in files where the last enclosures are more recent, and files can only be released when the most recent enclosure is thirty years old. The good news is that you will not have to wait until 1997: it is not our practice to comment in detail on material that has not yet been released, but I understand that two files . . . are due for release in January 1994. I suggest that you contact the Public Record Office early next year.[2]

I find Pope's statement that '. . . prior to 1967 it was not felt that UFO material was sufficiently important to be kept . . .' somewhat perplexing. It is at odds with the stance taken by the Air Ministry in earlier years, particularly in 1953, 1956 and 1957, when there are clear indications that UFOs were viewed with the utmost seriousness.

Nevertheless, I followed Pope's advice and in January 1994 contacted the Public Record Office. They subsequently forwarded me copies of the two aforementioned files, which cover the period 1961 to 1963 and amount to an incredible 611 pages! Whilst the papers certainly give us a rare glimpse into the workings of the Air Ministry in the early 1960s, they seem to raise more questions than they answer.

The majority of the papers are concerned with routine matters: responding to enquiries from UFO researchers regarding details of Air Ministry policy on UFOs and analysing UFO reports forwarded to Whitehall by members of the general public. Indeed, save for one solitary report which was possibly the result of a genuine mis-identification of an air-to-air refuelling operation, there is a complete absence of UFO reports filed by military personnel.

The sceptic would argue that this is because no such reports existed. Had the previously cited encounters at Topcliffe, Gaydon, Lakenheath and Odiham, among others, not taken place, then I would be tempted to agree. Is there an adequate explanation as to why there should have been an abundance of UFO reports filed by the military in the 1940s and 1950s, yet so few in the 1961–1963 period?

It becomes apparent from examining the two files that both originated with a particular Air Ministry secretariat known as S6. In turn, S6 received occasional assistance from another division, S4. Although S4 was involved in the analysis of the gun-camera footage which showed a UFO in flight over England in 1956, it appears that by the 1960s its role in UFO investigations had been greatly reduced.

Now, according to a two-page memorandum the Air Ministry announced, on November 14, 1962, that a decision had been taken to 're-write the Standard Operating Procedures' concerning reports of unidentified flying objects. A brief extract from the memo reveals the following: 'Reports from civilian sources and replies thereto are dealt with by S6, and reports from service sources, including unidentified radar responses, are dealt with by A.I. (Tech) 5(b).'[3]

No wonder the files of S6 are so lacking in quality UFO reports from military sources such as Royal Air Force pilots and ground radar operators: the investigation of such encounters was never a part of S6's official remit. Moreover, a study of a number of internal papers generated by S6, following an enquiry by a member of the public, reveals that the department was completely unaware of the official RAF Intelligence investigation into the UFO incident at Topcliffe in 1952. This leads me to believe that staff within S6 did not possess the necessary 'need to know' to have access to the more sensitive UFO reports. So S6 was little more than a collection point for UFO sightings of no security importance, reported by the public at large.

It is apposite here to relate an encounter described to me by a Royal Air Force officer, 'K.R.' He witnessed a UFO while flying from El Adem in Libya to Nicosia in Cyprus on September 11, 1962, and filed a report with RAF Intelligence, as did his commanding officer. Needless to say, the files of S6, which cover the September 1962 period, make absolutely no mention of the experience.[4]

It has already been established that serious involvement on the part of the Deputy Directorate of Intelligence (Technical) (DDI (Tech)) in UFO studies dates back to at least 1953. I have also revealed that in December of that year new reporting procedures were implemented to ensure that all UFO reports filed by service sources reached that department.

We now have evidence that AI (Tech) 5b was exclusively responsible for the study of UFO reports received from the military in the early 1960s. What do their files tell us? Curiously, they have not surfaced. However, during the course of conducting enquiries into the workings of the department, I have unearthed several interesting facts.

Sec (AS) 2a, a branch of the Ministry of Defence involved in the investigation of UFO encounters today, flatly refuses to discuss AI (Tech) 5b beyond saying that it was 'a specialist military division which cast an expert eye over UFO reports, as part of its normal duties concerned with the air defence of the UK. As is the case today, it is not our practice to discuss details of the role and duties of such branches'.[5]

Therefore, I determined to contact the MOD's Records Management Division in an attempt to ascertain what the official MOD position was regarding possible public access to the files of AI (Tech) 5b. Situated within St Christopher House, Southwark Street, London, the Records Management Division fulfils three main functions:

(a) to advise MOD branches, service and civilian establishments on good registry practices;

(b) to provide accommodation for records that have both administrative and potential historical value;

(c) to review records with the view to selecting those worthy of preservation in compliance with the terms of the Public Records Act of 1958 and 1967.

There is also a liaison with the Public Record Office, ensuring that departments comply with the act. To identify records for preservation the MOD has adopted a two-stage review process, called first and second review. Files are initially reviewed some six years after closure. At this stage, two things can happen. Files that are perceived as having no historical or administrative value are automatically destroyed. Where there is some administrative but no historical value, papers are usually retained for a period no longer than twenty years. However, on occasions when the records are seen as having historical value, they survive for a second review, which takes place after twenty-five years.

At this point, files are either transferred to the Public Record Office for preservation or are destroyed. Records that are selected for permanent preservation are carefully assessed for any remaining sensitivity that might preclude release at the normal point, i.e. at the start of the thirty-first year.

Should any records be deemed not releasable, for reasons such as defence of the realm, the Lord Chancellor's approval is sought to keep the records closed from public viewing. Requests for continued closure of records are scrutinized by officials from both the Public Record Office and the Lord Chancellor's Advisory Council before submission to the Lord Chancellor.[6]

Is it possible that action has been taken to ensure that the files of AI (Tech) 5b which concern military-originated UFO encounters remain exempt from public disclosure? According to I.D. Goode, the Deputy Departmental Record Officer at the MOD's Records Management Division, this is not the case:

> I am sorry it has taken so long to provide a response to your letter of the 19 May 1994 in which you asked about surviving Air Intelligence, Technical Branch 5b files . . . We are in an identical position to the Public Record Office in that we also do not carry out research on behalf of the public on material that is freely available at Kew, i.e. the examination of lists of records selected for permanent preservation. Notwithstanding this, and in an attempt to be helpful, I have asked my staff to make a cursory examination of our own copy of the PRO listings. These lists not only include open records but also those selected that are currently closed to the public. I regret to advise [you] that whilst there are a few A.I. files preserved at the PRO none appear to have originated from AI5b. It would therefore seem to be the case that papers from this particular branch appear not to have survived the selection process. You will recall . . . that records not selected for preservation are destroyed, we must therefore assume this is what happened to the records of AI5b.[7]

I am quite sure that this reply is sincere, but it does leave us with a singular puzzle. We have seen that the UFO files of S6, which only concern reports filed by members of the public, were deemed worthy of preservation since they are now openly available for study at the Public Record Office. Yet the papers of AI (Tech) 5b – which one would imagine to have been of greater importance since they dealt with encounters between UFOs and the military – are reported to have been destroyed. Would the MOD really have permitted this? Is there an alternative explanation?

The only other possibility is this: the records of AI (Tech) 5b which do deal with UFO sightings submitted to the Air Ministry by forces personnel have not yet been forwarded to the Records Managemement Branch for possible future declassification. By their own admission, staff at the RMB can only review MOD documents some six years after the date of the last recorded action on the file in question. If AI (Tech) 5b did investigate some truly bizarre UFO encounters in the early 1960s – which involved Britain's military and which also had implications for the defence of the realm – it may be that those files are still routinely examined in the continuing search for answers to the UFO question.

If this is so, then these records would still be awaiting 'last recorded action' and would not have been passed on to the Records Management Branch. This theory provides a reasonable explanation as to why there is a complete lack of high-calibre UFO reports in Government files for the period 1961 to 1963, in contrast to those for the 1940s and 1950s.

Are we then to remain in total ignorance regarding the work of AI (Tech) 5b? Not completely. While that department's crucial files are hidden or lost, a study of the papers of S6 reveals that, on a number of occasions when UFO reports submitted to Whitehall by members of the general public could not be readily identified, S6 would ask for assistance from AI (Tech) 5b. By necessity, this inter-branch collaboration resulted in the generation of some paperwork which was permanently retained by S6. That paperwork shows that staff assigned to AI (Tech) 5b displayed considerable knowledge in areas such as astronomy and meteorology, and often, though not always convincingly, offered explanations for UFO sightings forwarded to them by S6. But, for that period, we shall not know the essential facts of our Governments' knowledge of and response to UFOs until the authorities see fit to release the relevant documents.

* * *

Throughout August 1963, S6 found itself overrun with UFO reports. On August 11, Mr T.J. Brack of the Air Ministry advised S6 that on the previous evening he had received the details of several UFO sightings from people in the London area. '. . . I regret that I was unable to dissuade two of the callers from requesting an official Air Ministry acknowledgement of and comment on their reports,' wrote Mr Brack in a memorandum to S6 which concerned the sighting of a 'bright light which moved . . . in a step like manner' over the city of London.[8]

At 11.55 p.m. on August 26, a 'bright round white light' was seen over Southampton. 'It was moving fast from S. to N. when first sighted. Then remained stationary for about 10 minutes before moving off N. at high speed,' wrote Mr D.E. Saunders in a letter to Mr R.H. White of S6.[9]

At 1.50 a.m. on August 27, Mr W. Hooper of Beckenham, Kent was awakened from his sleep by his wife, who had been watching 'a ball of incandescent gas, red and black [which] was about a foot in diameter, and gave the impression of intense heat . . .' In a letter written to the Air Ministry on September 9, Mr Hooper wrote: '[The UFO] started moving at an incredible speed in a northerly direction and was out of sight in a matter of about 4 seconds . . . I hope you will not try and persuade me that the object was a Meteorological Balloon as these as far as I know could not possibly travel against the wind.'[10]

In retrospect, the UFO sighting which garnered the most attention from S6 in 1963 took place on August 1. 'For the second night in succession scores of people rang the Air Ministry to report a mysterious triangular object in the sky over the London area. The Ministry could not explain it,' reported the *Daily Herald*.[11] A similar account appeared in the *Daily Express*: 'People in Kent and Essex phoned the Air Ministry in London last night asking about a "mystery object" seen in the sky and described as triangular or diamond-shaped. But official spokesmen could give no positive explanation.'[12]

Shortly afterwards, the Air Ministry issued the following statement: '[The UFO] was in fact a cosmic radiation research balloon, tetrahedral in shape, some 70 feet across . . . Several of these were released on the Continent in connection with the International Year of the Quiet Sun and one or two of them drifted over this country.'[13]

One of those who informed the Air Ministry that he had seen the UFO was none other than Timothy Good. He told me in 1994: 'I have checked my records regarding the object I (and many others) sighted on 1 August 1963. In fact, I did not receive a letter from the Air Ministry, nor did I write one to them. I reported the incident via phone the following day, and later, the AM spokesman phoned me back to give the "explanation".'[14]

There are several reasons for believing that the official explanation may have been erroneous. First, as Good points out, the object he saw was of a markedly different shape to that of the cosmic radiation research balloons.[15]

Second, according to Flight Lieutenant B.J. Skibinski of RAF Wattisham, the sightings of August 1 were the subject of a 'Confidential Signal' dated August 6, 1963.[16] If the object was deemed to be terrestrial in nature, why the need to classify the case at 'Confidential' level in the first place?

Third, and most notably, on November 8, 1963, Flight Lieutenant A. Mackenzie Hay of Headquarters Fighter Command issued a 'Confidential' memo to the Air Ministry which mentioned that, 'RAF Trimingham have full records of the occurrence . . .' Why would this be so? Since the only papers presently available for scrutiny which refer to the August 1 sighting are those generated by S6, it seems odd that a Royal Air Force station on the coast of Norfolk would have had in its possession 'full records' of what took place.[17] I can only assume that there must be other documentation in existence, perhaps generated at 'base level', which has still not seen the light of day.

There are good grounds for believing that the Meteorological Office also played a role (at least peripherally) in the August 1 encounter. A one-page memo concerning public interest in the case was sent by Mr G. Clark, the Meteorological Officer at New Ranges, Shoeburyness, Essex, to the Director-General of the Meteorological Office: 'This seems to fall within your orbit, or should I say trajectory?' Mr Clark jokingly wrote on October 26, 1963.[18]

Paul Greensill retired from the British Army in 1962 after having served with the 9th Independent Parachute Regiment of the Royal Engineers. In 1963, with a satisfying and successful military career behind him, he enlisted in the Territorial Army, inadvertently setting himself on course for an encounter which has left an indelible impression.

In August of that year, Greensill had been posted to the Ripon area of Yorkshire where, along with some forty colleagues, he was due to take part in a night-time exercise on the moors. Initially, it had been the intention that the unit would parachute into the area but this was abandoned, and they were eventually driven by lorry.

At about 11.30 p.m., as the unit settled into its pre-planned activities, something extraordinary occurred. With no prior warning, a circular object, lit by a dazzlingly bright white light, appeared in the sky as if from nowhere and hovered above the amazed TAs for around two minutes. Again without warning, the object suddenly accelerated away at an incredible speed and came to a sudden halt some distance away from its original position. There it stayed for another two minutes, after which it 'shot away' at an amazing velocity. No official report was filed, but Greensill has never forgotten the experience.

To this day he has no idea what was seen, but emphasized to me that it had been neither an aircraft nor a helicopter. The object operated in complete silence, and its fantastic manoeuvrability rules out a conventional vehicle as being responsible.[19]

The description given by Greensill sounds not unlike that made by Mr D.E. Saunders, who saw a 'bright round white light . . . moving fast' over Southampton during that same month. I prefer not to deal in speculation, but cannot help but suspect that both men were reporting independent sightings of the same UFO.

For some reason, the Ripon area of Yorkshire seems to get more than its fair share of outstanding UFO encounters. We shall see that an incident very similar to that reported by Greensill occurred in 1987, again in the midst of an army exercise on the moors, at the nearby village of Bishop Monkton. To my mind, this is beyond coincidence and I can only guess as to why the UFOs are skulking around mainland Britain in the dead of night, during military operations no less . . .

Following the mass of encounters reported in August 1963, the Air Ministry received an invitation to take part in a proposed television

documentary on the subject of UFOs which was being produced by
Associated Rediffusion. This presented the Air Ministry with a number
of problems, as a recently declassified memorandum from September
1963 shows:

1. The Associated Rediffusion programme, 'Here and Now',
who will transmit on October 1, a valuable programme on the
Officers and Aircrew Selection Centre at Biggin Hill, have asked
us for help in connection with another programme which will be
recorded next week at their Kingsway studios.
2. The programme will deal with 'Flying Saucers' and they will
have a number of the so-called 'experts' explaining why they are
sure such objects exist.
3. I have discussed this with Mr Langton of S6 who naturally
would have preferred it if we were not asked to take part at all.
However, since the T.V. company have said that if an official
cannot be made available they would like a statement of Air
Ministry views, Mr Langton is prepared to agree that it might
be better to appear willing by providing someone to speak (to
a prepared brief) rather than appearing to dodge the issue. He
would himself agree to take part, or Flight Lieutenant Bardsley
of Air Intelligence provided we could stipulate with the television
producer the following points:

(a) The official should be recorded apart from others taking part
in the programme;
(b) He does not have to meet the 'experts';
(c) He is not named.

4. The reason for the above is that we do not wish to get into an
unreasonable argument with these 'experts' and we do not want
them to know who deals with the subject at Air Ministry so that
telephone calls and letters are addressed direct to these officials or
officers.
5. Apart from my desire to help a television producer who is
helping us on another matter, I feel sure we could gain something
from taking part by explaining some of the known causes of

sightings. By educating at least part of the public we might cut down some of the reports we receive. There is no doubt that if we do not do something to mitigate the effects of the programme, S6 stands to receive a further flood of letters on the subject.

6. May I have your instructions please, after consulting D.U.S.2, as I am under some pressure from Associated Rediffusion for an answer.

11 September, 1963. R.C.Moody.[20]

On September 13, a decision was made that the Air Ministry would not participate directly in the documentary. Instead, the use of an official statement was authorized which, in part, mentioned that 'about ten per cent of flying objects reported to the Air Ministry are not explained and they remain unidentified because the evidence given about them is not sufficient . . . a vivid imagination is no substitute for accurate observation'.[21] Wisely, the Air Ministry chose not to inform Associated Rediffusion of the many UFO reports filed in the 1940s and 1950s by RAF pilots and ground radar operators . . .

It is interesting to note the desire to 'mitigate the effects of the programme'. This may be an innocent comment but it is a sad reality that the British Government's involvement in the UFO subject attracts very little serious coverage in the media. Having already established that the Government brought pressure to bear on one British newspaper in 1957 for reporting on the issue of UFOs, I do not discount the possibility that similar tactics may have been used against other papers and other media.

At noon on November 22, 1963, the *Thrift*, an Aberdeen-based collier ship, arrived in Blyth eight hours overdue after an unsuccessful search for a 'mystery object' off Girdleness.

The *Thrift* had been heading south for Blyth the day before when shortly before 6.00 p.m. four members of the crew, including the skipper, Captain J. Murray, saw a 'flashing red light' which passed within a mile of her port side. At a point three miles astern of the ship, the light vanished.

Captain Murray quickly alerted Stonehaven radio, put his vessel about, and made for the spot where the light was last seen. As the *Thrift* closed in, two distinct radar contacts were picked up on her screens – at a distance of about a quarter of a mile, they suddenly vanished. For three hours the *Thrift* searched, circling the area in vain. At one point a Shackleton aircraft from RAF Kinloss was dispatched and dropped flares onto the surface of the sea. Nothing was found.

'We could not make out what the light was,' said Captain Murray. 'It passed about three quarters of a mile off our port side, flashing brilliantly until it disappeared. It made no sound at all, yet we could hear the Shackleton when it was miles away. Judging by the way the radar contacts disappeared from our screen it seems that whatever was there must have sunk before we could get to it. We found no trace of wreckage during our search, but something definitely fell into the water.'[22]

On April 1, 1964 the Air Ministry and its associated branches, plus the War Office and the Admiralty, were unified into one centralized body – the Ministry of Defence. As a result, both S6 and S4 ceased to exist and their work was transferred to two new divisions. S4 Air and Defence Secretariat 8 (DS8). I have come across no evidence to suggest that the involvement of S4 Air and DS8 with respect to the UFO mystery was in any way different to that of their two predecessors; both continued routinely to analyse UFO reports received from members of the general public.

Neither division could accurately be termed 'UFO HQ', as the former head of DS8, Ralph Noyes, recalls:

Although Jenny Randles (among others) has frequently paid me the exciting compliment of supposing that I was 'the former Head of the MOD's UFO department', my Division, DS8 ... was nothing of the kind. DS8's job was to act in support of RAF operations. We only received reports of unidentified aerial phenomena lest they should, perchance, indicate that our air defence capabilities were less adequate than we hoped.

A sister Division (though I trust I shall not be thought sexist in so describing it) also received such reports whenever the clerks responsible for the distribution of papers considered that the report reaching the MOD indicated a complaint about low flying rather than a possible Russian intrusion. In consequence, there was often something of a muddle between DS8 and its colleagues about which of us should deal with the latest 'ghost story'. But neither of us was a 'UFO department'.[23]

Noyes' recollections appear to clarify the early activities of S4 Air and DS8, but what of AI (Tech) 5b, responsible for the receipt of UFO reports submitted by military personnel in the early 1960s?

Following the creation of the Ministry of Defence, Air Intelligence, of which AI (Tech) 5b was a part, was combined with the intelligence divisions of the Admiralty and the War Office to create the Defence Intelligence Staff.[24] Although the DIS primarily operates out of the MOD's Main Building at Whitehall, testimony now available suggests that, at some point during the 1960s, certain investigations into UFO encounters were undertaken by intelligence operatives at a wholly separate location.

According to at least three sources – an air traffic controller in the RAF in the 1980s, known to Jenny Randles, a retired Air Force mechanic interviewed by myself in mid-1996, and Cyril Townsend-Withers – one particular military facility which was (and possibly still is) deeply involved in the study of the UFO controversy is RAF Farnborough, Hampshire.[25]

Relevant to this matter is an account related to author and investigator Arthur Shuttlewood by the wife of a former Royal Air Force employee. According to the woman, in the period 1965–1966, her husband was employed at the Royal Aircraft Establishment (RAE) at Farnborough, where he specialized in the field of telemetry (the process of recording readings of instruments and transmitting them by radio). As she recalled: 'One day he met me and was unduly quiet. I asked what was the matter and he told me I must not tell anyone.'

As the woman listened, her husband revealed what was troubling him so much. Apparently, unusual radio transmissions had been monitored by staff at Farnborough, the origin of which could not be identified. It was clear, however, that the transmissions were some form of 'signal' or 'language'.

Although the signals were never 'decoded', Shuttlewood was advised that analysis had shown that the signals were most definitely not human in origin. 'What he told me was a lot more detailed than this,' the woman confided. 'I think he keeps a lot to himself about his true feelings . . . but something of great importance happened that day they snatched those special signals from space, I feel sure!'[26]

If, at some point during the 1960s, the Ministry of Defence relocated certain UFO studies to RAF Farnborough, then the likelihood is that the work centred around the analysis of UFO reports filed by military sources. Why can we assume this?

Both S4 and DS8, who played a relatively minor role in UFO investigations at the time, operated out of Whitehall – there was no reason for them to have had a second base of operations at Farnborough. And as Cyril Townsend-Withers has stated, the project at Farnbrough was staffed by intelligence personnel, as was AI (Tech) 5b. What does the MOD have to say about this?

Nick Pope of Sec(AS)2a has informed me that he is unaware of any UFO investigations ever having been undertaken at Farnborough.[27]

Hence, if the project at Farnborough was considered to be so sensitive by the Government that members of the MOD today are totally unaware of its existence, then logic says that its activities must have been far more covert than those of S4 Air and DS8, whose involvement the MOD has always acknowledged.

Known instances of Ministry of Defence officials visiting UFO witnesses are somewhat rare. Such a visit was made in 1966 following the sighting of a UFO by Police Constable Colin Perks of Wilmslow, Cheshire. In the early hours of a January morning in that year, Perks, who was engaged in a routine patrol of Wilmslow, viewed an unusual aerial object which immediately caught his attention.

It was about 4.10 a.m. when I heard a humming noise. I turned round and saw a greenish glow in the sky. It was about thirty-five feet off the ground and one hundred yards away, hovering above a field adjoining a car park. It appeared to be oval and about the size of a bus. It looked solid and had a definite shape about it.

It stayed in the same position for about five seconds with this high-pitched whine coming from it. Suddenly it moved off over the house tops at a very fast speed.

Following his encounter, PC Perks returned to Wilmslow Police Station and, with the incident still fresh in his mind, prepared an official report and drew a sketch of the UFO, both of which were passed on to his superior officer, Superintendent H.O. Kenworthy. In accordance with Ministry of Defence regulations, Supt. Kenworthy then forwarded a copy of PC Perks' report to Whitehall.[28]

Shortly afterwards, an investigator from the MOD travelled to Wilmslow to interview the Constable. In response to enquiries from the media, an MOD spokesperson assigned to the case remained typically tight-lipped, stating only that there was not enough evidence available to gauge with any accuracy what it was that PC Perks had seen.

Despite the MOD's stance on the case, PC Perks remained convinced that the UFO had been neither a conventional aircraft nor a figment of his imagination: 'I was scared stiff. People always laugh about these things. Most of the reports about flying objects are found to be phoney, but there was no mistaking the object I saw. It gave me a fright.'

Full support was also given to PC Perks by Supt. Kenworthy: 'I am reasonably satisfied that this man has seen something very unusual and we have treated it quite seriously. We do not know what conclusions the Air Ministry investigators came to.'[29]

Curiously, a journalist from the *Evening News* learned that a 'security curtain' had been enforced following the incident which was not lifted until the case was brought to the attention of the media, a full two months after.[30]

Had the Ministry of Defence learned something which demanded such secrecy? It is doubtful that we will learn the answer until the official papers on the case are declassified. In the meantime, I find it interesting that the Ministry of Defence chose not to reveal to

Superintendent Kenworthy their conclusions after the investigation of Perks' UFO encounter.

There is no reason to doubt Perks' account. I suspect that the MOD's silence was due to the fact that any endorsement of the encounter would have been seen as an admission that, once again, British airspace had been intruded upon by a genuine UFO.

In addition to the Ministry of Defence's official UFO investigations undertaken in the 1961–1966 period, a variety of other Government agencies and departments were involved in co-ordinating such studies.

Early in 1996 I conducted an interview with a retired police officer who was previously attached to the War Department Constabulary. Although cautious about revealing too much, he did advise me that at some point in the early 1960s an 'in-house' UFO project operated from the Proof and Experimental Establishment at Shoeburyness, Southend-on-Sea. According to the officer, the project was created in response to several baffling UFO sightings which had occurred in the vicinity of the P&EE. Furthermore those attached to the project did not report to the Air Ministry, but rather to the War Department Constabulary Office at Lansdowne House, London. My efforts to uncover the records generated by this particular project are ongoing.

There is more evidence to support my conviction that other Government departments conducted UFO studies in the 1960s. It comes from the late Waverney Girvan, a past editor of *Flying Saucer Review* magazine. In 1995 I was fortunate enough to obtain copies of much of Girvan's private – and very illuminating – correspondence from the 1960s.

I was particularly struck by a January 30, 1964-letter from Girvan to investigator Wilfred Daniels. He states that he is aware of a quasi-official body of people, some seemingly with Government ties, who would meet on occasion to muse on the UFO issue. I quote from a section of Girvan's letter:

> There is in existence a number of prominent men who meet occasionally in London for dinner to discuss UFOs. They are in no sense a group, nor will they join any group. Their names

are quite well known in one field or another and they have never come forward in any way to proclaim their interest or belief. These men include an Alderman of the city of London (a possible and likely future Lord Mayor); a Foreign Office Barrister; an M.P.; a theologian; a scientist and one or two prominent businessmen. They are men of honour and would not betray any confidence placed in them. As they themselves wish to keep their names out of the public eye in this connection they would be the last people to talk out of turn about UFOs.

Whatever the true identity of the 'prominent men' to whom Girvan was referring, the fact that their number included both a Member of Parliament and an individual with ties to the Foreign Office suggests to me that their interest in UFOs may not have been as unofficial as Girvan believed.

CHAPTER 8

INVASION!

DOCUMENTATION MADE AVAILABLE TO ME BY THE MINISTRY OF Defence shows that between 1959 and 1966 the British Government received details of 446 UFO incidents. The peak year was 1966, when ninety-five reports reached MOD staff. This total, however, was dwarfed in 1967, when the MOD was inundated with 362 reports – almost one per day.[1] The publicity generated by media interest in the encounters, many of which were filed by police officers, caused a sudden shift in the MOD's policy on UFOs and led a number of MPs to raise the UFO issue in Parliament.

In the first six months of 1967, the MOD studied more than 150 accounts of unexplained aerial activity.[2] But it was not until October of that year, that matters came to a head.

It was just a normal tour of duty for Police Constables Clifford Waycott and Roger Willey as they drove through the picturesque Devon countryside on October 24, 1967 – at least until 4.10 a.m. Waycott and Willey were nearing the hamlet of Brandis Corner, fifteen miles from Okehampton, when a highly unusual flying object loomed silently into view. 'It looked like a star-spangled cross radiating points of light from all angles. It first appeared to the left of us, then went into an arc and dipped down and we thought it had landed,' said twenty-nine-year-old Constable Willey. In a press conference organized the following day, PC

Waycott informed the media that at one point the craft appeared to stop over a field. 'When we got out to look,' said Waycott, 'it started moving again. It was not an aeroplane or a helicopter, but it was as large as a conventional aircraft.'

'It seemed to be watching us and wouldn't let us catch up. It was at various altitudes all the time, but mostly just above the trees. It had terrific acceleration. It seemed to know we were chasing it,' added Constable Willey who at times drove up to 90 mph in a vain attempt to keep up with the UFO.

The constables continued to chase the UFO for almost an hour and, at one point, actually stopped their car in a lay-by and woke up a sleeping motorist, Christopher Garner of Luton, to ask if he would confirm the presence of the UFO. Garner, at first believing that he was in the middle of a bizarre nightmare, asserted that he too could see the mysterious craft, which was by then at a distance of about 400 yards.

At about the same time, an entirely independent sighting of the same UFO was made by Mrs Stella Crocker of Brandis Corner. Describing the object as a 'starry cross', Mrs Crocker said that she had watched it through a window as it hovered under a cloud at an altitude of about 400 feet.

Shortly afterwards, an almost identical UFO was seen by Mrs Ursula Dommett, the wife of the rector of Caister-on-sea, Norfolk. Mrs Dommett said that as the craft travelled out to sea over the Norfolk coast, it gave off a bright light from four points which created a cross-like appearance. This description, it will be remembered, sounds very much like that made by Mr John Smith of the Royal Observer Corps of a UFO over Kessingland, Suffolk, fourteen years before. Although the UFO seen in 1967 was somewhat larger than that witnessed by John Smith, the similar configuration of lights that both objects displayed suggests to me that they may have had a common point of origin.[3]

In the days following Willey and Waycott's encounter, an avalanche of similar reports reached both the Ministry of Defence and the media. Notably, many of the sightings were made by qualified observers. Retired RAF Wing Commander Eric Cox of Hyde viewed 'seven brilliant lights' whilst driving at night through Hampshire on October 25. 'They were three miles away at treetop height, flying in a V-formation,' said Wing Commander Cox. 'After about three minutes, they broke off and three went away. They just faded. Then the other four formed a perfect formation – just like a plus sign or a cross. They were certainly under some sort of control because the formation was so tight.'[4]

Later on the same day, Mr G.W.R. Terry, the Chief Constable of East Sussex, called a conference of police officers at his Lewes Headquarters to discuss five UFO sightings filed at 4.45 a.m. by police crews throughout the country. All the reports were remarkably consistent, describing a particularly bright light travelling silently in a northerly direction. The officers concerned were later permitted to speak to the press 'in order to keep the incident in its right perspective'.[5]

On October 26, 1967, an amateur astronomer reported having seen an unidentified flying object at 6.45 a.m. the previous day in the skies over Hastings. Details of the encounter were reported to staff at the Royal Greenwich Observatory at Herstmonceux for comment. 'We are really interested in this report,' said a spokesperson at the Observatory. 'It is now quite obvious that there was something visible below the cloud cover. This is an advance. We now know that there is something up there and that something is not Venus.'[6]

During the twenty-four-hour period which followed the Royal Observatory's statement, more and more UFOs were seen across the length and breadth of the British Isles. Reports poured in from Dartmoor, Gloucester, Huntington and Somerset. On the Spelsbury–Chipping Norton road in Oxfordshire, two policemen encountered a pair of very dark, oval-shaped objects, both approximately fifty feet in diameter. The UFOs rapidly disappeared to the north at a height of around 600 feet.[7]

Shortly after the incident at Oxfordshire, six police officers from Derbyshire described seeing UFO over the town of Glossop. The officers revealed that as they watched the UFO hovering in the sky, it began to 'swing from side to side' before disappearing.[8] Reports of UFOs swinging in a pendulum-like manner have appeared time and time again, echoing that description by John Kilburn at RAF Topcliffe in September 1952: '[The UFO] maintained the slow forward speed for a few seconds before commencing to descend, swinging in a pendular motion during descent similar to a falling sycamore leaf.'[9]

*   *   *

'Nothing odd has been picked up all week on radar in this country,' said the Ministry of Defence in response to the events of October 24–26, 1967. Less than twenty-four hours after this statement, Whitehall was inundated with telephone calls from worried members of the public who had seen unusual craft in areas as far and wide as Brighton, Hertfordshire and Wigtown, Scotland. 'We are looking at them all,' said a representative of the MOD.[10]

As press coverage continued, Mr Peter Mills, Conservative MP for Torrington, Devon, tabled two questions in the House of Commons for the Minister of Defence:

(1) In view of the fact that an unidentified flying object has been seen in the Okehampton area, will he make a full statement on the circumstances of the report and what are his plans to deal with a possible recurrence of this flying object?

(2) In view of the fact that a flying object in the Okehampton area was described as a star-shaped cross larger than a conventional aircraft, will the Minister confirm that this is either one of our own aircraft or an unidentified flying object?

In an interview with the press, Mr Mills stated: 'I think the Minister ought to help clear up this business as to whether or not we are looking at our equipment or machines from another country, or indeed, another planet.'

Within two days of Mr Mills' questions in the House of Commons, the MOD announced that the matter had been partially resolved. The UFOs seen over Devon, Dorset and Sussex had simply been aircraft carrying out routine refuelling procedures. On October 24, said the MOD, nine F-100 aircraft belonging to the US Air Force were refuelled over Land's End and on the following evening, eight Phantom jets were involved in a similar operation over the North of England, all at a height of 26,000 feet. However, the MOD admitted that the object seen at Glossop, Derbyshire, remained unidentified.[12]

Less than a week after MOD staff issued these explanations for the UFO encounters of October 1967, they were forced to concede that their theory no longer held water – as the following report from the *Sunday Express* shows:

> The Ministry of Defence admitted yesterday that the emphatic and official explanation given on Friday – that the objects seen in the sky were US Air Force planes refuelling in mid-air – no longer stands up. There were no refuelling operations at the time of the sightings. A USAF spokesman said all the sightings were between five and nine p.m. and all the sightings of 'fiery crosses' in the sky were between midnight and dawn.[13]

On the day that piece was published an incident took place on the Sussex Downs which remains unresolved nearly thirty years on. At 6.45 p.m., twenty-one-year-old Paul Quick was pushing his broken-down motorbike through a heavily wooded area near Storrington when his attention was drawn to an unidentified aerial craft. 'There in the sky above me was an object like a rugby ball floating towards me,' said Paul. 'It was one and a half times the size of a double-decker bus and quite silent. It was about two hundred and fifty feet up. I was scared.'

Upon arriving home, Paul informed his family of what had occurred and, with his mother and sisters, proceeded to seek out the UFO again. Having caught sight of the object, the family watched awestruck as it descended onto the Sussex Downs at a distance of about two miles from their position. 'There is no question of a mistake or imagination. We called the police,' Mrs Quick told journalists. Police quickly arrived on the scene, equipped with tracker dogs no less, and conducted a thorough search of the vicinity but were unable to locate the UFO.[14]

'Police see UFO over Sussex' reported the *Daily Telegraph* at the same time. Recounting an incident of October 29, the newspaper stated that three policemen had seen the UFO whilst changing office duty at Lancing police station. PC Michael Sands said, 'It looked like a silver pinpoint of light, and was moving rapidly from south-west to north-east.' Other reports surfaced on the same day in and around the London area. Several independent sightings of a cigar-shaped UFO were made by people living in Islington, Ealing and Muswell Hill. One of the witnesses estimated that the UFO was 300 yards in length and fifty feet across. Two described it as exuding an orange glow, another that it appeared golden in colour.[15]

As a result of the sudden escalation in UFO reports in 1967, the media became much more willing to report on the issue in a non-discriminatory manner. For instance, newspaper reports between November 12–14 detailed a recently created Soviet study aimed at establishing the truth behind the UFO puzzle. The project had apparently been proposed following five well-authenticated UFO sightings within the borders of the Soviet Union.[16]

One month after this announcement, the British Government approached Moscow with a proposal that the countries combine their expertise and conduct a joint UFO study programme. It seems the 'October wave' had perturbed British authorities. In both letter and personal communication, I have been informed by MOD personnel that they have absolutely no knowledge of this proposal. Nevertheless, details of it can be read in a two-page document unearthed from the archives of the US Defense Intelligence Agency. Since this is a matter of some note, I shall set out the document in full:

SUMMARY:
Report includes information on Russian commission set up to study Unidentified Flying Objects. Of particular interest is the fact that at first the Russians publicised the commission, but now claim the commission has been disbanded.

REPORT:
1. In early November 1967 (exact date believed to be 10 Nov) Moscow TV presented a program on Unidentified Flying Objects. On 12 Nov 67 a Reuters release in the U.K. press (believe article was in Daily Telegraph) reported the TV program.

2. The essence of the TV program, and Reuters report based on the TV program, was that the Russians had recently set up a commission to study UFOs. The Chairman of the commission is retired SAF [*Author's note*: Soviet Air Force] Major General A.F.

Stolyarov, a former Technical Services Officer. The group consisted of 18 astronomers and SAF officers plus 200 observers.

3. A day or two after the TV program, the Reuters correspondent went to see General Stolyarov. The General was very polite, confirmed the information about the commission, the 18 astronomers and SAF officers and the 200 observers. In addition, he said five positive sightings had been made.

4. Approximately a week later the Reuters correspondent went back to see General Stolyarov. However, this time the correspondent could not get past the General's secretary, was politely but firmly told the General was no longer available for interview.

5. On 12 December 1967, the British Embassy was directed by London to further investigate the subject with a view to cooperating with the Russians in observation teams for UFOs.

6. The Scientific Counselor of the British Embassy went to the State Committee for Science and Technology and inquired about the UFO Commission and the possibility of British–Russian cooperation in observation of UFOs. The British Counselor was politely received and the Commission was freely discussed. The British were told they would receive a reply to their request about cooperation.

7. The British did not receive an answer and did not pursue the subject. However, on 6 January 1968 while on a routine visit to the Soviet State Committee for Science and Technology, the British Scientific Counselor was told the following: The Commission for investigating UFOs had been set up in response to a popular demand. The Commission had met twice, but since there was insufficient information to sustain it the Commission would be disbanded after the next meeting.

8. The British Scientific Counselor believes that the original announcement of the work of the Commission on TV was an oversight on the part of the censors because the Commission has

not been reported or referred to anywhere else. Mr [Censored] believes the Commission has not been disbanded, but will continue under cover. This information was sent to London.

COMMENT:

1. The preceding information was given to RO by source. RO also read confidential British files on this subject. RO did not approach Reuters correspondent because of delicate position of source. RO was unable to find anyone in Moscow who saw TV program or read article in UK press.

2. On 10 or 11 November 1967 the U.S. Science Attache received a telephone call from the Reuters correspondent and was asked if he had seen the TV program. When the Science Attache replied that he had not seen the program, the correspondent described it and asked the Science Attache if he thought the information was worth reporting. The Science Attache said yes. The Science Attache, like the RO, has not seen the UK press report. The U.S. Science Attache will receive two copies of this report and will forward one copy to the appropriate S & T [*Author's note:* Science and Technology] Agency in Washington.[17]

It is a pity that the DIA report, which was prepared by Colonel Melvin J. Nielsen, does not expand on the reference to 'confidential British files on this subject'. However, a number of interesting deductions can be made from this material.

According to the report, London directed the British Embassy in Moscow to approach the Russian authorities on December 12, 1967, only two months after the 'October wave'. There is no doubt in my mind that the many UFO reports studied by the MOD in 1967 greatly troubled the Government of the time, hence the desire to uncover details of Soviet findings on the subject. Although the Soviets ultimately proved reluctant to respond to the British proposal, the allusion to 'confidential . . . files' suggests that the Embassy did finally succeed in obtaining information on the Russian Commission. What is the Ministry of Defence's position on this matter today? '. . . we do not co-operate with other Governments on this subject,' I was informed by Kerry Palmer of the MOD in 1991.[18]

A further indication that the 1967 incidents struck a chord with the MOD is shown by the fact that, also in that year, a decision was taken to permanently preserve the UFO files of S4 Air, DS8 and the by-then-defunct S6. Prior to that time, I have been informed, all of the UFO records generated by those departments were routinely 'weeded out' and destroyed at five-year intervals.[19]

Come 1998, at least some of the Government's UFO papers dating from 1967 should be available for inspection at the Public Record Office. In light of the Ministry of Defence's stance that there is no overseas collaboration on UFO matters, I am rather pessimistic that anything of substance will surface with respect to their proposal to the Soviet Union. Moreover, had it not been for the two-page DIA report, released under the terms of the American Freedom of Information Act, we would still be completely ignorant of this aspect of the MOD's activities.

Of the 508 UFO reports studied by the MOD in the final two years of the 1960s, very few details have surfaced. However, I am aware of one credible report which was submitted by PC Donald Cameron of St Helens, Lancashire. At home at the time of his sighting, PC Cameron reported seeing six glowing objects hovering in the sky. He said at the time: 'I thought I was seeing things and called my wife. We watched them for about thirty seconds before they disappeared at speed towards Manchester. They were about a mile away. I could see them clearly even though it was a dull day. They were white and glowing. One was bigger than the others with a cup-shaped dome.'

As he made out an official report, PC Cameron added, not without some humour: 'I suppose I will get some ribbing from the lads, but that is not what worries me . . . it's what the Chief Constable thinks. I hope he believes me.'

'I am awaiting his report with interest,' responded Chief Constable Archibald Atherton. 'It is like seeing the Loch Ness Monster.' Contacted by the *Daily Sketch* for comment, the Ministry of Defence responded: 'It sounds strange, but we can't comment until we know all the facts and they have been investigated.'[20]

During October 1968 a strange object was seen over the village of Boosbeck, Cleveland, by at least four people, one of whom, 'Mrs B', gave an account to investigator Gloria Dixon. On the day in question, Mrs B was waiting at a local bus stop when, along with the other witnesses, she heard an unusual noise, 'like a high-pitched whirring'. Looking up, all four saw a dark, torpedo-shaped object flying overhead, emitting flames from its rear.

The UFO was first seen incoming from the North Sea and proceeded to head westward over the surrounding moors at a low altitude. The entire incident was over in no more than a minute.[21]

By all accounts, 1970 was a relatively quiet year for the Ministry of Defence, with only 181 reports logged by S4 Air and DS8. In the following year, things were quite different. During 1971 the MOD received details of nearly 400 UFO encounters, a figure which was not surpassed until 1977.[22] In contrast with the situation in 1967, the MOD was largely able to minimize the media attention given to the sudden increase in UFO incidents in 1971. Despite this, a number of reports from that year have surfaced into the public domain.

Bob Boyd, a Plymouth-based researcher, has uncovered details of a UFO encounter reported by British military personnel based at a facility on the island of Cyprus in 1971. Boyd's source, an ex-Royal Marine regimental sergeant, told him that he had been leading a night exercise on the island with 1,400 men when a 'burning ball of light' suddenly appeared out of nowhere.

'It was as if the sun had been lowered to the ground,' said the sergeant. 'We watched for 20-odd minutes, training powerful binoculars and night glasses on it until it disappeared out of sight.' Bob Boyd has also learned that more than a hundred rolls of film showing the strange object were forwarded to the MOD for inspection.[23]

Eighteen years after Flying Officers G. Smythe and T.S. Johnson saw a circular-shaped UFO in the vicinity of RAF West Malling, Kent, another encounter took place in the same area. At 8.45 a.m. on August 27, 1971,

Garry Harrison, a freelance draughtsman of Gillingham, was driving to his office when he was suddenly distracted by a light shining in his eyes as he approached the turning for West Malling. Looking to his right, Harrison was amazed to see an unusual-looking object hovering above the trees in a nearby field. Thinking that the object was possibly a helicopter, he brought his car to a standstill and got out for a better view. At that moment, Harrison knew that he was looking at no helicopter . . .

'. . . the sun had come off it and I could make out an oblong-shaped object with rounded ends. It had a silver metallic finish with a black rim around the bottom. I would think it was about fifty feet long, but it is hard to say how far away it was. When I first saw it, it was completely stationary. Then it started to come down very slowly behind trees and I lost sight of it. I would like to have searched further but I did not have the time. It was definitely not a balloon or any type of conventional aircraft.'[24]

Neither Malling Police nor the County Police Headquarters had received any other reports of UFO sightings in the area, but a County Police spokesman said: 'Whatever these things are, they are no laughing matter. I saw one myself once in Malaya.'[25]

As we have seen, there is strong witness testimony to suggest that during the 1960s covert investigations into UFO activity were undertaken by specialist staff based at RAF Farnborough. If this continued into the 1970s, then those investigators would have seen their quarry come to the doorstep. The prime witness was a Mr Ruck-Keene of Farnborough, a former Royal Air Force pilot with thirty years' military service to his credit:

At about 11.45 p.m. I was looking out of the window of my bedroom, having just extinguished the light, when I saw a very bright light in the sky, I watched it for about twenty seconds, wondering what it could be. It suddenly started to move so I realised it could not be an aircraft or a star, though it was too far away to make out any shape.

It was emitting a very bright yellowish/white light which was pulsating. It moved across the sky maintaining a steady height but not making steady progress because it would stop or slow down, and now and then there were very abrupt changes of direction

– small ones, but made very sharply. The light continued at the same intensity and 'sparkling' is as good a word as I can think of to describe it.

It moved through an arc of about thirty degrees from left to right – or in a westerly direction, and then it stopped again and remained stationary for perhaps twenty to thirty seconds, then returned along the same path, carrying out the same manoeuvres, until it had got back approximately to the starting point, where it again stopped for about twenty to thirty seconds and exactly repeated the same manoeuvre, and it went on doing this for the nineteen or so minutes that I watched it. At one point the light that it was emitting suddenly turned red for a short period, and then it went back again to its previous yellowish/white. The light was extremely strong, much stronger than could possibly be emitted by a star or heavenly body of any kind.

I managed to get a pair of binoculars on it – 7 by 50 binoculars, which are the best for use at night – but it showed nothing else. The intensity of the light was such that it just increased the dazzle. One could still not make out any shape or form behind the light. After about nineteen minutes it suddenly disappeared altogether, when at one end of its orbit. From the general movements of . . . whatever it was . . . it looked to me as if it were orbiting some object on the ground but that is purely supposition and based on flying experience.

When he was questioned, Mr Ruck-Keene said that he was unable to judge the distance of the object without knowing its size, but estimated that it was around five miles from his location and at an altitude of 3,000 feet.

Mr Ruck-Keene's nephew, Jonathan, also caught sight of the object. 'What I saw was exactly the same,' said Jonathan. 'I trained a pair of binoculars on it and I watched its irregular elliptical orbit. I could not pick out any shape at all because it was far too bright. I also noticed that it changed colour into a reddish-orange for some seconds, and then changed back again, I cannot speculate upon it as I know nothing about this sort of thing at all.'[26]

*   *   *

On the morning of September 8, 1972, housewife Sally Pike of Hilperton was relaxing in a deckchair in her back garden when, at 11.45 a.m., she noticed a transporter aircraft flying overhead to the nearby Keevil airport. As she watched, Mrs Pike noticed something decidedly out of the ordinary:

> Just behind [the aircraft] I noted a silvery object flashing in the sun. This was chasing round the body and tail of the aircraft. I picked up my husband's binoculars, which were close by, and observed that the object was bell-shaped and certainly resembled no other craft I had seen before. My estimation is that it was between six and eight feet across. It made no sound that I could hear, although the noise of the transporters would probably have drowned it, anyway. The object seemed to be playing 'tag' with the plane. The pilot gave no visible indication of having observed the object, which really glinted brightly.
>
> I trained my binoculars upon him at one stage to see if there was any reaction. The aircraft was low enough for me to see the pilot quite well through the binoculars . . . After a minute or so the plane moved across the estate and I gradually lost sight of both it and the bell-shaped object. I rushed indoors to phone my husband and tell him of the extraordinary sight. When I went outside again . . . I glanced up and caught sight of a brilliant glint high in the sky. I did not have time to get the binoculars on this occasion, but watched as this flashing object — which may have been the same thing I saw playing tag with the transporter — moved rapidly off and disappeared from view.[27]

If the pilot of the aircraft had witnessed the UFO, then it is all but certain that an official report would have been forwarded to the Ministry of Defence. Both civilian and military pilots are required to submit details of unusual aerial phenomena through official channels.

Mrs Pike's description of the UFO seeming to play 'tag' with the aircraft is something which is often reported in UFO encounters, and is best exemplified by the incident over the Isle of Wight in 1956. I can offer no definitive explanation for this curious habit which many UFOs repeatedly display. But it seems logical that any visiting alien intelligence would wish to keep a close watch on the developing technology of the natives.

One thing which sets this account apart from many others is the apparent small size of the UFO. Unless the occupants were diminutive to the point of absurdity, the probability is that the object was unmanned and piloted remotely. This is not an uncommon feature in UFO incidents. Two UFOs, which sound astonishingly similar to the one seen by Sally Pike, were sighted over Arizona in 1947. A report of July 7, 1947, made available to me by the FBI, discloses:

> On 1 July 1947, Lt. William G. McGinty, USN . . . was interviewed by this Agent, and stated in substance: That on 30 June 1947, at about 0910, MST, he was flying at 25,000 feet over Grand Canyon, Arizona, in a P-80 type aircraft. He stated that he was heading south towards Williams Field, Arizona, when he saw two round objects going at inconceivable speed, straight down. He further stated that his reactions were to turn away from the objects. He further stated that one of the unidentifiable objects followed the other seconds apart. He further stated that due to the speed of the objects, he could only see that they were circular, and that they were possibly light gray in color. He further stated that it was his opinion that the objects were approximately eight feet in diameter. In conclusion, he stated that the objects would have probably hit the ground approximately twenty-five miles south of the South Rim of Grand Canyon, Arizona.[28]

A similar account comes from the late Leonard Stringfield, a pioneering researcher who specialized in the field of UFO 'crashes'. One such incident brought to Stringfield's attention concerned the crash (and subsequent recovery by a special team of US operatives) of a UFO on Mexican soil on August 25, 1974. In an operation which was not altogether legal, the US team crossed the border into Mexico and removed the UFO before the Mexican authorities had the opportunity to conduct their own detailed analysis of the mystery vehicle. In this particular case, the UFO was a mere sixteen feet, five inches in diameter. Notably, the colour of the UFO was silver, much like polished steel – just like the object described by Sally Pike.[29]

On September 24, 1992, the Ministry of Defence admitted to me that 201 UFO reports had been filed with the Government in 1972, all of which are now archived and unavailable to the general public until 2003. If the sighting near Keevil Airport was reported officially then, one hopes, the MOD's analysis of the case will come to light when that year's papers are eventually declassified.

That a number of the UFO encounters studied by the MOD in 1972 were considered somewhat 'sensitive' seems to be supported by the testimony of investigator and author Arthur Shuttlewood. In January of that year an acquaintance of his attempted to obtain confirmation of a UFO event which had taken place over the North Sea. As a consequence of his enquiries, Shuttlewood's source was duly visited by two gentlemen from CID who requested that he advise them of how he had obtained his information.[30]

During 1973, figures were slightly up on the previous year, with DS8 and S4 Air logging some 233 UFO reports. Despite the MOD's most welcome decision to reveal the number of UFO encounters reported during that year, they have yet to comment officially on the series of baffling, country-wide incidents which began in mid-1973 and came to a climax in Wales in January 1974. Before examining the evidence, however, it is worth making mention of the experience of Mr R.O. Reynolds of Exeter since it amply sets the scene for the events that followed.

In the period 1973–4, as a serving member of the RAF, Mr Reynolds was stationed at Coltishall, Norfolk. He recalls that at some point during that time, 'a request was put onto the SRO [Station Routine Orders] asking personnel seeing unidentified objects or lights in the sky near the airfield to report the sighting[s] to the Station Air Traffic Controller.'

As Mr Reynolds has stated, 'I thought the request was odd at the time, as nearby was, and still is, the radar stations at RAF Neatishead and Watton, both of whose job [it] was to monitor the airspace, which included Coltishall.'[31]

Odd, perhaps, but far stranger things were to come . . .

CHAPTER 9

THE 'COPTER AND THE CRASH

OF ALL THE VARIOUS ELEMENTS WHICH MAKE UP WHAT IS popularly known as the 'UFO phenomenon', there can be few so strange as the so-called 'phantom helicopters'. For at least four decades numerous people throughout the world have reported seeing helicopters, very often black in colour and with no identifying markings, in areas which have been subjected to intense UFO activity. This has led a number of investigators to speculate that the helicopters are operated by a covert arm of the American Government which is involved in a surreptitious UFO monitoring programme.[1]

One of the most confounding features of many such reports is the ability of the helicopters to operate in almost complete silence. To many, the idea of a 'silent helicopter' must seem far-fetched. However, in early 1995 the much-respected US publication, *Aviation Week and Space Technology*, reported that, '. . . the U.S. military has been working for years on at least two helicopter projects. The more recent is development of a light, very quiet helicopter with a mast-mounted sight.'[2]

It went on: 'The program's existence was under scored on Apr. 9, 1991, during an . . . interview with a former Lockheed official. When asked if he had heard of something called a "quiet helicopter," the official responded, "Absolutely . . . a very quiet helicopter. But I can't talk [about it]; that's getting into very sensitive [areas]."'[3]

Although it is undoubtedly the case that the majority of 'phantom helicopter' accounts originate in the United States, a wave of sightings of such craft – which culminated in the crash of an unknown object atop a Welsh mountain – occurred in Britain in the winter of 1973/4. Before looking at these reports, let us examine a number of similar incidents which have been reported elsewhere.

One of the earliest episodes on record dates from October 11, 1966, and concerns a helicopter–UFO event at the Wanaque Reservoir, New Jersey, USA. The encounter began with the sighting of a disc-shaped UFO by a number of policemen as it passed over the reservoir. Emitting a dazzling white light, the object then headed towards an area of forest where it was eventually lost from view. As soon as the UFO vanished at least ten aircraft and six or seven helicopters suddenly appeared. The point of origin of the vehicles was never determined.[4] If this had been a one-off case then it would be reasonable to assume that the presence of both the helicopters and the UFO was due simply to coincidence. Yet such incidents occur time and time again.

On the night of September 26, 1974, a father and son, Walter and Dan Richley, saw a strange object hovering high above their farm at Lynchburg, Ohio. As there was a powerful searchlight mounted on the family's pick-up truck, Walter and Dan decided, 'as an experiment', to try to get a better view of this object which was taking so much interest in their farm.

As the beam of light touched the UFO the Richleys found themselves bathed in an equally bright beam of red light which emanated from the UFO. Naturally frightened out of their wits, both father and son ran for the safety of their home. As they did so the UFO began to retreat over the horizon until it finally disappeared from view.

At 11.00 p.m. on the following night Dan was sitting up reading alone when he was suddenly jolted by a loud noise coming from outdoors. On running to the window he was amazed to see a large helicopter descending. 'I then got Dad out of bed,' said Dan. Mr Richley quickly assessed the meaning of the helicopter's presence: 'I think I put my light beam on something that was a military secret. That 'copter came here to warn me.'

Leonard Stringfield, who conducted a personal investigation of the case, asked Walter Richley if he had received an apology or renumeration for the damage caused by the helicopter as it blew debris around his yard. 'No, and I'm not about to press it, I'd rather forget it,' replied Richley.[5]

Since at least 1967 the USA has been beset by a disturbing phenomenon: cattle mutilations. Exactly who, or what, is responsible for the widespread killing of cattle under very bizarre circumstances is far from clear. On many occasions farmers, policemen and veterinarians throughout North America have come across cases where a significant number of cattle have been subjected to unusual surgical procedures. A report which originated with the Federal Bureau of Investigation, dated February 2, 1979, lends credence to the possibility that the phantom helicopters are involved in the animal mutilation mystery to some degree:

> For the past seven or eight years mysterious cattle mutilations have been occurring throughout the United State of New Mexico. Officer Gabe Valdez, New Mexico State Police, has been handling investigations of these mutilations within New Mexico. Information furnished to this office by Officer Valdez indicates that the animals are being shot with some type of paralyzing drug and the blood is being drawn from the animal after an injection of an anti-coagulant. It appears that in some instances the cattle's legs have been broken and helicopters without any identifying numbers have reportedly been seen in the vicinity of the mutilations. Officer Valdez theorizes that clamps are being placed on the cow's legs and they are being lifted by helicopter to some remote area where the mutilations are taking place and then the animal is returned to its original pasture ... Officer Valdez is very adamant in his opinion that these mutilations are the work of the US Government and that it is some clandestine operation either by the CIA or the Department of Energy and in all probability is connected with some type of research into biological warfare.[6]

Is the CIA operating an undercover germ-warfare experiment which involves the use of unmarked helicopters to carry out testing on privately owned herds of cattle? Although this theory is entirely possible, it suffers from one crucial flaw. If the CIA is conducting such experiments, why does it do so on open farmland where there is a better than average chance of being shot at by an irate farmer? It would be much simpler for the CIA to carry out its research in the surroundings of a secure governmental facility. Those responsible for the mutilations appear entirely oblivious to the outrage that their actions provoke.

Linda Moulton Howe's remarkable book, *An Alien Harvest*, published in 1989, documents her investigations into cattle mutilations, phantom helicopters and unidentified flying objects. Howe, an Emmy Award-winning television producer, has presented a convincing amount of evidence which suggests that the three subjects are inextricably linked. Howe cites a number of cases where apparent extra-terrestrials have been seen in the immediate vicinity of mutilation sites. She suggests the possibility that the aliens may derive some form of sustenance from the removed body parts of the unfortunate cattle.[7]

If extra-terrestrials are responsible for these grisly attacks then what role is played by the unidentified helicopters? A number of researchers have mused on this puzzle, including Tom Adams, a long-time student of the cattle mutilation mystery. He has suggested one particularly plausible scenario to explain the helicopter link: '. . . The helicopters are of military origin. The government of the United States possesses a very substantial amount of knowledge about the mutilators, their means, motives and rationale. The government may be attempting to persuade mutilation investigators and the populace as a whole that perhaps the military might be behind the mutilations, a diversion away from the real truth.'[8]

That the cattle mutilations continue is amply demonstrated by the following report which appeared in 1993 in the *Albuquerque Tribune*:

Mysterious cattle mutilations, which seemed to stop in the 1980s, have resumed in this southern Colorado valley and a neighboring valley west of Trinidad, authorities confirm. Again, as during their peak in the 1970s, circumstances surrounding the killings are unexplained: lack of footprints, vehicle tracks or any sign of a struggle; selective, surgical-like removal of certain parts of the animals; and a lack of witnesses.[9]

This account prompted retired Costilla County Sheriff, Ernest Sandoval, to comment that he had received many reports of unusual lights from 'all over the county' during the earlier years of cattle mutilation activity, including the following which, once again, implicated the mystery helicopters, as Sandoval recalled: 'This young couple coming into San Luis passed a property where seventeen cattle had been mutilated. And there was this chopper that had a cow in a harness hanging from it, right across the highway.'[10]

In 1975 a torrent of reports of UFOs, mysterious lights and unidentified helicopters originated with, no less, the US Government themselves. Numerous sightings were reported in the vicinity of Malmstrom Air Force Base, Montana, Loring AFB, Maine, Wurtsmith AFB, Michigan, and at many other Government establishments throughout North America. Although, in a number of cases, it was definitely established that real, tangible helicopters had been in evidence, no agency was willing to admit to ownership of the craft. Nor was any explanation given regarding their relationship with the many UFOs seen during the same time-frame.[11]

At the height of the wave of such reports in the USA, similar incidents began to be reported in the United Kingdom. It is generally accepted that the British wave began around September 1973. However, I include the following encounter since it displays many of the characteristics of later reports.

At 9.15 p.m. on May 10, 1973, a young couple were parked in their car at Hartshead Pike Hill, a local beauty spot on the moors near Oldham. Both saw what they initially thought to be a helicopter. As it drifted towards them the couple were able to see that the object appeared dome-like in shape, with an abundance of what seemed to be window-space. Approaching in total silence, the UFO first hovered above the Pike, rotated in a clockwise direction and then reversed. Emanating from the object were beams of red, green and white lights. After several minutes of floating barely a hundred feet above the mystified couple, the object moved away, accelerating rapidly as it disappeared.[12] A few sporadic incidents, similar in type, were reported periodically through the summer of 1973, but it was not until later in the year that matters escalated.

Despite the fact that a number of sightings of unidentified helicopters and unidentified flying objects were filed by people living in and around the area of Buxton, Derbyshire, in September 1973, the media largely ignored the accounts until early 1974.[13] It was revealed on January 15, 1974, that police forces throughout the North of England had been alerted to look out for any unusual helicopter movements in their vicinity. For six months, night sightings of unidentified helicopters had been filed in both Cheshire and Derbyshire, something confirmed by Cheshire police:

> We don't know of any reason why the helicopter should make these trips at night. Obviously we are anxious to find out. Apart from anything else the helicopter crosses one of the main flight paths to Manchester airport. There is an obvious danger to the aircraft going into the airport. We are very interested to know what is happening. We hope to be able to trace the pilot and put some suggestions to him. It would appear the pilot is in breach of civil aviation laws. A special licence is needed to fly a helicopter at night.[14]

A spokesperson for Derbyshire police added: 'All sorts of things spring to mind but we have pretty much ruled out that it is anything to do with illegal immigrants, and nothing appears to have been stolen in areas where the aircraft has been sighted.'[15]

It appears that the Cheshire police believe only one helicopter was involved in the night-time sorties. But on the following day, Staffordshire police admitted that they too had received details of unidentified helicopter activity in the dead of night. Although they declined to give details of specific locations, police informed the media that they were aware of at least fifty sightings in Staffordshire, Derbyshire and Cheshire. (Interestingly, it was also stated that both Special Branch and the Royal Air Force had been alerted to look into the matter.)[16] Fifty sightings over three counties? I find it highly implausible that a solitary helicopter could have been responsible for all the reports.

Although the reasoning behind this conclusion has never been disclosed, Staffordshire police said their enquiries had led them to believe that the helicopter mystery originated in the London area, adding that whoever was flying the craft was either highly skilled or 'completely crackers'.[17]

Still more helicopter reports surfaced in Staffordshire, this time near Newcastle-under-Lyme. In response to enquiries made by the *Birmingham Post*, police confirmed that they had received 'several reports . . . of it being heard in the north of the county. All traffic controllers report that no flight plans for a helicopter have been filed. We do not know what it is up to.'[18]

Darley Moor, Derbyshire, was the site of a strange incident in the early hours of January 18. An unnamed person informed police that they had seen a 'single, bright light' flying at an unspecified altitude over the Moor. Derbyshire police declined to speculate as to whether there was a connection with the helicopter sightings, but confirmed that an investigation had been set in motion.[19]

The probability that a number of helicopters were responsible for the many accounts we have on record is supported by the fact that a multitude of other reports surfaced on January 18. Cheshire was the location once again, and reports poured in from Bramhall, Prestbury and Scholar Green.[20]

The reader will have noted that Officer Gabe Valdez of the New Mexico Police was 'very adamant' that, of the phantom helicopter–cattle mutilation cases which he had investigated, most were the work of '. . . some clandestine operation either by the CIA or the Department of Energy . . .'

Strangely enough, at the very time that the UK was being subjected to its own invasion of mystery helicopters, rumours were rife in the media that somewhere between thirty and forty US intelligence agents – from the CIA and the National Security Agency – had been posted to Britain on a security matter. Ostensibly, this was to gather information on 'subversive elements' within the British Trade Union movement.[21]

It must be remembered, though, that both the CIA and the NSA have had long-standing involvement in the investigation of the UFO mystery. Also, it was stated in the *Times* that the American agents were believed to be based at a number of 'U.S. civilian and military research offices in

London' – where Staffordshire police believed the unidentified helicopters came from.[22]

In response to the *Times* article, an official statement was issued to the press from the American Embassy: 'As a general policy, the U.S. Embassy does not comment on news articles dealing with intelligence matters. The story in today's Times, however, is so far outside the area of truth that it must be denied categorically. There is absolutely no truth in the allegations that there has been an influx of American intelligence men into Britain in recent weeks or months.'[23]

Nevertheless, rumours of such an influx persisted. And it is perhaps illuminating to note that the Embassy's statement was only issued after a morning of intensive consultation with officials in Whitehall and transatlantic telephone calls to Washington.[24]

More sightings of unusual aerial lights and unidentified helicopters were reported throughout mid-January, 1974. Possibly one of the last recorded encounters took place on the evening of January 24, 1974, when Paul Gelling, sub-editor at the *Birmingham Evening Mail*, saw a 'white descending light' in the sky at Aston Catlow, near Stratford-upon-Avon. 'The light fell from the sky and seemed to explode into blue and green,' said Gelling.[25] This particular sighting received little coverage in the press since it was overshadowed by an altogether more mysterious event which had occurred on the previous evening.

At approximately 8.30 p.m. on January 23, an unidentified aerial object impacted on Cader Bronwen, a 2,000 foot peak in the Berwyn Mountains between Bala and Corwen, Wales. One of the first people to see the object as it travelled overhead was Mrs Anne Williams of Bro Diham, Llandrillo.

'I saw this bright light hanging in the sky,' said Mrs Williams. 'It had a long fiery tale which seemed to be motionless for several minutes, going dim and then very brilliant, like a dormant fire which keeps coming to life. It would have been like an electric bulb in shape, except that it seemed to have rough edges. [The object] then fell somewhere behind the hills at the back of my bungalow and the earth shook.'[26]

That the crash of the object caused a considerable earth tremor was something also confirmed by Police Constable Gwilym Owen who was off duty at the time and having a drink in the nearby Dudley Arms public house: 'There was a great roar and a bang and the glasses shook. The sky was lit up over the mountains. The colour was yellowish but other people in the valley described seeing blue lights.'[27]

Five miles from the scene of the crash, Police Sergeant Gwyn Williams was at home in Corwen when the object hit Cader Bronwen. 'The walls shook and the mirror swung away from the wall,' recalled Sergeant Williams. 'My first thought was that a big lorry had hit the cinema – it was that kind of a roar and bang. Everyone ran into the street.'[28]

Remarkably, the force of the impact caused tremors to be felt much further away than Corwen. Police stations as far as sixty miles from the mountain received calls from members of the public who had felt the 'quake'.[29]

In fact, at 8.38 p.m. on the same night, the Global Seismology Unit of the Institute of Geological Sciences at Edinburgh recorded an earth tremor measuring between 3.5 and 4 on the Richter Scale. In response to questions from eager journalists, Dr Roy Lilwall, the Senior Scientific Officer at the institute, said that he had been told that a meteorite had come down on Cader Bronwen. He added that, to have been responsible for the 'earthquake' recorded at Edinburgh, the meteorite would have had to have weighed several hundred tons.[30]

Prior to the explosion on the Berwyn Mountains, the object had also been seen by a number of amateur astronomers based both in Cheshire and on the Isle of Man.[31] That two inexplicable phenomena – the mysterious helicopter wave and the object that crashed in Wales – should both have been seen in the same time-frame over Cheshire cannot be mere coincidence.

Approximately ninety minutes after the crash, Mr Ken Haughton of Betws-y-Coed viewed a 'luminous sphere', some 400 feet across and travelling at an approximated height of 15,000 feet. It was Mr Haughton's opinion that, as he watched the UFO, it descended into the sea in the area of Ryhl or in the Dee estuary.[32]

On the following day, a Royal Air Force mountain rescue team from Anglesey was sent to the area and, along with personnel from Gwynedd police, searched for any sign of the object or its impact point. In turn, they received assistance from the RAF station at Valley, Anglesey, who dispatched two aircraft to conduct a photographic survey of the area. Nothing was found.[33]

That day an unusual craft was seen by David Upton of Gobowen. As he went out of the back door of his home at about 7.15 p.m., David was struck by the brightness of an object in the western sky and quickly ran back into the house for a pair of field glasses. To his complete amazement, these revealed a disc-shaped object which seemed to be divided up into four distinct sections, each of which was of a different colour – red, green, yellow and purple. David's sister, Elizabeth, a twenty-year-old bank clerk, then took over the glasses, followed shortly after by their mother, Mary Upton. Both verified David's description.

'I had been watching it for about ten minutes and thought perhaps I should tell someone about it,' said Elizabeth. She telephoned the local police and they said that they would dispatch someone to the area. A minute or so after the call, the UFO disappeared behind a cloud. 'We waited for the cloud to pass and when it did the disc had gone too,' said Elizabeth. 'When I first came out of the house the light from the object was dazzling, like a street lamp. When we looked through the field glasses we could define its overall disc-shape and the four sections.'[34]

Was this yet another unidentified aerial craft, perhaps searching for the remains of the vehicle which struck the Berwyn Mountains?

Two people known to have been involved in the investigation of the 'crash site' of the object were Doctors Ron Maddison and Aneurin Evans of Keele University. Both expressed the opinion that a meteor had been the culprit.[35] This theory, however, does not satisfactorily explain the testimony of Mrs Anne Williams who recalled that the object was 'hanging in the sky', and '. . . seemed to be motionless for several minutes . . .' And one would imagine that – if a meteor had impacted into the side of a Welsh mountain with such force that the subsequent shockwaves were felt at least sixty miles away, and possibly as far away as Scotland – it would have left a fairly noticeable crater. Yet according to Dr Maddison, 'the only changes we could see were recent disturbances of surface soil in some areas, but we were hampered to some extent by light snowfall'.[36]

The 'meteor' theory also fails to explain the 'luminous sphere' seen by Ken Haughton to descend into the sea near Rhyl, and the multi-coloured

UFO witnessed by the Upton family at Gobowen. If the object was not a meteor, then what was it?

Respected researcher Margaret Fry has interviewed a number of people who had involvement in the Cader Bronwen crash and has uncovered a telling amount of information which negates the accepted theory that the object had been a meteor.

One interviewee was a nurse who, on the evening of January 23, received a telephone call from the police at Colwyn Bay informing her of the possibility that an aircraft had crashed on Cader Bronwen. She quickly packed her nursing bags and, with her two teenage daughters, drove to the scene to lend any assistance that was deemed necessary.

Upon arrival at Cader Bronwen, all three were amazed to see a huge, circular object positioned on the side of the mountain which radiated an orange glow. The nurse and her daughters remained 'quite close' to the object for more than ten minutes, at which point they noticed a number of people climbing the peak and carrying torches. Having had the opportunity to see the UFO at close quarters, the nurse was convinced that it had not crashed. Quite the reverse, the object appeared fully intact, as if it had landed there.

As her daughters' nerves were quite shattered, and there was no evidence of a fatal accident, the nurse quickly led her family back down the mountain. As they descended they were met by a group of police officers and army personnel who hustled them away saying that no-one was allowed on the mountain. The nurse regretted leaving the landing site when she did, but felt that it was necessary for her daughters' sakes.[37]

If, as now seems likely, a team of army personnel had been deployed to secure the UFO landing site on the night of January 23, then one might ask, Where did they come from? The speed with which they arrived at the scene suggests that they must have had warning that the UFO was likely to make a 'touch-down'. If the curious helicopter wave of 1973–4 was evidence of some 'rapid deployment' unit designed to monitor UFO activity – as seems to have been the case in the American incidents – then one cannot ignore the the possibility that the two matters were related. More so when it becomes apparent that, after the

UFO landing on Cader Bronwen, sightings of the mystery helicopters largely ceased.

There was no evidence of the presence of either the UFO or the unit of soldiers on the peak by the time that Doctors Maddison and Evans and the mountain rescue team arrived on the following day. So one can only assume that, unless the UFO exited the area under its own volition, it was removed at some point late on the evening of January 23, or in the very early hours of January 24.

Two days later it was stated in the local press that 'police and RAF rescue experts' had come to the conclusion that the strange lights seen throughout the area were due to the actions of a number of men who were out at the time hunting hares! Any link with the strange explosion was merely coincidental . . . RAF search team leader, Sergeant H. Oldham, said that another search of the area was unlikely to occur unless further information surfaced which attributed the 'lights' to another source.[38]

Where the 'hare' explanation came from is something of a mystery. Not surprisingly, it received short shrift with the local witnesses, as can be seen in the following extract taken from a letter to the *Wrexham Leader*:

> Regarding your front page article 'Mystery Tremor' in the issue of January 25, I find the explanation given absolutely ludicrous. The tremors shook houses over a 60 mile radius, and the lights were seen clearly miles away – this was reported by the national press and radio.
>
> I know nothing about 'Hare hunting' but unless the hunters use aircraft searchlights and kill their prey by lobbing a small atom bomb at them, then I fail to see how anyone can accept such an explanation.[39]

Was all the talk of 'hares' designed to discredit speculation that the object had been something other than a meteorite? It is certainly true that press coverage of the incident declined rapidly when this very novel theory first surfaced. Oddly enough, when a similar encounter took place in December 1980 at Rendlesham Forest, Suffolk, it was remarked by some commentators that what were believed to have been landing marks left by a grounded UFO were possibly quite down-to-earth indentations made by the local rabbit population![40]

Are we any closer to learning what actually took place in those winter months of late 1973 and early 1974? The existence of the 'phantom helicopter' wave is proven, as is the appearance of the many unusual 'lights' seen in the same time-frame and in the same areas, namely Staffordshire, Derbyshire and Cheshire. That something other than a meteorite touched down on Cader Bronwen on the night of January 23, 1974, also appears likely.

There is, however, one point which remains unresolved. According to the majority of the witness reports, the object had hit the mountain with considerable force. Yet the UFO seen on the peak at close range by the nurse and her daughters appears to have landed normally and there was no evidence of a crash.

Were there two separate incidents? Given that a number of UFO sightings were reported after the initial explosion, perhaps we should consider it a possibility that the object which was responsible for the incredible blast on the mountain was a different one to that seen by the nurse and her family.

What of the rumoured CIA links to these incidents? Admittedly, there is no hard evidence to suggest that the CIA were in any way implicated in the retrieval of the object from Cader Bronwen. Yet a link between the CIA and the mystery helicopters has been postulated, in official FBI documentation, no less. Is it merely coincidence that while Britain was being plagued by its own 'helicopter invasion', rumours were rife within the media that CIA and NSA personnel were operating on mainland Britain? Perhaps the idea of a joint CIA-Ministry of Defence project designed to respond on a quick reaction basis to UFO incidents should be considered . . .

One such 'quick reaction' unit known to exist in the USA is Project Moon Dust, although it now goes under a different, still-classified name. A document which originated with the US Air Force in 1961 reveals that: 'Peacetime employment of AFCIN intelligence team capability is provided for in UFO investigation . . . and in support of Air Force

Systems Command (AFSC) Foreign Technology Division (FTD) Projects
Moon Dust and Blue Fly. These . . . projects all involve a potential
for employment of qualified field intelligence personnel on a quick
reaction basis to recover or perform field exploitation of unidentified
flying objects . . .'[41]

Had a CIA-controlled Moon Dust team been dispatched to the British
Isles in late 1973 to perform 'field exploitation' of a downed UFO? If so,
this would provide a reasonable explanation for the many UFO-helicopter
reports in circulation at the time, not to mention the rumoured influx of
CIA agents to the country.

Another link suggesting that the phantom helicopter phenomenon may
be tied to a Government-controlled project to retrieve crashed UFOs
came from Leonard Stringfield. In a 1982 status report, Stringfield
related the account of a US lieutenant colonel who professed to have
intimate knowledge of the mysterious helicopters. Dubbed 'Colonel
X', the source confided the following in Tommy Blann, a dedicated
researcher of Stringfield's acquaintance: '. . . underground installations, as
well as isolated areas of military reservations have squadrons of unmarked
helicopters, which have sophisticated instrumentation on board, that are
dispatched to areas of UFO activity to monitor these craft or airlift them
out of the area if one has malfunctioned.'[42]

There is an interesting epilogue to the events of 1973–4. During the
course of her enquiries into the UFO enigma, Jenny Randles learned from
a former British Government official that one such 'device', namely a
crashed UFO, was kept under wraps at a military base somewhere in
South Wales.[43] If this was a reference to the object which fell to earth
on Cader Bronwen, then the British Government has had in its possession
irrefutable proof of extra-terrestrial visitation since at least 1974.

CHAPTER 10

UNIDENTIFIED VISITORS

LESS THAN THREE MONTHS AFTER THE CADER BRONWEN EVENT, an equally astonishing, though substantially different, encounter took place at a highly sensitive military establishment in southern England. Although the witness has requested anonymity (largely due to the fact that she still believes the incident to be covered by the Official Secrets Act), I have interviewed her at length, and have confirmed that her credentials are indeed bona fide. Her account is certainly provocative.

The date was early 1974, and the setting, the Marconi facility at Frimley. At the time the witness was employed as a draughtswoman in the 'Central Services' branch – having previously served an apprenticeship in a particular division of the Royal Navy – something which ensured she had access to much of the establishment.

On arrival at work one particular morning, she was surprised to see an inordinate number of MOD personnel swarming around one specific building which had been cordoned off. Although she was aware that something of significance had occurred, it was not until later that she was able to tackle a trusted colleague who was himself a manager at the base.

'Something very serious has happened, hasn't it?' she enquired. 'Yes,' came the response, 'we've had a break-in. I can't say any more.' Over the course of several weeks, however, further pieces of the puzzle began to fall into place. It transpired that the 'break-in' was far more than simply an unauthorized entry. What occurred was nothing short of the penetration of one of the British Government's most guarded research stations by a living, breathing extra-terrestrial creature!

I was cautiously advised that the incident had occurred at night, and the prime witness was a security guard who had been patrolling the building as part of his routine duty. Whilst walking along a corridor, the guard was startled by a dazzling blue light which emanated from a room. But this was no ordinary room – it was a storage facility for top secret documentation generated by Marconi as part of its work on behalf of the British Government, much of which related to classified radar-related defence projects.

Realizing that no-one should have been in the area at that hour of the night, the guard burst into the room, only to be confronted by a shocking sight. There, literally sifting through pages of top secret files, was a humanoid (but decidedly non-human) creature which quickly de-materialized before the shocked guard's eyes. Although severely traumatized by the event, he was able to give a brief description of the being to his superiors and noted that the blue light emanated from a helmet which encompassed the head.

By the following morning the guard had suffered a near-complete nervous collapse and was taken (under military guard) to an unspecified hospital for intensive therapy. He was not seen again. Some weeks later, my source had occasion to overhear snippets of a conversation which took place in the office of her superior, a Mr Bevan. I have been advised that the following is an almost word-for-word transcript of the relevant section of the conversation: 'We have no way of keeping these beings out; we just don't know what to do next. If they can get in here, they can get in anywhere.'

Are 'James Bond-type' extra-terrestrials infiltrating our most protected research stations and stealing our defence secrets? As outlandish as such a theory may sound, it does receive a degree of support from official sources. For example, consider the following extract taken from a 1972 report titled 'Controlled Offensive Behaviour – USSR' which was prepared for the US

Defense Intelligence Agency. (As we shall learn later, the DIA has a close working relationship with opposite numbers in Whitehall.)

> ... before the end of the 1970s, Soviet diplomats will be able to sit in their foreign embassies and use ESP (extra-sensory perception) to steal the secrets of their enemies ... a spy would be hypnotised, then his invisible 'spirit' would be ordered to leave his body, travel across barriers of space and time to a foreign government's security facility, and there read top-secret documents and relay back their information ... the Soviets are at least 25 years ahead of the U.S. in psychic research ... [and] have realised the immense military advantage of the psychic ability known as astral projection (out-of-the-body travel).

Bizarre? Most definitely, but military agencies throughout the globe are keen to exploit new and radical intelligence-gathering techniques. The method described above is simply one of many which have been examined in the past quarter of a century by the governments of the UK, USA and USSR. Perhaps, somewhere else in the universe, such techniques have already been perfected, to the extent that a living organism can now literally come and go at will, completely unhindered by our seemingly rigid physical laws.

Interestingly enough, my source for the 'Marconi story' still lives in the vicinity. She has informed me that, in the years following the incident at Frimley, more and more unusual aerial craft made their presence felt in the area and at the nearby RAF Farnborough – including one object, dubbed 'the bat', which continues to make repeated intrusions into Farnborough airspace to this day.

In late November 1975, researchers Peter Bottomley and Gordon Clegg conducted a detailed investigation of an incident which had reportedly occurred on June 23 of that same year in the Atlantic Ocean.

'The first point that must be made concerning this report is that although the witnesses' name, address and full occupation [are] on file, none of these details can be made public,' reported Bottomley and Clegg.

'This is because he was at the time under the strict jurisdiction of the Ministry of Defence, to whom a full report was made. We are most fortunate therefore, that he has seen fit to brave the Official Secrets Act by relating the story to us.'

At the time of the sighting the witness was on board a ship off the west coast of Ireland, where he was operating radar equipment in thick fog. An echo was suddenly picked up on the screen which was presumed to be a surface vessel closing in on the ship.

The captain was quickly notified of the object's presence, where-upon it began to accelerate at a 'totally impossible' rate. Being well acquainted with all types of natural phenomena and anomalous propagations (which can easily confuse an inexperienced radar operator), the witness realized that whatever he was tracking, it could only be classed as an unidentified flying object, and not any form of sea-based craft.

In keeping with standard procedure, the captain filed a report which was channelled through to the Ministry of Defence for study. Following the encounter, Bottomley and Clegg had several opportunities to interview their source, and on each occasion his account was related without any internal inconsistencies. Moreover, both were highly impressed with the man, who appeared to have a keen understanding of radar and electronics, and was both 'level-headed and open-minded'.

Throughout the duration of the sighting, Bottomley and Clegg learned, the ship had been stationary, and there had been no temperature inversions and no surface turbulence reported. Unfortunately, the witness failed to wind up the vertical aerial as the object began to disappear out of range – as a consequence he was unable to say whether the object was simply lost over the twenty-two-mile horizon of the equipment, or if it also ascended into the sky.

In conclusion, Bottomley and Clegg formed the opinion that their informant was sincere; he believed that he had seen a genuinely anomalous unidentified flying object; but could offer no conclusive explanation as to what the UFO had been.

'The possibility of a hoax seems remote, because of the character of the witness and the fact that he is insistent on personal details not being revealed,' commented the two researchers. 'Owing to the close supervision of the ship's crew by the MOD, the investigators feel that there is little more progress that can be made on this case.'[1]

At 12.40 a.m. on the morning of January 14, 1976, Mr Rod Riddell, a thirty-five-year-old Pilot's Assistant resident on the Isle of Wight, was in his garden when he noticed a bright, stationary light in the western sky. As Mr Riddell watched the light, which was estimated to be at cloud height, it seemed to grow brighter. As it did so, the light began to move in an easterly direction, albeit at a speed of no more than 30 mph.

Mr Riddell quickly called his wife, Jenny, and both watched as the light travelled over their heads at a considerably lower height than when first seen. At that point, the Riddells were able to see that the light was attached to a rectangular object around a hundred feet long and fifty feet wide. Despite their proximity to the strange vehicle, the Riddells reported that it operated in complete silence. After passing overhead the UFO continued to move eastwards, accelerated to a 'fantastic speed', and disappeared at an upward angle into the early morning sky.

Mr Riddell subsequently reported details of the encounter to staff at the Royal Air Force facility at Thorney Island, who ventured the possibility that the object had been nothing more than a helicopter (a theory which was later negated when checks revealed that no helicopters had been flying at the time in question). Interestingly, Mr Riddell was informed that he would 'probably hear shortly from the Ministry of Defence': this was something of an understatement!

Within five minutes of his conversation with staff at Thorney Island, Mr Riddell received a telephone call from the MOD, who requested details of the encounter. The speed with which the MOD followed up on this matter is almost unparalleled, at least as far as civilian witnesses to UFO sightings are concerned. It was later discovered by Richard Nash, an investigator who looked into the matter, that there had been good reason for the Ministry of Defence's immediate interest in the case: at 10.30 p.m. on January 13 – that is about two hours and ten minutes before the Riddells' sighting – an entirely independent report of a very similar object had been filed with the MOD by the Meteorological Officer at RAF Thorney Island.

Despite this corroboration, Mr Riddell received a 'non-committal' letter from the MOD, offering no explanation for what he and his wife had viewed in the Isle of Wight skies.[2]

Of the thousand or so pages of UFO-related documentation declassified by the United States' Central Intelligence Agency, very few make any reference to UFO encounters involving British witnesses. There is one document in particular which stands out as an exception. Dated November 18, 1976, the one-page report is titled 'Aerial Observation of Intense Source of Light' and was prepared by the CIA's Domestic Collection Division.

Since all of the 200 UFO reports examined by the Ministry of Defence in 1976 are still classified, this particular report may give us some indication of the types of UFO encounters which the MOD was obliged to investigate during that year.

1. An unusual incident was observed during a 10 September 1976 British European Airways (BEA) flight (number 831) Moscow to London. Between 1800 and 1900 hours, the aircraft was cruising at an altitude of approximately 33 thousand feet (9,900 meters), apparently inside the border of Lithuania, when a blinding light was observed off the starboard flight path of the aircraft. The light's distance was estimated to be approximately 10 to 15 miles (16 to 24 kilometers) off of the aircraft's path and approximately five to six thousand feet (1,500 to 1,800 meters) below the aircraft, somewhat above a lower cloud layer. The light, which resembled a sodium vapor lamp (yellowish in color), and which was too intense to view directly for any period of time, completely lit the top of the lower cloud layer, giving it a glowing cast.

2. The light was of such interest that the BEA pilot came onto the aircraft's intercom network, stated that he was somewhat concerned over its presence, and said he had asked the Soviet authorities for an identification of its source. The Soviet authorities came back with a negative identification response, suggesting that he should not ask questions. The light was observed for

approximately 10 to 15 minutes, until the aircraft had flown past and left the light source behind.[3]

I have been unable to glean any further information on this matter from the CIA, and my enquiries with Russian authorities remain unanswered. Hopefully, the MOD will see fit to release its papers on the incident in due course. Notably, a similar UFO, also emitting an extraordinary amount of light, was seen in British airspace by pilot D.W. Sweeney in late 1957.

Shortly after midnight on Sunday, August 28, 1977, a large object, variously described as being 'triangular-shaped' or 'diamond-shaped', was seen by more than ten police officers and several members of the public in and around the Windermere area of Cumbria.

At 12.10 a.m. Police Constable Ian Mackenzie, on duty at Bowness, noticed two very bright, horizontal lights in the sky which were flying to the right of the nearby Langdale Pikes and heading in his direction. The lights moved slowly – so slowly that PC Mackenzie dismissed the possibility that they were attached to an aircraft – and became brighter, but travelled in total silence. PC Mackenzie continued to watch the lights until they disappeared behind an area of trees.

At that same time, thirty-nine-year-old Police Sergeant John McMullan was walking through the town of Keswick when he too saw the UFO. Fortunately, as it manoeuvred overhead, Sergeant McMullan (who was with three other policemen at the time) was able to make out the outline of the object: the shape of a 'hang glider or [a] diamond'; the only attendant noise was a 'quiet hum'.

Ten minutes later, Police Sergeant James Trohear and Police Officer John Fishwick reported that, along with a number of other officers, they too could see the UFO from their position, which was the Fallbarrow Park Caravan Site on the shores of Lake Windermere. It was Sergeant Trohear's opinion that the craft was 'triangular or slightly diamond-shaped', while another officer commented that the outline of the object 'resembled the shape of a stingray fish'.

At 12.22 a.m., Police Officer Alexander Inglis was driving home to

Carlisle from Keswick on the A591 Keswick-to-Bothel road with three colleagues, when all four noticed the mystery lights travelling over the hills to the north-west. When it became apparent that the object was heading in their direction, Officer Inglis brought the car to a halt for a better view. Aside from seeing two 'extremely bright lights', none of the officers could make out a distinct shape, but a very faint 'purring' noise was in evidence.

A mere three minutes after that, PC Joseph Maw and a colleague reported that they too could see the lights, heading in the direction of Buttermere, and travelling low over the fells. PC Maw commented that a slight buzzing noise could be heard. At the same time, Mrs Mary Mortlock of High Portinscale near Keswick, watched as an object passed over her house, after first having approached from the direction of Bishop Rock in the north-west. Her attention had first been drawn to two horizontally positioned lights, which, she said, were accompanied by two amber-coloured lights. It was impossible to make out the size of the object, explained Mrs Mortlock, but she continued to watch its movements until it was lost from view near Helvellyn.

Shortly after Mrs Mortlock's experience, a UFO was seen by Police Constable David Wild, who was out on foot patrol on the A592 Rayrigg road at Bowness. He estimated that the UFO was at a height of around 1,500 feet, and had come to a complete stop over a nearby hill. Although unable to accurately distinguish the shape of the UFO, Constable Wild said that it had appeared to be 'kite-shaped, or like a skate fish', adding that the object was 'very large . . . and solid in construction'.

At 12.30 a.m., twenty minutes after the initial sighting by PC Mackenzie at Bowness, sixty-three-year-old John Platt, his wife and several relatives saw the same strange craft moving towards Cartmel Fell. As they watched, the object halted its forward motion, then 'floated' away noiselessly in an easterly direction. The whole experience had been 'uncanny and rather weird' said Mr Platt. Meanwhile, a husband and wife (who have requested anonymity) at Silverdale also caught sight of the craft. Grabbing a pair of binoculars, the husband reported: 'I was looking up into what appeared in shape like a giant ocean-going catamaran with twin hulls. A large transom at the front supported what appeared to be two giant lights [without beams].' His wife described the lights as 'large bulkhead areas intensely illuminated'. The moonlight did not appear to reflect from the surface of the object, which was a 'dull, shadowy, charcoal colour'.

At the exact moment of their sighting, a report to the effect that there was an unusual aerial craft in the area was broadcast over local police radio. Two of those who responded to the message were Constable Ronald Jones and Sergeant Geoffrey Merckel. From their position near Skelwith Bridge on the A593 road, they watched a 'diamond, kite-shaped object' move silently towards Grange and disappear out to sea over Morecambe Bay. Unless there were other witnesses who have yet to come forward (which is entirely possible), the UFO was lost from view at that point and never returned. Or did it?

On September 30, 1977, at 7.30 p.m., a very similar craft was seen by a motorcyclist driving on the A2 road from Sittingbourne towards Newington. 'Two very bright white beams, like headlights' emanated from the object, which was described as being similar in shape to 'a flatfish – a skate', a description virtually identical to that reported by PC David Wild at Bowness.

The fact that the 'Cumbrian' case has so many supporting witnesses who attested to the strange shape of the object, not to mention its size, ability to hover, and capacity to operate in almost complete silence, convinces me that something manifestly extraordinary was in evidence in the Windermere skies on August 28, 1977.[4]

By now, it will have become apparent that UFOs have a curious tendency to make their presence felt during large-scale military manoeuvres. Sightings of highly unusual objects were reported during Operation Bulldog in 1949 and throughout Operation Mainbrace in 1952. A similar incident took place on the Yorkshire Moors in 1963, as Paul Greensill, formerly of the British Army, has verified. Fifteen years after Greensill's experience, history almost repeated itself.

The year was 1978, and the place was, once again, the Yorkshire Moors. Whilst taking part in a night exercise, Mike Perrin and 'Titch' Carvell of the Royal Armoured Corps were driving their Land Rover across the Moors when they caught sight of a dome-shaped, silver-coloured object hovering some fifty yards from their position. Both reported that the craft made a 'strange buzzing' sound.

'It was about the size of five Land Rovers and had portholes,' said Perrin. 'Lights inside were flashing red and white. I tried to start our vehicle, but the engine was totally dead. We watched the UFO for five minutes, then it shot off and all the power returned to our engine. It's army policy to dismiss UFO reports, but when we went back to the area next morning with a sergeant, we found a large circle of burnt grass where the object had hovered.'[5]

I find it particularly striking that the UFO exhibited the power to render the Land Rover completely inoperable. Was this an unintentional side-effect of the UFO's presence, or was it a demonstration of the power that the UFO intelligences possess? Let us hope the former.

Although the British Government had been used to dealing with large-scale 'UFO flaps', such as those which occurred in 1967 and 1971, nothing could have prepared the Ministry of Defence for the huge increase in UFO reports with which it was swamped in 1978. No fewer than 750 encounters involving unidentified aerial objects were investigated by MOD staff in that year, a figure which has never been bettered, before or since. Also, via an academic source involved in secret research for the MOD, Timothy Good has learned that £11 million in Defence funds was appropriated in 1978 to ensure that in-depth investigations were undertaken.[6]

By the end of 1979, a further 550 UFO sightings had been filed with the MOD, making a total of 1,300 reports for that two-year period. I should stress that this does not mean that the United Kingdom was blessed with visitations by thirteen hundred extra-terrestrial spacecraft during that time, but it does suggest that the MOD's investigative teams certainly had their work cut out.[7]

Combined 'radar-visual' sightings of unidentified flying objects over the UK, and indeed throughout the world, date back to the 1940s. It is this type of report which carries most weight, and is among the hardest to explain as a mere figment of an over-active imagination. One incident in particular which falls into this category took place in early April 1980.

The event began during the evening, when an uncorrelated target was picked up flying over Nottingham by radar personnel at the nearby East Midlands Airport. As the UFO was following a line of flight which was to take it close to Birmingham Airport, a civilian radar operator at Birmingham was apprised of the situation by staff at East Midlands.

It was not long before the UFO made its presence known to Birmingham Airport. Most remarkable of all, as the radar operator at Birmingham locked onto the UFO he was amazed to find that, whilst travelling in a south-westerly direction, it did so at a mere 44 mph! Naturally puzzled, the operator resolved to keep a close watch on its movements.

At a point between Birmingham and Coventry, the UFO was sighted visually by the pilot of a light aircraft which was also in the vicinity. The UFO appeared to resemble 'a car headlight shining through mist' reported the pilot. Staff at Birmingham Airport continued to track the object until it reached the Bristol area, whereupon it was lost from their radar scopes.

According to the radar operator at Birmingham (who related the above to Jenny Randles), the UFO had also been tracked at other facilities. None would admit to this, however, and they merely referred enquirers to RAF West Drayton, Middlesex. It was at West Drayton that the trail went decidely cold.[8]

Most probably, fully aware that they had a genuine UFO incident on their hands, the authorities at West Drayton contacted the Ministry of Defence who assumed control of the matter. This theory is supported by the following statement made to me by Flight Lieutenant J. Bosworth of West Drayton in 1988: 'With reference to reports of UFOs here at the Aeronautical Information Section (Military), which is a part of my flight, we act only as a convenient "post-office" for receiving these reports, and take no further action other than passing them on to the MOD.'[9]

'For the first time in twenty years I was stumped for an explanation,' admitted the radar operator at Birmingham Airport to Jenny Randles.[10] Whether or not the Ministry of Defence was equally stumped, I cannot say. I can say that no official denial of the incident has been forthcoming from the MOD, which is surely suggestive of something.

As we have seen, one particular Royal Air Force installation which has been implicated in a number of UFO encounters since the early 1950s is

RAF Neatishead, Norfolk. Malcolm Scurrah, now employed as a systems analyst for West Yorkshire police, has gone on record as stating that, during his tenure with the Royal Air Force which lasted from 1979 to 1986, he was involved in a UFO event at the base which was cloaked in official secrecy. The encounter has a number of parallels with the 1952 and 1956 incidents at Neatishead.

Malcolm is unsure of the exact date of the occurrence, but has been able to confirm that it took place in either the latter part of October or early November 1980. As on August 13, 1956, the UFO was tracked on ground-based radar at Neatishead, executed a number of aerial manoeuvres which 'defied all convention', and was seen by the pilot of a Royal Air Force Phantom fighter aircraft, who described it as a 'very bright light in front of him'. As was also the case in 1956, the UFO vanished as quickly as it had arrived. Malcolm has also stated that a number of high-ranking Royal Air Force personnel arrived at Neatishead to question those involved, and that other senior RAF figures departed with the relevant radar tapes which displayed the movements of the UFO.[11]

Within a month of the experience at Neatishead, a 'glowing orange ball' was seen manoeuvring around the 'Northern', an oil platform in the North Sea. The date was November 25, 1980, and the time was 6.40 a.m. It is not known for how long the object was seen, but the event was apparently not transitory. The object was of sufficient size to be seen from another platform in the Brent field which was approximately twelve to fifteen miles from the Northern. An RAF Nimrod aircraft was dispatched to the area, and the Royal Air Force was put on standby. Derek Smith, offshore installation manager for Chevron Oil and an ex-Royal Navy Commander, duly entered details of the encounter into the platform's log book. So far as is known, no firm conclusions were ever reached.[12]

The final months of 1980 also saw an abundance of UFO encounters reported throughout the rest of the planet. I have chosen to reference the following case – which I have selected from the released UFO files of the United States' Department of State – because the description given of the UFOs is not wholly dissimilar to that reported by the Royal Air Force pilot involved in the 1980 experience at RAF Neatishead.

In February 1981 the State Department prepared a three-page 'Confidential' memorandum titled 'Close Encounters in Afghanistan' which was circulated to a number of official bodies. Between September 1980 and January 1981, the document revealed, several reports had been received of 'strange lights' which illuminated large portions of the Afghan countryside:

> Accounts have in common the brightness of the lights, the distance from which they are discernible, and the size of the areas they appear to illuminate (more – perhaps much more – than 5 miles in diameter). Accounts differ in that some speak of narrow beams, which are compared with laser or search lights, as a part of the phenomenon. Most, though, speak of more diffused illumination. Accounts differ as to whether lights slowly wax and wane, or reach maximum intensity and turn off instantly.

The report continued with a description of the lights given by a firsthand witness:

> . . . first impression was that [the light] was borne by a helicopter which was searching for them. It did not move. However, nor was any aircraft (or other) motor noise discernible. They left the area as quickly as possible but were sure that the light remained visible and stationary for at least 20 minutes.
>
> I asked [censored] if the light might have come from something like the hand-held magnesium parachute flares such as are used by the U.S. Army. He was quite sure not, as there was no movement and the duration was much too long. As for mortar-launched flares, there was no explosion and again no drift.
>
> Interestingly, a night light phenomenon . . . was seen by diplomats and others a few months ago and reported in the press. We think this was probably of the moving light, classic UFO school, and not related to the Afghan sightings.[13]

Was there a connection with the encounter at RAF Neatishead? Quite naturally, the State Department suggested that the sightings had more to do with the activities of 'the Red Army' – which may well be true, but we should not simply reject the case out of hand, particularly in light of what took place in the final month of 1980 . . .

CHAPTER 11

THE RENDLESHAM AFFAIR

LATE IN DECEMBER 1980 A SERIES OF ALMOST SCIENCE FICTION-LIKE happenings took place in Rendlesham Forest, a densely treed area adjacent to the joint USAF/RAF military complex at Bentwaters–Woodbridge, Suffolk. Essentially, what occurred was nothing less than the landing of a structured craft of unknown origin. It was seen by a variety of USAF personnel, was tracked on radar, deposited traces of radiation with the forest, avoided capture, and created a controversy which rages to this day.

The case is supported by an army of military witnesses, a number of official documents, and an eighteen-minute audio cassette recording made 'live' as the events unfolded. Since early 1981 the incident has been the subject of numerous magazine articles, several books and a number of television documentaries.[1] Probably no other UFO case has attracted so much publicity, at least not in the British Isles, and there has probably been no other UFO encounter which has caused so many headaches for the British Government.

That something took place, the MOD has never disputed. Yet, as I have been reminded on a number of occasions, it is the considered opinion of the British Government that the entire matter is without defence significance. Based on what you are about to read, I beg to differ with this assertion.

One of the most interesting things about the Rendlesham affair is the vicinity in which the events unfolded. Until their closure in late 1993, Woodbridge and Bentwaters served as 'front-line' defenders of Britain's security. At the peak of the Cold War there were more than 13,000 US servicemen at the twin bases, plus an undisclosed number of nuclear weapons. In addition, several thousand Americans lived off-base, in rented cottages scattered throughout the communities of Alderburgh and Wickham Market.[2]

Some five miles from the now-vacated Woodbridge base is a small strip of coastal land known as Orford Ness, home to Britain's early radar-based research in the 1930s. As the Second World War loomed, much of that work was transferred to RAF Bawdsey, several miles south of Orford Ness but still on the outskirts of Rendlesham Forest. Historically important for its imposing manor house built in the 1880s by Sir Cuthbert Quilter, Bawdsey's work proved crucial in supplying Britain with adequate radar coverage during the war.[3]

As noted in chapter two, Canadian resident Ronald Anstee has stated that a UFO, some fifty feet in diameter, was seen in the vicinity of Rendlesham Forest in the summer of 1947. More interesting, the encounter was somehow connected with a new type of radar system that had been put to use in the area.

Sensitive radar projects continued to be developed in Suffolk for many years. In the late 1960s an 'Over the Horizon' radar system known as 'Cobra Mist' was established at Orford Ness, essentially to monitor the airspace of potentially hostile nations, and to give an advanced warning of any attempted aerial attack on the British Isles.[4]

To this day, that particular OTH project is considered a highly sensitive issue. The MOD's Defence Intelligence Staff, for example, are currently withholding from public access two files which concern the activities at Orford Ness; namely, 'Scientific and technical: OTH detection systems project' and 'Orford Ness, OTHR detection systems project'. Graham Stanley of the Public Record Office's Government Services Department has advised me that both files are classified and exempt from disclosure because 'they contain information relating to the security and intelligence agencies and are obviously highly sensitive'.[5]

In light of all this, one would imagine that the presence of a landed

UFO only a few miles from Orford Ness would have had the Ministry of Defence in a state of consternation. Apparently not, if the MOD's public stance is anything to go by: '. . . the witnesses described the object as being 3 metres wide and 2 metres high and that it illuminated the area with a bright white light,' Clive Neville of the MOD told me in 1988. 'In view of its reported small size, it is considered highly unlikely that the object was a piloted vehicle. In addition, I think you will agree that it is highly improbable that any violation of UK airspace would be heralded by such a display of lights. I believe that it is equally unlikely that any reconnaissance or flying activity would be announced in this way. As such we are satisfied that the incident is of no defence significance.'[6]

Now, what about the facts . . .

Much has been written about the extraordinary series of encounters which occurred in Rendlesham Forest in December 1980. Perhaps the most telling account comes from Airman Larry Warren, who was stationed at RAF Bentwaters at the time and claims intimate knowledge of the events which took place. As Warren recalls, the incident occurred during the early hours of December 27 when, along with a convoy of military personnel, he was driven by jeep to the edge of the forest. From that moment on, matters took a startling and seemingly fantastic turn:

> We were all told to hand in our weapons. I had an M16 rifle. Then we took lights into the woods. Amazing things seemed to happen even then. I noticed animals running in panic from the forest. Fuel gauges on the vehicles registered empty when we knew they were full.
>
> As we approached a clearing we could see some very bright lights. We were a bit shook up to come across a U.S. medic treating one of our security police who appeared to have broken down and was crying. The clearing was full of RAF and USAF security people – about 200 of them. Several movie cameras had been set up and choppers were flying above.
>
> Then we saw an object. It appeared to be resting on the ground and looked like a giant aspirin. It was transparent. We were in awe,

never having seen anything remotely like this. Nearby, there was an airman carrying a radio. Suddenly we heard a chopper pilot telling him: 'Here it comes.'

We looked up and saw a red ball of light coming towards us from over the trees. In the distance, it looked about 100 feet high and appeared to be coming in to land. It came down right over the transparent aspirin on the ground. There was no sound at all. We were all mesmerised. All of a sudden, the red light exploded. The place was filled with an explosion of all kinds of colours.

We were blinded. When the colours died down, we looked again, and there was a machine there. It appeared to have a triangular shape and was covered with pipes and valves and things. It was about 20 feet across the bottom with sloping sides up to the top 12 feet to 15 feet high . . . certainly big enough to handle people.

A captain motioned us to approach the ship. We walked up close enough to touch it. It was giving off a metallic bluish light. There were three groups of about four security men each circling the thing. I could see our shadows on the craft. As we walked, they moved. But when we stopped, the shadows seemed to take another pace. It was weird.

Suddenly, a green light came on at the top of the spaceship. It moved down the sides of the craft until it reached our heads then bounced from one to the other along the side. Just like the ball bounces in a video game. Then I realised the spaceship was inhabited. There were beings aboard. I didn't see them because I was on the wrong side of the craft. But others did. They said there were three, and they were wearing silver suits. I had a strange feeling and seemed to black out.

The next thing I knew, it was about 5.00 a.m. and I was waking up lying half across my bunk. I still had my uniform on and was up to my knees in mud. To this day, I don't know how I got back to the barracks, or what happened after I saw the green light bounce off our shadows. My room-mate said I'd been brought into the room by some people – he didn't know who – and just dumped on the bed.

Later that day, myself and several of the guys who had been at the field were given the once-over with a geiger counter but we were never told why or what the results were. We were all called to the base security office at Bentwaters and told what we'd seen had been classified top secret.

Several civilians were doing all the talking. We took them for CIA. They said if we ever told the story, no one would believe us. One guy added that if we did talk, then bullets were cheap. I thought, 'This guy is actually threatening our lives. He obviously meant it.' Looking back, the one thing that bothers me is that the officers and civilians present seemed to know all about it – they weren't all that surprised.[7]

There ends Larry Warren's remarkable acount. Of course, this is simply one man's testimony to an event which occurred more than fifteen years ago. Fortunately, however, Warren's testimony does not stand alone – others have come forward to confirm that something truly 'other-wordly' did indeed occur.

On January 13, 1981, the Deputy Base Commander at RAF Woodbridge, Charles Halt, prepared an official report concerning the events within Rendlesham Forest which was duly forwarded to the Ministry of Defence for inspection.

What the MOD thought of the report, we can only guess at, but in the weeks and months that followed, the Ministry proved highly reluctant to discuss the Rendlesham affair. To illustrate, it was not until April 13, 1983, that an official admission was made to Jenny Randles that a few 'lights' had been seen in the vicinity of Rendlesham Forest which remained 'unexplained'.[8]

Almost two months later to the day, a copy of Colonel Halt's memorandum was declassified in accordance with the American Freedom of Information Act, and forwarded to US researcher, Robert Todd. In a June 14 letter to Todd, Colonel Peter Bent, Commander of the 513th Combat Support Group (CSG), made a stunning admission: 'It might interest you to know that the U.S. Air Force had no longer retained a copy of the 13 January 1981 letter written by Lt. Col. Charles I. Halt. The Air Force file copy had been properly disposed of in accordance with Air

Force regulations. Fortunately, through diligent inquiry and the gracious consent of Her Majesty's government, the British Ministry of Defence and the Royal Air Force, the U.S. Air Force was provided with a copy for you.'9

Curiously, during the course of an interview with MOD spokeswoman Pam Titchmarsh on August 18, 1983, Jenny Randles was specifically told that, contrary to the statement of Colonel Bent, the Ministry of Defence had not supplied the Americans with a copy of Colonel Halt's memo. Notably, Titchmarsh was extremely wary about discussing the case with Jenny, who had made a special visit to Whitehall with colleagues Brenda Butler and Dot Street. 'I wouldn't know,' was Titchmarsh's uneasy reply when Jenny asked her if the MOD's 'operational staff' had built up their own files on the case.

Nevertheless, since a copy of the Halt memo had been released to Robert Todd by American authorities, Titchmarsh was obliged to admit that her department (DS8) did have a copy of Colonel Halt's report on file, but denied that the events of December 1980 were of any defence significance – a stance from which the Ministry of Defence has never wavered.[10] At this juncture, let us turn our attention to that one piece of paper which the MOD felt so compelled to deny any knowledge of until 1983 – Colonel Halt's memorandum of January 13, 1981:

1. Early in the morning of 27 Dec 80 (approximately 0300L), two USAF security police patrolmen saw unusual lights outside the back gate at RAF Woodbridge. Thinking an aircraft might have crashed or been forced down, they called for permission to go outside the gate to investigate. The on-duty flight chief responded and allowed three patrolmen to proceed on foot. The individuals reported seeing a strange glowing object in the forest. The object was described as being metallic in appearance and triangular in shape, approximately two or three meters high. It illuminated the entire forest with a white light. The object itself had a pulsating red light on top with a bank(s) of blue lights underneath. The object was hovering or on legs. As the patrolmen approached the object, it maneuvered through the trees and disappeared. At this time the animals on a nearby farm went into a frenzy. The

object was briefly sighted approximately an hour later near the back gate.

2. The next day, three depressions 1½" deep and 7" in diameter were found where the object had been sighted on the ground. The following night (29 Dec 80) the area was checked for radiation. Beta/gamma readings of 0.1 milliroentgens were recorded with peak readings in the three depressions and near the center of the triangle formed by the depressions. A nearby tree had moderate (.05–.07) readings on the side of the tree toward the depressions.

3. Later in the night a red sun-like light was seen through the trees. It moved about and pulsed. At one point it appeared to throw off glowing particles and then broke into five separate white objects and then disappeared. Immediately thereafter, three star-like objects were noticed in the sky, two objects to the north and one to the south, all of which were about 10 degrees off the horizon. The objects moved rapidly in sharp angular movements and displayed red, green and blue lights. The objects to the north appeared to be elliptical through an 8–12 power lens. They then turned to full circles. The objects to the north remained in the sky for an hour or more. The object to the south was visible for two or three hours and beamed down a stream of light from time to time. Numerous individuals, including the undersigned, witnessed the activities in paragraphs 2 and 3.[11]

One year after Pam Titchmarsh admitted to Jenny Randles that Colonel Halt's memorandum was on file, a copy of an audio-tape recording made within Rendlesham Forest that night also surfaced, under somewhat odd circumstances. Lasting for around eighteen minutes, the tape is basically a running commentary attesting to the accuracy of Halt's written report. The reader should note that the eighteen minutes of recorded data covers a period of several hours. Nevertheless, we are left with a vital source of corroborating evidence for the events detailed in paragraphs two and three of Colonel Halt's memorandum:

HALT: The light's still there and all the barnyard animals have gone quiet now. We're heading about 110, 120 degrees from the site out through to the clearing now, still getting a reading on the meter . . . Everywhere else is just deathly calm. There is no doubt about it – there's some type of strange flashing red light ahead.

HALT: . . . We see strange strobe-like flashes to the er . . . well, they're sporadic, but there's definitely some kind of phenomenon. At about ten degrees, horizon, directly north, we've got two strange objects, er, half-moon shape, dancing about with coloured lights on 'em. That, er, guess to be about five to ten miles out, maybe less. The half-moons are now turning to full circles, as though there was an eclipse or something there, for a minute or two . . . One's moving away from us.

UNIDENTIFIED VOICE: It's moving out fast!

UNIDENTIFIED VOICE: This one on the right's heading away too!

HALT: . . . Now we're observing what appears to be a beam coming down to the ground. This is unreal! . . . And the objects are still in the sky although the one to the south looks like it's losing a little bit of altitude. The object to the south is still beaming down lights to the ground.

HALT: O.K., were looking at the thing; we're probably about two or three hundred yards away. It looks like an eye winking at you. It's still moving from side to side, and when you put the starscope on it, it sort of has a hollow centre; a dark centre. It's, you know, like the pupil of an eye looking at you, winking. And the flash is so bright to the starscope that it almost burns your eye. We passed the farmer's house and crossed into the next field, and now we have multiple sightings, of lights with a similar shape and all. But they seem to be steady, now, rather than a pulsating or glow with a red flash.

HALT: At 0244 we're at the far side of the farmer's, second farmer's, field. And made sighting again, about 110 degrees. This looks like it's clear out to the coast; it's right on the horizon. Moves about a bit, and flashes from time to time . . . We're turning around, heading back towards the base. The object to the south is still beaming down lights to the ground. 0400 hours, one object still hovering over Woodbridge base at about 5 degrees off the horizon, still moving erratic . . .[12]

What is particularly surprising about the audio-tape recording is the fact that it was released for public scrutiny not via the United States' Freedom of Information Act, but rather via former Woodbridge Base Commander Colonel Sam Morgan, USAF, who supplied researcher Harry Harris with a copy in August 1984. A second copy of the tape was sent to Jenny Randles by an anonymous source: 'I was in hospital at the time,' Jenny told me, 'and one copy reached me without cover letter and was waiting two weeks when I got out. To my knowledge, nobody ever got [a copy of the tape] via [anyone] but Morgan in the first instance – and in all cases, via Britain.'[13]

As well as being extensively edited (internal references on the tape suggest that the original recording lasts for at least two hours), the tape contains two very unusual audio intrusions which appear completely unrelated to Halt's commentary. One is a short extract of piano music, whilst the other is an unidentified voice which utters the words, 'He took this long to dock.' There may be a rational explanation for this, as Jenny Randles explains: 'The interruptions on the tape have nothing to do with its status. The Base Commander, Sam Morgan, recorded it in his office by playing the original (later lost) on another deck and recording it onto his [deck] with no direct link, thus picking up all [of] the room's ambient sounds. A cough is heard at one point! The two interruptions occur, I suspect, when a couple of small bits were hastily edited out in this rough and ready way, because some things were said that it was preferred not to release. But that last thought is my "guesstimate".'[14]

There is possibly a very good reason why Pam Titchmarsh of the MOD responded in an 'uneasy' way to Jenny Randles' questioning in 1983. Evidence suggests that Colonel Halt's involvement in the incident was just a small part of a very large jigsaw. Shortly before the UFO was seen at close quarters in Rendlesham Forest, its movements were tracked in the East Anglian skies by staff at RAF Watton, Norfolk.[15] Not without some personal risk, one member of staff at Watton entrusted East Anglian author, Paul Begg, with the details.

Begg's informant had not been on duty on the night of the encounter but a colleague had, and it was this person's account that finally reached Begg. According to the source, an unidentified target had been picked up by the radar operators at the base and was tracked heading towards Suffolk, specifically a region to the east of Ipswich. The target was duly reported to other facilities, both civilian and military, and was checked against all known air movements. No identification was forthcoming; the target was uncorrelated.

So far as is known, the base took no further part in the encounter (although it was generally known that other bases had tracked the UFO's movements), yet within days representatives from the US Air Force arrived at the base and removed all of the relevant radar tapes.[16]

Those radar tapes have not resurfaced, at least not outside official channels. However, Squadron Leader E.E. Webster of RAF Watton has admitted to me that the base was implicated in the later encounter of December 28: 'Our log book for the period does indeed say that a UFO was reported to us by RAF Bentwaters at 0325 GMT on 28 December 1980 but that is all the information we have.'[17]

Having been informed of this, I was determined to resolve the issue, and was later given the actual details of Watton's log entry written at the time, which reads as follows: 'Bentwaters Command Post contacted Eastern Radar and requested information of aircraft in the area – UA37 traffic southbound – UFO sightings at Bentwaters. They are taking reporting action.'[18] To clarify, 'UA37' refers to 'Upper Air Route, Upper Amber 37' which runs approximately north–south some forty miles east of Bentwaters and is used by civilian airliners.[19]

An intriguing account, which may well be related to the Rendlesham affair, comes from Graham Birdsall, one of Britain's leading UFO researchers and editor of *UFO Magazine*. Birdsall's source of information is George Wild, a former senior prison officer at Armley Prison, Leeds. While attending a seminar in the Midlands some years ago, Wild learned from a fellow officer who was then based at High Point Prison, Suffolk, that instructions had been received advising staff to prepare for a potential evacuation of all persons within the jail – there was a possibility that some form of 'incident' was going to take place later on the same night. When the staff at High Point queried the instructions, they were advised that the matter was one of 'national security'. The date of the 'incident'? December 27, 1980.[20]

Birdsall has also related hitherto unknown details concerning the December 1980 encounters: 'It is our understanding that a group of heavily armed US personnel left their base at Woodbridge in Suffolk, and were later confronted by an armed British detachment from nearby RAF Bentwaters.

'We are told by [an] excellent authority, that the British demanded the Americans disarm as they had no legal right to handle firearms under any circumstances. After a brief, but nerve-jangling few minutes, and after the American detachment had consulted via radio with their seniors, they withdrew to their base.'[21]

I was also determined to learn what the local police knew of the Rendlesham affair. 'I will be writing to you in the near future once I am aware of the full circumstances of the incident,' I was told by an inspector from Woodbridge Police Station. Soon after, I received the following reply from Superintendent S.M. Pearce of Felixstowe police: 'I can inform you that, at shortly after 4.00 a.m. on 26th December 1980, the police did receive a call reporting unusual lights being seen in the sky near RAF Woodbridge. The police responded to this call, but there was no evidence to substantiate or indicate the presence of an unidentified flying object.'[22]

This seems relatively straightforward, but the story does not end there. Early in December 1984 an investigative team with America's Cable News Network (CNN) came to Britain, intent on getting to the bottom of the incident. As part of their enquiries, the team had arranged to conduct an interview with a Suffolk policeman who, it was claimed, '. . . could be the key witness in the so-far unexplained UFO mystery of Rendlesham Forest'. Unfortunately, the interview did not take place, as the following extract from the December 7, 1984 edition of the *East Anglian Daily Times* shows:

> Chuck de Caro, director of the [Cable News Network] unit told the EADT yesterday they believed they had been close to uncovering a major new lead.
>
> 'We were near the base and had a local bobby with us and were about to talk to him, when two USAF officers approached. The bobby was put off from talking then but quite willingly arranged to meet us later. For no apparent reason that appointment was cancelled. That seems strange to us,' said Mr de Caro.
>
> Suffolk police said the policeman concerned had approached them to ask permission to talk and this had been given. 'The appointment was cancelled for personal reasons. The film crew were allowed to talk to another policeman.'[23]

Without doubt the most controversial and, it has to be said, tenuously supported aspect of the Rendlesham case has to be the allegation that, as well as the unknown craft seen near to RAF Woodbridge, unearthly creatures were also witnessed by at least some of those involved.

One of those who maintained that there was an alien presence within Rendlesham Forest was the pseudonymous 'Steve Roberts', an airman at the base whose account was made public by the Randles/Street/Butler team. Roberts' information suggested that the creatures were around three feet in height and wore 'all-over' silver suits. Supposedly, they were hovering close to the ground and were suspended in a shaft of light which projected from the underside of the craft.

Roberts recalled that Wing Commander Gordon Williams approached the aliens while everybody else present was ordered back, at which point some sort of communication was alleged to have taken place. Of course, this is highly sensational and largely uncorroborated. Moreover, despite the fact that an abundance of information on this case now exists, Roberts' true identity remains cloaked in mystery, which surely undermines the reliability of his account.[24]

A second source who has commented on the alien aspect is Larry

Warren, whose testimony we have already examined: '. . . I realised the spaceship was inhabited. There were beings aboard. I didn't see them because I was on the wrong side of the craft. But others did. They said there were three, and they were wearing silver suits'.[25]

For his part, Charles Halt has stated unequivocally that, 'The stories about holographic aliens emerging from their craft are pure fiction.'[27] Were Warren's colleagues in error? I do not know, but I am impressed by Warren's account, as is investigator Timothy Good.[27]

For the record, the 'alien' angle has also been disputed by others who were directly involved. John Cadbury advised Jenny Randles that no contact with aliens took place, and that Wing Commander Gordon Williams was not present. 'I knew [Williams],' said Cadbury. 'If he had been there I would have known about it and it would have changed everything.'[28] A second airman at the base, commenting on the stories that alien creatures were seen, advised Randles: 'No way. There is no way that happened . . . That is all absolute bull.'[29]

It should also be remembered that Charles Halt's memorandum refers to an object '. . . two to three meters across the base and approximately two meters high'. It seems unlikely that such a small object would have been able to comfortably contain up to three humanoid creatures, even if their stature was somewhat slighter than our own.'

In the final analysis, I am not altogether certain that extra-terrestrial entities were in attendance, but am satisfied that the various phenomena witnessed by Charles Halt and others were under some form of intelligent control.

What is the official opinion on the Rendlesham affair today? I put this question to MOD spokesman Nich Pope in 1994.

> That's difficult. The sighting, of course, occurred in 1980, but as far as I've been able to tell, our papers pretty much start following a *News of the World* report. I've not been able to turn up where we originally received [Colonel Halt's report] which, I think came under a covering note from Squadron Leader David Moreland, the RAF Base Commander. I've not been able to turn up the

letter that Squadron Leader Moreland wrote, nor have I been able turn up anything that indicates what we did, when, and if we received it in December 1980 or early in '81.

I'm aware from the file that's built up since, that the incident was looked at at the time and was judged to be of no defence significance, but I don't have many more details than that. It's not disputed, I don't think, that something strange was seen there by Colonel Halt and by some of the other personnel. What's obviously in dispute is what it was, and I know that although some people have some more exotic theories, there was a chap who put forward the theory it was simply Orford Ness lighthouse reflected through the trees and all sorts of lights and shadows as a result of that.[30]

Commenting on the audio-tape recording made by Colonel Halt, Pope added:

UFO researchers talk about it a lot. Now, my initial opinion was that I thought that that was a fake, but I understand since then that Colonel Halt was asked directly about it and said that the tape is a genuine recording. My problem with all this is that I joined Sec (AS) 2a in 1991, some ten years-plus after this had all taken place. With all the best will in the world, the trail had gone cold. By then there was very little I could do except look at the file of correspondence which, as I say, pretty much kicked off after the *News of the World* article, so it's been a very difficult case for me to form an opinion on.

One of the main reasons that I thought the tape was a fake was, I found it a bit difficult to imagine the concept of people actually going out to investigate something on guard duty and having a recorder and pressing 'Play' in the first place; I found it a slightly bizarre concept. I try to stay open-minded on it. The problem is that, as with most UFO cases, unless you solve them very quickly and get to speak to the people straight away, the trail goes cold.

Exactly what is contained within the 'Rendlesham file' held in Pope's office? 'It's simply a correspondence file. It starts with the *News of the World* article and everything since then is, "I have read that in 1980 X, Y and Z happened. What do you think?" What we don't have is anything that shows what, if any, consideration was given to the case by the MOD at the time in 1980. I'm not even clear that the report got through to us.'[31] What can be said of Pope's comments? It is curious that the file is made up solely of correspondence between members of the public with an interest in the case and staff from within Pope's division, Sec (AS) 2a. According to Pope, '. . . the incident was looked at the time and was judged to be of no defence significance'. Yet also by his own admission, Pope has been unable to uncover any paperwork which would lead to an understanding of how the 'no defence significance' judgement was reached. Moreover, until I supplied him with a copy, Pope was also unaware of the existence of the audio-tape made by Colonel Charles Halt.

Are we to believe that – following their receipt of an official USAF document concerning the landing of a structured UFO adjacent to a strategic military base – the Ministry of Defence merely 'looked' at Colonel Halt's report and assessed that it was of no particular concern? Even if this was the case, surely the MOD would have produced at least some paperwork? Yet according to Pope, Sec (AS) 2a have nothing, not even a solitary piece of paper, to indicate what action was taken by the MOD at the time. Even the covering letter from Squadron Leader David Moreland of the Royal Air Force appears to have vanished.

All this leads me to believe that the official investigation carried out by the MOD at the time is still considered classified, and that Sec (AS) 2a have been specifically excluded from learning the results of that investigation. As I will shortly demonstrate, Sec (AS) 2a is not the only branch of Government monitoring the ongoing UFO situation.

Returning to the missing 'cover letter' written by Squadron Leader David Moreland, which accompanied Colonel Halt's report to the MOD, Jenny Randles has informed me: 'Moreland told me, when we met, that it was simply an endorsement of the credibility of Halt, as he himself, i.e. Moreland, saw and knew nothing firsthand.'[32]

An example of the high regard that Moreland had for Halt can be seen from the following statement made to journalist Keith Beabey in 1983: 'The first I knew of these events was when [Halt] came to me and related

what he had seen. I know Colonel Halt well and respect him and I fully
believe he was telling me the truth. Whatever it was, it was able to perform
feats in the air which no known aircraft is capable of doing. I put the
events the Colonel related to me down to inexplicable phenomena.'[33]

Trying to gauge what actually took place in Rendlesham Forest back in
December 1980 is a daunting task. Most perplexing is the issue of when
the various encounters really occurred. For instance, Colonel Halt's memo
states that the initial encounter occurred 'early in the morning of 27 Dec
80'. Yet in a lengthy interview with writer A.J.S. Rayl, Halt stated that
he had heard about the incident 'Just after Christmas, about 5.30 a.m.,
December 26, 1980 . . .'

Then there is the matter of RAF Watton. Squadron Leader E.E.
Webster advised me that Watton's log book showed that they had
been contacted at '0325 GMT on 28 December 1980', presumably
when Colonel Halt and his men were scouring Rendlesham Forest. In
his official report to the MOD, however, Halt stressed that he was
present in the forest on '. . . the following night (29 Dec 80)'. To cap
it all, there is Superintendent S.M. Pearce of Felixstowe police who has
gone on record as stating that Woodbridge police responded to a report
of '. . . unusual lights . . . in the sky near RAF Woodbridge . . .' at 4.00
a.m. on December 26! I find it most improbable that all those involved
would knowingly give a false date, and therefore suspect that there were
multiple UFO incidents in and around the Woodbridge area in the latter
part of December 1980.

I also suspect that when and if the facts are finally revealed to us, they
will prove to be far stranger than we have imagined thus far. George Wild's
account that the nearby High Point prison was primed for evacuation
because of an incident involving national security; the confiscation of
radar tapes from RAF Watton; and the tense stand-off between British
and American forces in Rendlesham Forest; all this suggests to me that
a massive truth is being withheld from us.

Whatever the future may bring, we should never forget that were it
not for Charles Halt's memorandum to the Ministry of Defence, which
fortunately surfaced via the American Freedom of Information Act, our

knowledge of the Rendlesham affair would be greatly diminished. I leave the final words to former MOD official, Ralph Noyes: 'Whatever "intruded" at Bentwaters/Woodbridge in December 1980 has possibly done so often before in human history ... If Colonel Halt has done nothing except to draw attention to it in undeniable form, we shall probably have to put up a statue to him some day in some leafy square.'[34]

CHAPTER 12

THE 1980s AND BEYOND

I HAVE BEEN GRANTED PERMISSION TO RELATE THE FOLLOWING account on the understanding that I do not divulge any compromising information concerning my source. Whilst I appreciate that this may affect the credibility of the account, I am satisfied with the claims of my informant, and stand by his revelations.

For a period of months in 1981 my source was employed as a radar operator at a particular facility on the island of Cyprus. On August 16 an object, described as being 'vast', was tracked approaching the island at a height in excess of 30,000 feet, and at a speed of 900 mph. It was initially believed that this was a conventional aircraft, albeit of unusual dimensions. This theory quickly evaporated when the object reportedly came to a sudden stop and hovered over the base for around three-quarters of an hour. To the astonishment of those who saw the object, it was triangular in shape, sparkling white in colour, and over 700 feet in length!

My source also states that prior to the sighting, an encrypted message was sent to the base from the Ministry of Defence in London ordering a 'complete stand-down' of aircraft in the event that any strange 'aerial phenomena' was sighted in the vicinity of the base airfield. Note also that the term 'aerial phenomena' was one which the British Government had employed as an alternative to 'UFO' at least as far back as 1953 – when military personnel were warned not to discuss UFO sightings outside of official channels.

Numerous photographs were taken of the UFO and were held under lock and key along with the relevant radar tapes and log reports. On the following day, two people, a middle-aged woman and an elderly man, rumoured to be from the Ministry of Defence, arrived at the base and, after six hours, left with all of the available evidence concerning the event. Needless to say, those involved were sworn to secrecy and reminded of their obligations to the British Government.

My source also later learned, via a colleague with intimate knowledge of the encounter, that a meeting to discuss the case was held at RAF Lakenheath in Suffolk at some point during August 1981. Present were representatives from the Ministry of Defence and the US Air Force Office of Special Investigations (AFOSI).

Curiously, I have been advised that other similar sightings occurred at the base throughout the summer of 1981, but my informant refuses to discuss them in detail – despite assurances of confidentiality on my part. I should stress that my source admits to feeling uneasy about breaking his security oath, but feels that there is no justification for the Government withholding such information if, as is officially maintained, UFOs present no threat to the security of the United Kingdom.

Perhaps the most puzzling aspect of this affair is the fact that the Ministry of Defence appeared to have prior knowledge that something unusual was likely to take place. I enquired of my source if he had considered the possibility that the object had been some form of experimental aircraft. If that was the case, it would go a long way towards explaining the MOD's order that all military aircraft be stood down at the time that the UFO appeared. This brought forth the following reply:

Whatever we saw, it was not man-made; I can guarantee that. This thing was seven hundred feet long, and was over the base for three-quarters of an hour. I'm pretty sure [that] we don't have the technology to build something like this, nor the Americans (sic). And if it was Russian, why weren't we allowed to intercept it?

Plus, you've got to remember that it isn't easy to hide a seven-hundred-foot-long aircraft on the ground! You'd think that it would have been seen taking off and landing if it was something of ours that was being regularly tested. Now, I know that we do test-fly some weird things now and again, but no, this was something else.

Then there's the Lakenheath meeting; I know that [the representatives from the MOD and AFOSI] were really bothered about it. I don't really have much else other than what I've already told you, but you can take it from me, this thing was really alien. How did the MOD know that [the UFO] was going to arrive? Well, your guess is as good as mine. Maybe it's not a good idea to ask questions like that. Don't forget, it was all graded Top Secret.[1]

In view of my source's statements and the cageyness of both British and American authorities, I find it most unlikely that an official confirmation of the reality of this encounter will be forthcoming for many years, if at all. In 1992 the Ministry of Defence admitted to me that 1981 had been an extremely busy year: no fewer than 600 UFO reports poured into Whitehall.[2] Unfortunately, due to governmental restrictions on public access to official records, none of these reports are likely to see the light of day much before the year 2012.

On March 25, 1982, it was announced in the press that the Ministry of Defence had ordered a 'top-level probe' into a UFO sighting made by Police Sergeant Ian Victory and PC Anthony Underwood as they drove through Milton Keynes at 4.35 a.m. on the previous morning. On Saxon Street the officers' attention was drawn to a 'lozenge-shaped' object in the sky. Not surprisingly, the patrol car was brought to a 'screeching halt'. The officers then sat and watched the mystery craft as it sailed overhead. Both described it as being yellow in colour, with surrounding red and blue flashing lights.

'They all laughed at us when we told them back at the police station,' said Sergeant Victory. 'But I definitely saw it – and I've never seen anything like it before.' Milton Keynes' Police Chief, Superintendent John Burton, backed the claim of his officers: 'These are two experienced officers and I've no reason to doubt their integrity.'

The MOD admitted that a report had been received, but did not speculate about the object, only saying: 'We are making a full investigation.'[3]

Almost two months after the incident at Milton Keynes, another lozenge-shaped device was seen moving steadily over the Clent Hills, West Midlands, by Michael Jones, a thirteen-year-old schoolboy. The date was May 30, 1982, and the time was 12.45 p.m. According to Michael's account, the top section of the object appeared to be silver in colour, whilst the bottom part was red. He was unable to estimate the speed or distance of the UFO, but believed that it was about ten feet thick and twenty to thirty feet in diameter. After having watched the UFO for about three minutes, Michael commented, '[The object] was moving in various directions as if on a spindle.'[4]

In the latter part of October 1983, almost three years after the incredible events at Rendlesham Forest in December 1980, the nearby hamlet of Hollesley received a night-time visitation from an unidentified, triangular-shaped craft which hovered over the area for approximately twenty minutes, projecting three powerful white lights down to the ground. One of those who saw the UFO was forty-one-year-old Ron Macro of Kesgrave.

'We froze,' he recalled. 'The lights were in a triangle and remained perfectly still.' Mr Macro continued to watch for several minutes, at which point the object began to move. 'Whatever was in the sky flew over us. The lights beamed down and we heard a high-pitched whine,' added Mr Macro.

A further sighting was made by Debbie Foreman and Pauline Osborne, who were driving past Hollesley at the time and chanced to see the object. As they neared the craft, Debbie's car began to malfunction: 'The headlights on the car dimmed and the engine cut out. Until then the car had behaved quite normally. But everything seemed to go wrong.'

As a result of the incident, villagers demanded a meeting with representatives from RAF Woodbridge. One, John Button, said: 'If they are experimenting then we ought to be told. And if there's something flying around here which comes from outer space, we ought to be told about that too.' Unsurprisingly, RAF Woodbridge stayed tight-lipped. 'Nothing was seen on radar. I cannot say more than that,' said Captain Kathleen McCollom of Woodbridge's Public Affairs Division.[5]

Ten months after the experience at Hollesley, a Britten-Norman Trislander freight aircraft actually collided with an unidentified flying object whilst flying over Rendlesham Forest. Damage to the aircraft was not too severe, but an immediate investigation was launched by the Civil Aviation Authority, as the following report on the case shows:

24 AUGUST 84 IPSWICH – UK REPORTABLE ACCI-DENT: A/C struck object in cruise. Propeller, fuselage, cowling & control runs damaged. The A/C was flying in slight turbulence when a bump was felt. Just before descent the right hand engine control was found to be seized so an asymmetric approach & landing was executed. On inspection it was apparent that the left propeller had struck an unidentified object, propelling it through the cabin roof, with a piece exiting through a window. There were several holes in the fuselage & damage to the engine, aileron & rudder trim cables. Three pieces of foreign metallic object were found, including a small cylindrical magnet. The UFO has not been identified. No information received concerning nature or origin of UFO.[6]

The principal responsibilities of Britain's Civil Aviation Authority (CAA) are the economic and safety regulation of the nation's civil aviation, and the operation of the National Air Traffic Services (NATS) (the latter is co-ordinated jointly with the Ministry of Defence). Established in 1962, the function of NATS is to secure the safe flow of air traffic within Britain's airspace and to provide air traffic services for aircraft flying over the north-east quarter of the North Atlantic.[7] Early in 1995, I obtained a number of reports originating with the CAA, which leave me in no doubt that staff attached to the Civil Aviation Authority are well-acquainted with the UFO enigma. Several of those reports cover the period 1979–1983 and are reproduced below:

19 SEP 79 VICENZA – UFO observed passing 200 feet below aircraft. Milan control reported no traffic.

11 JUN 80 VICENZA – UFO passed close to subject aircraft. Object appeared to be like a fighter aircraft drop tank.

13 FEB 81 LYON – Unidentified foreign object seen on aircraft radar. A sizeable oval shaped target appeared on radar centre-line at limit of range tracking towards aircraft at very high speed. No visual sighting made.

12 JUN 82 DINKELSBUHI – Large translucent object 500 feet long at 41000 feet. ATCC (*Authors note:* Air Traffic Control Centre) requested subject aircraft to investigate this object which was found to have the form of a double rectangle surmounted by a globe (egg shape) crowned by a silver cone. Object observed by all on board.

21 JUN 82 BRINDISI – Unidentified object sighted by pilots. Object passed down left hand side at same height as aircraft (FL230) & 2 miles away. Black shiny doughnut shape about the size of a car. Object was tumbling & judged to be stationary.

18 AUG 83 FLORENCE – Unidentified flying object seen by crew. Large black object, balloon shaped with large white spot on it, observed 10 NM SE of Firenza. No attachments to object. SUPP. INFO: Italian CAA replied no met balloon could possibly have been present at the indicated place or time.

Between 1984 and 1986 (during which time the Ministry of Defence received more than 500 UFO reports), at least four more encounters involving UFOs were investigated by the CAA, as the following records show:

26 OCT 84 READING – Unidentified flying object: bright light 65 Deg Elev, 200Deg T, duration 7 minutes.

20 DEC 84 HERALD – Bright white lights arced across A/C track. No range activity in channel. Lights also seen by another A/C.

5 FEB 86 5427N 0530W – Bright light passed upwards in front of A/C. A/C was crossing east coast of Ireland on descent. Light travelled towards A/C from a 2.30 position range approx 1½ miles and passed 1000 ft above travelling right to left 1 mile ahead. Burst of green light observed at peak of its ballistic flight. A/C ht 1450 ft. CAA closure – possibly flare fired at about time of OCC by Aldergrove. Pilot considered this unlikely but no other explanation has emerged.

21 AUG 86 Belgrade – Non UK Airmiss missile type object passed 500 ft above on reciprocal track A/C heading 290 MAG at FL 390. Object was black, cigar shaped, without wings. Belgrade radar informed on RTF. CAA closure – foreign authority advised.[8]

All airports which operate under the authority of Britain's Civil Aviation Authority are required to forward the details of any UFO sightings which they receive direct to the Ministry of Defence, as an extract from the 'Manual of Air Traffic Services' demonstrates: 'A controller receiving a report about an unidentified object must obtain as much as possible of the information required to complete a report . . . The completed report is to be sent by the originating air traffic service unit to the Ministry of Defence.'[9] Hence, we can safely assume that the MOD remains fully informed of UFO encounters involving both military and civilian pilots.

One of the dilemmas facing anyone who is fortunate, or possibly unfortunate, enough to see a UFO is whether or not to report their account to some form of official body. Nobody wishes to be labelled a crank or a liar. Unfortunately, such prejudices still exist and those who do believe that they have seen something truly extraordinary either have to stay silent or, if they do choose to go public, run the risk of outright ridicule.

The following incident, never filed through official channels, was reported to Jenny Randles and concerns the sighting of a UFO by a British Army communications officer. During the early hours of a March morning in 1987, 'Mr B' was alone on the moors near Bishop Monkton, North Yorkshire, where he was taking part in a twenty-four-hour military exercise. At around 3.00 a.m., the witness noticed a strange red light in the sky above the moors. He continued to watch the light for approximately twenty minutes, during which time it completed three 'circuits' of the immediate area. Mr B told Jenny that the light was steady and seemed relatively near to him.

Soon afterwards, the witness noticed two aircraft closing in on the UFO. Identifying the aircraft as 'Phantoms', Jenny's informant watched as they proceeded to give chase. As if in response to the approaching aircraft, the UFO began playing a game of 'cat and mouse' with the pilots. 'One moment it was in front of the pursuers, the next it would move at speed behind them,' Mr B confided in Jenny. This aerial dogfight continued for another five minutes, at which point the UFO accelerated away at an incredible speed. Both jets remained in the area for a short while before also departing.

The following day, without saying why, the witness discreetly asked his colleagues if there had been any problems with communications during the exercise. It had been a trouble-free night, he was advised. Mr B elected not to file an official report.[10]

Since it is all but certain that the Phantom crews would have been obliged to submit a detailed account of what had taken place, it is unlikely that Mr B would have suffered adversely by doing likewise. Rather, independent corroboration from a ground-based source could have proven invaluable to those given the task of evaluating the encounter. However, this case does serve to demonstrate that, even in official circles, there is a reluctance to discuss the subject of unidentified flying objects. We can only guess at the amount of UFO incidents involving military personnel which have, for whatever reason, gone unreported. But among the general public it is estimated that perhaps nine out of ten UFO sightings remain unacknowledged.

During 1988, the Ministry of Defence found itself inundated with some 397 reports of unidentified aerial activity and, as in 1967, many of the encounters were reported by police officers.

At 9.17 p.m. on the night of February 16, 1988, Sergeant Stuart Griffiths and PC Michael Powell of Willenhall police were on duty in the Rosehill area of the town, when they saw a 'large object' flying high in the night sky. 'There were red and green lights around its circumference which were either flashing on and off or the whole thing was spinning,' said Sergeant Griffiths at the time. 'I've never seen anything like it. What amazed me was there was no sound at all.'

It was later revealed by police that, seven minutes prior to the sighting at Willenhall, a separate sighting of the same object was made by Sergeant Steve Godwin and Inspector Roger Clarke, who were on patrol in the nearby town of Walsall. As a result of media interest in the encounters, Willenhall police stated that they had received several anonymous telephone calls from members of the public reporting much the same thing, and that a full report was being submitted to the Ministry of Defence.[11]

As October 1988 drew to a close, a puzzling encounter was reported by Tony Silvestri, a mechanic from Ciliau Aeron, Wales. In an interview with the *Western Mail,* Mr Silvestri recalled the encounter which occurred whilst driving with his wife and daughter.

'Gwendoline, my wife, and Allana, who is eight, were both scared stiff by it,' said Mr Silvestri. 'The whole interior of the car was lit up by a brilliant greenish light . . . It was so bright that I could not see through the windscreen or out of the windows. Fortunately it only lasted for a few seconds. It couldn't have been caused by the headlights of other cars because it was too bright and the wrong colour. I pulled up and stopped at the side of the road but could see nothing that might have caused the strange light inside the car.

'Next day I gave the car a complete electrical check and there was nothing wrong with it. I didn't think there would be because the light was too brilliant to be caused by an electrical fault.'

On October 27, Mr Silvestri was interviewed by Flight Sergeant Dave Pengilly of RAF Brawdy, Pembrokeshire. 'Each report of this kind is always investigated,' explained Sergeant Pengilly. 'I make checks and then pass it on to the powers that be in the Ministry of Defence who are now looking into this case. We don't like unidentified things in our airspace.'

'Until now,' said Mrs Silvestri, 'we've had no time for UFO stories. We didn't really believe in them. But nothing like this ever happened to us before and we hope it won't again. We were terrified.'[12]

The latter part of October 1988 also saw an inordinate amount of UFO activity in the areas of both Kent and Sussex. One incident in particular which stands out was reported by Police Constables Norman Sells and Robin Buxton, who had been driving through High Halden at 3.45 a.m. on an autumn morning when 'the whole of the night sky became as bright as daylight'. The curious light display lasted for three or four seconds before normality was restored. The officers quickly filed a report with police headquarters at Maidstone. Notably, other unusual events had been reported by people in the same area for several days.

Teenagers Joanna Dickinson and Julie Jessop were walking near to Julie's home at Woodlands Caravan Park, Biddenden, when they saw an oval-shaped object displaying four bright white lights, with a red light in the centre. Both girls estimated that the object was at a height of around 500 feet and emitted a deep hum. As they watched, the object suddenly climbed vertically into the evening sky.

Shortly after the sighting at Biddenden, Stephen Button, the brother of a Tenterden policeman, reported seeing a strange device while driving his car in the area. When Mr Button first caught sight of the object, which was likened to a 'blue ball', it was at a height of between fifty and a hundred feet, but began to descend as Mr Button looked on. He finally lost sight of the object as it disappeared behind a line of trees. Staff at RAF Manston were duly informed and details were passed on to the MOD for analysis. To date, the results of that analysis have not been made public.[13]

In 1989, the Civil Aviation Authority once again found itself caught up in the UFO controversy. The first indication of CAA involvement comes in the following report made available to me in 1995:

11 NOV 89 BELFAST – UFO passed above aircraft at height of 11200 feet & burst into cascade of lights. UFO heading approx due west – aircraft heading 310 deg. UFO burst less than

500 metres from left hand side of aircraft. Proximity of cloud intensified brightness of light. Confirmed by another aircraft and tower.[14]

A still-unresolved case, involving the Ministry of Defence, the Civil Aviation Authority and police, took place in the early hours of a December morning in 1989. The incident began at around 5.00 a.m. when air traffic controllers at Manchester Airport spotted a 'static blob' on their radar screens which they were unable to identify. Thinking that the object was possibly a helicopter, controllers at the airport contacted Kidsgrove police and enquired if the force's helicopter was in operation at the time. The answer was no. However, since it did appear that some form of aerial craft was in the area, a number of officers from Kidsgrove were dispatched to Mow Cop, a local beauty spot in North Staffordshire, where the strange phenomenon was reportedly hovering.

On arrival at Mow Cop, the officers were somewhat surprised to see a green and white light in the morning sky which appeared to be the same object reported by radar operators at Manchester Airport. As the officers continued to watch the UFO, they found that their portable radios were rendered inoperable.

Shortly after, Chief Superintendent Peter Grocott arrived on the scene to assess the situation: 'We didn't get to the bottom of it . . . The traffic controllers called us because they thought it could have been the county's helicopter but it was not flying that night,' said Chief Superintendent Grocott at the time. He added, 'We checked the Air Force too and they said it was nothing to do with them.'

Police at Kidsgrove did reveal that several other people had telephoned them to report seeing the UFO at approximately 5.00 on the same morning, and that those reports had been written up in the station log book. In response to media questioning, Chris Mason of the Civil Aviation Authority blamed the radar blip recorded at Manchester Airport on unusual weather conditions.

In the *Stoke-on-Trent Evening Sentinel* of December 7, it was confirmed by a Ministry of Defence spokesman that a copy of the police report on the encounter had been received, and that an inquiry was to be carried out. Considering that this was an interesting case – with both radar and visual confirmation that something out of the ordinary was seen, as well as the apparent disturbance to the police officers' radios – I naturally contacted the MOD to ask if it would be possible to obtain a copy of the official report on the matter. I expected the MOD to sit tight on the documentation, but was somewhat taken aback by the reply given to me in March 1990: 'A search of our files has revealed that, contrary to the press reports, the Ministry of Defence did not receive any details of these incidents.'[15]

So we have a blatant contradiction. On the one hand, the statement of the MOD, made to to the press at the time, that a report from the police had been received, and that an investigation was underway. On the other hand, I was assured that the MOD was completely unaware of the case. Personally, I do not doubt that the MOD did receive a copy of the police report, primarily because all police stations have standing orders to submit the details of any UFO sightings directly to the MOD at Whitehall. Moreover, all airports which operate under the jurisdiction of the CAA are obliged to keep the MOD informed of any UFO sightings brought to their notice.

It seems obvious, therefore, that the MOD would prefer to keep any conclusions reached in this case strictly in-house. I suspect that the reason for the MOD's about-face is that when first contacted by the Stoke-on-Trent *Evening Sentinel*, the full implications of the matter were not wholly apparent, and it was literally a case of the Ministry being caught with its guard down.

During October and November 1990, literally dozens of reports of unusual aerial objects surfaced in the British Isles and throughout Europe. At around 10.00 p.m. on October 14, Mr Roger Hadley was travelling along the A591 Kendal bypass when his attention was drawn to a cigar-shaped light in the night sky. 'It was as if it was above the car,' said Mr Hadley, who described the object as a 'fluffy light', some thirty feet across. Curiously, Mr Hadley added that at the time that he first saw it, the object was enveloped by some form of mist or cloud. According to a report in the *Westmoreland Gazette*, the Ministry of Defence chose to play down the encounter: 'Our sole interest in UFOs is if they have a military nature. Unless we have a report of something over one of our airfields we wouldn't bother about it.'[16]

On October 31, Paul Cowell, manager of the Red Cafe at Margate, reported seeing freak lightning and seven flashing lights over Kingsgate in the small hours of the morning. 'If I had only seen one of these things, I would have thought it was a helicopter. But there were seven of them. It was a very exciting experience, but shocking,' said Paul, whose girlfriend, Tracey Render, also saw the strange spectacle. Initially, their attention was drawn to the odd lightning display, which lit up the surrounding clouds making them appear golden in colour. As the couple watched the lightning, a 'little mass of lights' suddenly appeared and proceeded one by one to enter a black object which was manoeuvring within one of the clouds.

'We cannot shed any light on the matter,' said a spokesman for RAF Manston. 'We did have a helicopter flying that night, but much earlier on. It is nothing to do with us.'[17]

'I've never seen anything like it before and can't explain what it was,' said British Airways pilot Mike D'Alton, commenting on his sighting of a large silver disc-shaped object whilst piloting a Boeing 737 from Rome to Gatwick on the night of November 5, 1990. 'My co-pilot and I called in two cabin crew to see it and then it went out of sight. Ground radar couldn't pick it up, so it must have been travelling at phenomenal speed.'[18]

Thanks to an investigation carried out by Paul Whitehead of the Surrey Investigation Group on Aerial Phenomena, other credible witnesses have been located who had viewed anomalous objects on the same night: a second British Airways pilot who viewed 'two very bright mystifying lights' over the North Sea, and the pilot of a Royal Air Force Tornado aircraft. In the latter case, the pilot reported that his plane, which was flying with another Tornado, had been approached by nine bright lights. In fact, the lights came so close that the pilot was forced to take violent evasive action.[19]

Yet another account comes from Timothy Good: 'According to a highly placed RAF Germany source, two terrific explosions were heard on two separate occasions at night in the Rheindalen area. After the second explosion (at 22.00) the crew of a Phantom jet reported UFOs heading north in a "finger" formation.'[20]

On the night of April 21, 1991, the term 'close encounter' took on an altogether more significant meaning for the crew and passengers of a London-bound airliner. At 9.00 p.m. Captain Achille Zaghetti, who was piloting a McDonnell MD-80 aircraft, was amazed to see an unidentified flying object pass his aircraft as it flew over the coast of Kent at a height of more than 22,000 feet. As the UFO was no more than 1,000 feet above the airliner, and the incident was therefore classed as a 'near miss', an official inquiry was launched by the Civil Aviation Authority. Approximately two weeks after, the CAA issued a statement to the media:

> The pilot said the object was light brown, round, 3 metres long, and did not describe any means of propulsion. The aircraft was under the control of the London air traffic control centre who had no other aircraft in the vicinity but consistent with the pilot report, a faint radar trace was observed 10 nautical miles behind the Alitalia aircraft. The air traffic controller submitted an occurrence report and investigatory action began immediately. Extensive enquiries have failed to provide any indication of what the sighting may have been.[21]

One of the most interesting things about this particular incident is the attitude taken by the Ministry of Defence at the time. 'What happened is a mystery. It was yet another UFO,' said the MOD on the same day that the CAA issued its findings on the case.[22] In a statement to the *Independent*, the MOD elaborated: '. . . we do have quite a few UFO reports and often people who see these things describe them as missile or cigar-shaped, or else round, and sometimes they do appear to be travelling with no means of propulsion.'[23]

The speed with which the MOD dismissed the case as yet another unexplained incident led to suspicion that this was simply a cover story – intended to hide the fact that a missile, or pilotless 'drone' had gone astray and almost collided with a civilian airliner over a densely populated area of the British Isles. As fantastic as this scenario may seem, it is actually plausible. At the precise moment that Captain Zaghetti viewed the UFO, his aircraft was flying directly over Lydd Ranges, a Ministry of Defence firing range, run by the nearby Shorncliffe Camp – an area which is marked on aircraft navigational charts as 'Danger Zone DO-44'.[24]

Air traffic controllers at Lydd Airport admitted to the *Sunday Times* that weapons testing was undertaken at the army range directly under established flight routes. 'The MOD notify us when they're firing up to 6,500 feet with live stuff. We're never told of any missiles. It's all top secret,' said Cleo Proctor, duty controller at Lydd Airport.[25]

The Ministry of Defence worked quickly to squelch rumours that the UFO was an errant missile. 'Whatever [Captain Zaghetti] might have seen might have been something that was flying, but was certainly not anything that was fired. It was a Sunday. The only ranges we have in the Kent area are Lydd and Hythe, and they are concerned with small arms only,' the MOD told Stephen Ward of the *Independent*.[26]

The controversy continued unabated. Duncan Lennox, editor of *Jane's Strategic Weapons Systems*, said that the description of the UFO given by Captain Zaghetti was consistent with that of a target missile or drone of the type used for air defence practice. According to Lennox, although not usually primed with a warhead, such a missile could certainly destroy an aircraft: 'If it hit the cockpit, it would kill the crew and bring down the airliner.'[27]

Despite Lennox's statements, the MOD continued to assert that the object did not originate with the British military, as the following letter to me shows:

> The only surface-to-air missiles that could go as high as 22,200 feet are the Bloodhound (operated by the RAF) and the Sea Dart (operated by the Royal Navy). The Rapier missile is launched from the range at Benbecula in the Western Isles and the Aberporth range in Wales. Precise details of the operational ceiling of Rapier missiles is classified, but they could not go as high as 22,200 feet. The sighting in question would not be connected with the range at Lydd, as this has only anti-tank, light mortar, grenade and rifle ranges as well as limited field firing facilities.[28]

To this day, both the Ministry of Defence and the Civil Aviation Authority maintain that the entire incident remains unexplained. If so, this implies that the MOD is admitting that a genuine UFO has penetrated British airspace and almost caused a mid-air disaster. On the other hand, if the UFO angle was introduced to divert attention away from the allegations that the object was a missile, then this conjures up an interesting scenario: the MOD is exploiting the UFO phenomenon to cover up potentially embarassing incidents of its own making. As Graham Birdsall, editor of *UFO Magazine*, has said: 'Tell MPs that a missile almost brought down a civilian aircraft and all hell is let loose – tell MPs it was a UFO, and nobody wants to know.'[29]

Strangely, several similar incidents were reported to the CAA throughout the summer of 1991. As far as we know, the next such encounter took place on June 1 at 2.38 p.m., when a yellow-orange cylindrical object, ten feet in length, was seen by the crew of a Britannia Airways Boeing 737 en route to London from Dublin.

Sixteen days later, yet another cylindrical-shaped UFO was sighted, this time by Walter Leiss, a German engineer aboard Dan Air flight DA 4700 as it headed towards Hamburg. 'The object was slender, grey, and, so it seemed, sort of cigar-shaped,' said Leiss. 'It's flight path was on a parallel with ours but diametrically opposed. The object flew over the cloud-deck and under our aircraft; the object seemed to oscillate in altitude. It's possible the object was standing still and only gave the impression of movement. The object was estimated to be visible for two to three minutes.'[30]

On July 15, 1991, almost two months after Captain Zaghetti's experience over Essex, a Boeing 737 narrowly avoided collision with a 'small black lozenge-shaped object' as it approached Gatwick Airport. Once again, the Civil Aviation Authority launched an immediate investigation. According to the CAA report, the object was first seen by the co-pilot of the aircraft at an estimated distance of 500 yards and a height of around 15,000 feet. The report added:

Within the space of about 1.5 seconds it passed very close, less than 100 yards away, down the port side of the aircraft, and only 30 feet above the wing. Whilst members were unsure what damage could have occurred had the object struck the B737, the general opinion was that there had been a possible risk of collision. The object must be considered untraced. No impact or disturbance was felt on the aircraft and no damage was observed during a flight inspection. The pilot assessed the risk of collision as high.[31]

Although the matter received no media publicity at the time, the CAA was also obliged to investigate an incident which had occurred in 1992 on, of all days, April 1. An account prepared by the CAA states:

1 APR 92 ELBA – Unreported/unidentified high speed (estimated mach 3) return seen/untracked on weather radar. Return travelled towards reporting aircraft, eventually passed below (reporting aircraft at FL330) and 5 NM to left. Reported to Rome air traffic control.[32]

'A close encounter between a British Airways jet with 60 passengers on board and an illuminated, triangular-shaped unidentified flying object at 13,000 feet above the Pennines is under formal investigation by the Civil Aviation Authority . . .', it was stated in the *Times* on February 2, 1995.

The incident had actually taken place on January 6, as Captain Roger Wills and co-pilot Mark Stuart began their descent towards Manchester Airport in a Boeing 737 twin jet. Seventeen minutes before touchdown, all was normal until a mystery object flashed past the right-hand side of the aircraft at a distance described as being 'very close'. So close, that the crew actually 'ducked down' in their seats as the object sped past them. An immediate check with air traffic control at Ringway revealed that nothing had been picked up on radar, save for the 737 itself.

Fearing ridicule, Captain Wills and First Officer Stuart did not report their experience to their colleagues, but British Airways management were ultimately advised of what had occurred. In line with set procedures, a full report, complemented with sketches of the UFO, was sent to the Joint

Air Miss Working Group (JAWG), which is a part of the Civil Aviation Authority.

CAA spokesman, Chris Mason, said that any suggestion that the object had been a UFO was 'purely speculative', adding that the investigation could last up to six months. 'A very small proportion of near-miss situations involving untraced aircraft remain unresolved,' he added.

Neither witness expressed a desire to comment on the incident, but a colleague of Wills and Stuart informed the media: 'They are high-grade, sensible guys. Everyone's talking about what they saw and it is right that it is reported, so the experts can try to establish what it was.' At the time of writing, the details of the JAWG investigation are not known. Meanwhile, Kerry Philpott of the MOD has advised me that:

> As a matter of routine, the Ministry of Defence was notified by the Civil Aviation Authority of the report made by the British Airways pilots on 6th January. I consulted Departmental experts with responsibility for air defence matters, who confirmed that they were not aware of any evidence which would indicate that our air defences had been breached. As this is our only concern the MOD's interest in this particular incident concluded. No subsequent information has come to our attention, which would suggest that the original assessment was incorrect. The incident of 6th January [1995] remains a matter for the CAA.'[33]

There the matter stood until early 1996 when the Civil Aviation Authority released its findings on the case. In a remarkable three-page report, the CAA gave a graphic description of the events which almost ended in mid-air tragedy:

> The first officer reports that his attention, initially focused on the glare shield in front of him, was diverted to something in his peripheral vision. He looked up in time to see a dark object pass down the right hand side of the aircraft at high speed; it was wedge-shaped with what could have been a black stripe down the side. He estimated the object's size as somewhere between that of a light aircraft and a Jetstream, though he emphasised that this was

pure speculation. It made no attempt to deviate from its course and no sound was heard or wake felt. He felt certain that what he saw was a solid object – not a bird, balloon or kite.

The report continued with a fascinating extract taken from the actual conversation between the crew of the B737 and the radar controller at Manchester Airport:

B737: '. . . we just had something go down the RHS just above us very fast.'

MANCHESTER: 'Well, there's nothing seen on radar. Was it, er, an aircraft?'

B737: 'Well, it had lights; it went down the starboard side very quick [and] just slightly above us, yeah.'

MANCHESTER: 'Keep an eye out for something, er, I can't see anything at all at the moment so, er, must have, er, been very fast or gone down very quickly after it passed you, I think.'

B737: 'OK. Well, there you go!'

With a variety of 'conventional' suggestions found wanting, the CAA Working Group concluded thus: 'Having debated the various hypotheses at length the Group concluded that, in the absence of any firm evidence which could identify or explain this object, it was not possible to assess either the cause or the risk to any of the normal criteria applicable to airmiss reports. The incident therefore remains unresolved.'

As 1995 progressed, sightings of unusual aerial objects over the UK continued to proliferate. Indeed, during the summer months in particular, a number of intriguing cases came to light, including that of Mrs Helen Whitlock of Binsted, who witnessed a six-foot-long object manoeuvring approximately fifty feet above her garden.

'The thing was grey, shaped like a cigar, more rounded than a rocket, with a very hazy, white, frothy band around the middle, like you were watching it through a mist. There were two streams of red and green lights coming from this band.'

For fifteen minutes, Mrs Whitlock watched, mesmerized by the spectacle. Suddenly, the object was gone. 'It wasn't like it disappeared from view behind anything. It just vanished.'[34] I am reminded of the encounter of Roger Hadley, who in 1990 viewed a similar-shaped craft near the A591 Kendal bypass. Even more curious, in that encounter too it was reported that the object was enveloped by some form of mist or cloud. Perhaps next time we see an unusual cloud formation in the sky, we should examine it a little more closely . . .

To demonstrate that authorities in the UK recognize the serious nature of the UFO puzzle, on at least two occasions in 1995, police forces in both Essex and the West Midlands employed the use of helicopters in their attempts to locate evidence of UFO activity.

On August 4, a 'shuttlecock'-shaped UFO was seen in the skies at Westcliff, Essex, by at least five police officers and several members of the public. 'It looked like a shuttlecock – white with a red and yellow band and blue sparking from the back,' said Claire White of Westcliff.

'It made no sound and I'm sure it wasn't an aircraft or a star. It was much bigger,' commented PC Geoff Howell, who was fortunate enough to make an observation of the UFO through binoculars.

Since checks with Southend Airport, local military bases and the coastguard drew a complete blank, a decision was taken by police to dispatch the force helicopter to the area. Despite the fact that the crew were unable to locate the UFO, I find the actions of Essex police encouraging – their prompt response surely demonstrates that such encounters are viewed with mounting concern.[35]

Two weeks later, a similar occurrence took place in the Aldridge area of Walsall, West Midlands. At 1.00 a.m. three uniformed police officers were amazed to see a 'cylindrical object with a glowing, green haze' which appeared to travel through the sky in an arc, before landing near a local beauty spot, Stubbers Green pool.

As with the encounter at Westcliff the force helicopter was scrambled to investigate the mystery. Oddly enough, it was reported in the media that the helicopter crew were looking for 'burnt areas' on the ground. Quite what prompted this statement has never been revealed but it would seem to indicate that police believed some sort of object had made contact with the ground.[36]

At 7.30 p.m. on November 2, 1995, several people in the Sowerby Bridge area of Yorkshire viewed a 'very large', disc-shaped unidentified flying object in the vicinity of Scammonden Reservoir. According to witness testimony, at least seven aircraft and no fewer than three heli-copters appeared to be circling the object, which in turn departed after ten minutes. Prompt enquiries on the part of investigator Tony Dodd revealed that authorities at RAF West Drayton were aware of the event. They subsequently attributed the matter to low-flying military aircraft which had unfortunately caused a number of floodlights surrounding the reservoir to explode. Dodd, however, persisted in his enquiries, and learned from Yorkshire Water that no such floodlighting had been damaged in any way.[37]

Whatever was seen, it would appear that the explanation offered by RAF West Drayton was erroneous, and the presence of our old friend, the 'phantom helicopter', strongly suggests that something out of the ordinary occurred.

For the Ministry of Defence's part, 1995 was a fairly busy year, with one division in particular, Sec(AS)2a, logging some 373 reports of unexplained aerial activity in the skies over the UK. But it was 1996 that saw the release of some intriguing and previously unknown information.

On July 24, in answer to Parliamentary questioning, the Ministry of Defence revealed that on two occasions in the previous five years the Royal Air Force had been obliged to scramble or divert aircraft to 'intercept and identify uncorrelated radar tracks entering the United Kingdom air defence region'.

These two incidents were not elaborated upon, but an admission was made that records were on file concerning: (a) the November 1990 UFO encounters over the North Sea reported by the pilots of a patrol of RAF Tornado aircraft; and (b) a UFO report filed with the MOD by the meteorological officer at RAF Shawbury in the early hours of March 31, 1993. 'Reports of sightings on these dates are recorded on file and were examined by staff responsible for air defence matters,' the House was told. 'No firm conclusions were drawn about the nature of the phenomena reported but the events were not judged to be of defence significance.'

Also in 1996 a further 300-page batch of Ministry of Defence UFO reports, this time covering the period 1964–1965, was declassified in accordance with the Government's 'thirty-year ruling', and is now on open display at the Public Record Office. By far the most revealing entry in the file is a collection of correspondence between Lieutenant Colonel John P. Spaulding, Community Relations Division, US Air Force, and the Ministry of Defence.

On June 15, 1965 Lt. Col. Spaulding wrote to the MOD to enquire what the British Government's position was with respect to UFOs: 'Do you have a Government program comparable to our Project Blue Book? If so, do you have a scientific consultant? Are there civilian organizations in your country which are dedicated to the study of UFOs? How much UFO activity do you have in your country?'

Although Lt. Col. Spaulding directed his letter to Mr R.A. Langton of S4 AIR, the responsibility of replying was judged to be a matter for another MOD division (the name of which is deleted on the released papers – something which I deem to be not without significance). Denying that it had established a Blue Book-type UFO study programme, or that it employed a 'special scientific staff', the Ministry did reveal to the Americans that, '[UFOs are] normally handled as part of the routine work of our Air Force Technical Intelligence department . . . We investigate about 70 cases a year but there are others which are not reported to us, although sometimes reported in the newspapers.' And, demonstrating its awareness of the activities of the civilian UFO research community, the MOD confirmed that in the UK there existed 'a considerable number' of groups devoted to solving the UFO puzzle.

Whilst the above replies may be considered relatively standard, the MOD confided in Lt. Col. Spaulding something far more revealing: 'Our policy is to play down the subject of UFOs and to avoid attaching undue attention or publicity to it. As a result, we have never had any serious political pressure to mount a large-scale investigation such as Project Blue Book. Indeed, the matter has been raised only once in Parliament in the last 5 or 6 years, and then only in a perfunctory way.'[38]

Consider that first sentence: 'Our policy is to play down the subject

Nick Pope, who for three years (1991-4) investigated UFO sightings for the Ministry of Defence.

The Ministry of Defence Main Building at Whitehall.

RAF Rudloe Manor, Wiltshire, headquarters of the Royal Air Force's Provost and Security Services (P&SS).

Recently-declassified RAF documents show that P&SS involvement in the investigation of UFO encounters dates back to at least 1962.

In 1996, the Ministry of Defence admitted that RAF Rudloe Manor had served as the 'RAF coordination point for reports of "unexplained" aerial sightings'.

A panoramic view of RAF Rudloe Manor.

Frank Redfern (bottom row, far right) during his basic training with the Royal Air Force.

The team of radar mechanics involved in the tracking of a UFO at RAF Neatishead, Norfolk in September 1952.

Ernest Sears, who served with the Royal Air Force during the Second World War, and who, in 1960, witnessed two RAF Gloster Meteor aircraft pursue a UFO over the British mainland.

The first anniversary conference of the Staffordshire UFO Group. According to a number of sources, including Robert Dean, a retired US Army sergeant-major, such events are routinely monitored by the Intelligence services.

Cannock Chase, Staffordshire, the reported site of a UFO crash in 1964 and where numerous large, triangular-shaped UFOs were seen in 1988.

Elite helicopter-based units of the military are regularly dispatched to monitor UFO activity. Here, a military helicopter is caught on film while hovering over a crop circle formation in Wiltshire in 1996.

In the 1950s and early 1960s the Gloster Meteor was routinely deployed to intercept UFOs in British airspace.

'I draw a parallel between the way in which incredibly complex patterns appear in a field, with the way in which we broadcast through radio astronomy. Perhaps it is an attempt at communication.' Nick Pope, Ministry of Defence, 1996.

On 15 July 1991, Royal Air Force Police were seen monitoring crop circle formations found near RAF Lyneham, Wiltshire.

A close-up photograph of a 1996 crop circle formation.

of UFOs and to avoid attaching undue attention or publicity to it.' If the entire UFO mystery is without merit, then why the need for such extraordinary measures on the part of the MOD? Furthermore, the Ministry's admission that, by adhering to such a policy, it had succeeded in staving off any serious Parliamentary interest in the subject of UFOs, will not, I hope, go unnoticed by today's politicians. Indeed, in view of the above, it is my sincere hope that Parliament will now press for a full disclosure of exactly what has been learned about the entire UFO issue over the past half a century.

Having now examined some of the more credible UFO encounters investigated at an official level over the course of the past fifty years, let us take a look at a relatively recent addition to the evolving UFO mystery in the UK – one which is showing disturbing signs of increased activity.

CHAPTER 13

FLYING TRIANGLES

TO THE MAJORITY OF PEOPLE, ANY MENTION OF UNIDENTIFIED FLYING objects inevitably conjures up images of 'flying saucers', 'flying discs' and similar-shaped craft. This is no bad thing since it at least indicates an ongoing public awareness of the subject. However, it should be noted that while many people do report sightings of circular-shaped objects, UFOs come in a variety of designs, and in the last decade there has been a dramatic increase in the number of triangular-shaped vehicles seen over the United Kingdom. That the Ministry of Defence is aware of this there is no doubt. Many reports have been forwarded to Whitehall clearly indicating the presence of 'delta'-shaped objects in British airspace. If MOD staff have a view on this influx of reports then they are not saying, instead preferring to stand by their claims that none of the sightings brought to their attention have proven to be of concern from a defence standpoint.

An interesting series of reports of both triangular and diamond-shaped UFOs surfaced in and around Essex during September 1988. Many of the witnesses stated that they had seen a 'large black, sometimes triangular-shaped object, very low in the sky, with coloured lights, usually red, green or yellow and moving silently'. UFO investigator Ronald West revealed to the media that as a result of his enquiries he had received almost thirty telephone calls from people who had seen the mystery objects in the skies over Basildon, Laindon and Wickford.[1]

On September 4, four independent witnesses saw what they described as a multi-coloured square-shaped object, lighting up like a Christmas tree. This was seen over the Thames Estuary and Southend area.

We have had reports of white, red, green and yellow lights. One said there was a triangular shape and . . . another a square. I live in Clacton and when one person from Leigh rang I was watching the same thing. From here it looked like a small pea. From Leigh it must have been massive.

I checked with Southend Airport which gave out that Heathrow was overcrowded with aircraft and had to stack planes. But I do not believe that. If the lights had been in straight lines, yes. But they were doing all sorts of antics. There must be another explanation.[2]

That year also saw a similar cluster of sightings around the Cannock Chase area of Staffordshire, prompting local MP, Bill Cash, to raise the issue with Roger Freeman, Minister for Defence. 'I have written to Mr Freeman and given him details of the sightings and I have asked him to make inquiries and let me know his views,' said Mr Cash, adding that, '. . . several independent individuals in the constituency who can be regarded as reliable witnesses saw these things and were caused a great deal of concern. I don't know what they were myself.'

One of those individuals was police statistical officer Eileen Ballard who, at 10.00 p.m. on May 16, 1988, viewed a number of objects of a triangular configuration from her home in Stafford. Along with five friends, Mrs Ballard reported that the craft were resplendent with lights, moved very slowly and, most remarkable of all, were entirely silent.[3]

By November 1988, Mr Cash had received a response from the Ministry of Defence. 'The reported phenomenon is quite likely to be connected with civil air traffic going into Birmingham Airport which was exceptionally busy at the time,' said a Ministry spokesperson.

In response, Mr Cash countered: 'The question is how could it be civil aircraft? These were reliable people who actually saw things. And what they saw could not be explained by civil aircraft, that's the point. The reply did not tell us very much, but it is very difficult for MOD staff who haven't seen these things to actually know what they are.'[4]

It was reported on December 1, 1988, that a businessman, Robin Westcott of Combe Martin, had seen a very similar object to that viewed by Mrs Ballard. The event had taken place at 7.15 p.m. on the previous Friday evening.

'It all happened so quickly as we were driving along,' recalled Mr Westcott. 'My friend didn't see it as we were talking at the time, but I saw it clearly above the top of the hedges – though only for two or three seconds. It was much brighter halfway down the two sides of the triangle and was on the Exmoor side of the road about half-way between Combe Martin and Barnstaple.

'It was difficult to see how large it was or how high in the sky. I waited to see it again as we drove along, but it had disappeared.'[5]

Within two months of Mr Westcott's sighting, the strange craft was once again active in the Essex area. On January 28, 1989, a 'triangular or shield-shaped UFO' was seen over Tiptree. Changing colour from 'bright to a dull white', the UFO disappeared from view in the vicinity of Chelmsford. There several people saw three bright lights flying in what was described as an 'inverted triangle formation', at approximately 8.30 p.m. in the evening.[6]

Yet another sighting was made in Essex on a Friday night midway through 1989. One of the principal witnesses, Mr Edward Chard, a Tailoring Manager from Canvey, said: 'I saw these lights hovering around and I got the binoculars out and it certainly was not an aircraft. When I used the binoculars all I could see was a triangular shape and it was fairly big. I was quite taken aback.'

Similar reports were received at the local police HQ, and checks were made with air traffic controllers at both West Drayton and Stansted, neither of whom was able to explain what was seen. Police were similarly unable to give a qualified explanation, only suggesting the possibility that the sightings were due to 'aircraft stacking'. They did, however, reveal to the local press that a report was being forwarded to the Ministry of Defence for analysis.[7]

'A stunned woman rang Hessle police to tell them she had watched a hovering UFO for three quarters of an hour,' reported the *Hull Daily*

Mail on July 14, 1990. A police spokesman said that the woman had described the UFO as being 'triangular-shaped when viewed sideways and with a square rear end,' adding that, 'it hovered for 30 minutes and then shot off vertically until it disappeared from view. Flames were observed coming from the rear of the object.'[8]

Two wholly independent sightings of a low-flying and almost silent UFO were reported by people living in the Gelding and Arnold areas of Nottingham on the night of May 22, 1991. Mrs Elaine Buck of Gelding described seeing an array of lights in the pattern of an 'elongated triangle', resembling the outline of a Concorde passenger plane: 'I was closing the bedroom window when I saw the lights. I ran downstairs and told my husband, who thought I was going mad. When he saw them he couldn't believe it.'

Fifteen minutes later, the UFO was seen by Mr Jack Sergeant and his wife as they drove towards Arnold. 'There were two diamond-shaped lights, about 1,000 feet up. I ran into the house and got my binoculars, then I could see they were no more than a few feet apart. There was a low humming or pumping noise. The lights were much bigger than those of any aircraft.'[9]

By June 1991, the number of UFO reports received in the same time-frame by the Nottingham-based East Midlands UFO Research Organisation exceeded fifty. Checks were made with a variety of sources, including the MOD and East Midlands Airport, but no answers were forthcoming. Commenting on the reports that he and his colleagues had examined, the organization's secretary, Mr Anthony James, said that people were seeing two separate objects flying a tight formation: 'They have been decribed as very bright lights on two triangular-shaped objects, many times larger than any known aircraft.'[10]

Early on the morning of October 11 that year, two friends, Ann Barnes and Trudy Edgeworth, were returning from a night out when their attention was drawn to a triangle of bright lights in the sky between Eversham and Cheltenham. Mrs Barnes recalled that the UFO resembled 'two car headlights in the sky, shining down as if it was looking at us'. She continued: 'It was a triangle shape with curved edges, which started off as red, changed to green, then red and back to white before it flew off.'

'It was a bit scary,' added Mrs Edgeworth, corroborating the account of her friend. 'I am not sure I believe in this sort of thing or not, but it wasn't an aeroplane – it was definitely something else, and looked like a UFO. When you say that to people they think you have gone mad. It really made me go goosey.'[11]

An alarming case, in which a middle-aged couple's house was enveloped in a brilliant beam of light, was investigated in 1991 by Sterling-based UFO researcher, Ron Halliday. According to the *Lothian Courier* of October 24, 1991, the encounter had taken place on an evening in the previous month. The couple reported that a bright beam of light had swept through their house, lighting up the bedroom 'like daylight' before disappearing. Baffled by what they had seen, the couple received an explanation the following night when both viewed an unusual-looking craft suspended in the autumn sky. Shaped like a pyramid with a bright light on the apex, the object hovered and rotated in the air for twenty-five minutes before disappearing in the same direction as the light beam of the previous night. 'Basically, we haven't been able to explain what the pyramid was so it's been verified as an unidentified flying object,' said Halliday.[12]

'It was a massive triangular object with flashing lights all around it,' said Mrs Jackie Chown of Ellastone in response to her sighting of an unidentified aerial vehicle in the Ashbourne area of Derbyshire. 'It was very big, made no noise, and seemed to be coming down over Back Lane travelling towards Uttoxeter,' added Mrs Chown. So impressed were the Chown family by the encounter that Mrs Chown's son, Dave, set off in his car with a family friend to search for the object. Although they drove around the whole area, the UFO had apparently vanished. Nevertheless, Mrs Chown was quite convinced of the reality of the incident, which occurred in January of 1993. '. . . it certainly was not a helicopter or plane as it made no noise – but I cannot explain what it was,' she said at the time.[13]

During 1994, sightings continued unabated, and I am aware of at least one such sighting which was investigated by the Civil Aviation Authority. Their summary follows:

> 1 MAY 94 – Sighting of unusual object. Member of public reported seeing a black boomerang-shaped object, which appeared to hover over RAF Northolt, above 30000 feet, before tumbling approx 2000–3000 feet, while rotating through 180 degrees on its axis. No other reports of anything unusual received – possibly A/C in Bovingdon stack seen from odd angle in setting sun.[14]

The *Maldon & Burnham Standard* reported on December 15, 1994, that a motorist had claimed to have seen a strange object above Maldon, Essex, five days earlier: 'Sergeant Gary Heard of Maldon police said it was described as triangular, about the size of a football pitch and illuminated by lights, giving the impression of floodlights. The observer said it hovered in the sky for about two minutes at 11.30 p.m. before fading away.'[15]

'A triangle of strange lights could match up with an unidentified flying object sighted throughout Europe,' commented the *Kingsbridge Gazette* on January 6, 1995, in response to a sighting reported by Mr Mark Hulin of Lower Town, Malborough. 'Lots of stars were out and I was looking at a particular star when this thing caught my eye,' said Mr Hulin. 'There were three white lights in the shape of a triangle, with a light in each corner. The lights were moving very slowly as one object. As they moved they rotated so it was highly unlikely they were separate lights.'[16]

March 1995 saw an increase in 'triangle' activity in Derbyshire. On March 3, Ian Taylor and Ian Brooks caught sight of one of the elusive craft over moorland between Ashbourne and Wirksworth. 'It had no sound and through binoculars we could see it was of a triangular nature with green lights on each corner. Eventually it moved off in a westerly direction,' said Mr Taylor.[17]

On March 16, a Sinfin mother and daughter saw a remarkably similar craft at 7.15 p.m. near Stenson Fields. Although the mother expressed a desire for anonymity, she did agree to be interviewed by researcher Peter Edwards. Neither witness was traumatized by the event; in fact the mother described herself as being 'elated' by the whole experience. The object was reportedly of the now-familiar triangular variety, dark in colour, with three bright lights in each corner and one in the centre. Having interviewed the mother, Peter Edwards commented: 'I do believe this is a genuine sighting because of the way she came across – excited and truthful. She could hardly believe it.'

Omar Fowler, head of the Derbyshire Phenomena Research Association, added: 'We know the new Aurora spy plane is of a similar design but its minimum speed would be around 200–300 mph. There is no way it could hover or travel at 20 mph like some of the local sightings we have heard about. I believe it is an alien craft.'[18]

A highly impressive encounter with the elusive 'triangle', involving a former member of the Royal Air Force, took place during the small hours of July 23, 1995. On the morning in question, fifty-six-year-old Rob McDonald, who served in the RAF for twelve years as an aircraft fitter, had just left a barbecue at a house on West Common Lane, Scunthorpe, when he caught sight of a strange aerial spectacle.

'The sky was clear and there was no mist,' recalled Mr McDonald. 'The stars looked very sharp. There were approximately 24 bright orange lights and they were travelling in groups of eight. Each group of lights was joined together with a bar and the lights were mathematically spaced apart. The groups formed a perfect equilateral triangle.

'They were very high up and travelled over West Common Lane in the direction of Polaris. The lights took seven seconds to cross the horizon which means they must have been travelling at nearly 15,000 mph.'[19]

As 1995 progressed, the triangle phenomena seemed bent on making its presence felt once again in the Derbyshire area. On August 2 at 2.30 a.m. it was seen by Dennis Jackson of Matlock who was driving between Youlgreave and Tansley; while on November 4 the 'triangle' was out in force near Ashbourne where it was seen at 9.15 p.m. by Peter Gamble. As is typical in such cases, no sound emanated from the objects.[20]

Similar accounts to those I have cited continue to receive regular media coverage to this day. Unfortunately, I have seen no evidence to suggest that the Ministry of Defence is contemplating an about-face regarding its standpoint that the 'triangles' are of no defence significance. One can only speculate on how such a conclusion has been reached. That the MOD has taken, and continues to take, a keen interest in these developments, I do not doubt. Of the possibility that the MOD will see fit to consult us regarding its conclusions surrounding the enigma, I am rather more doubtful.

Reports of large, silent triangular-shaped machines are not exclusive to the British Isles. In the late 1980s, for example, the skies over Belgium were virtually saturated with such objects, some of which were seen by official sources, including factions of the Belgian Air Force. Notably, many of the accounts that surfaced in Belgium were practically identical in nature to those reported over Britain, leading me to believe that we are possibly witnessing the unfolding of a large-scale reconnaissance programme of extra-terrestrial origin. Keep this in mind as we turn to the Belgian wave of 1989.

One of the busiest nights for sightings in Belgium was November 29, when literally hundreds of people saw several UFOs in the Eupen area of the country. Of particular interest is one incident reported by two members of the local Gendarmerie, which has striking similarities to a number of the cases already examined. Both officers reported that as they conducted their nightly patrol, their car was suddenly lit up by a beam of light which emanated from a huge 'dark triangle equipped with three "projectors" and a winking red light'. As with the 'Concorde-like' craft sighted at Nottingham, the officers stated that the UFO made a faint humming sound, adding that the light beam which enveloped their car was so dazzling 'that we could read a newspaper under it'.[21]

Perhaps most notable about the 'Belgian wave' is the immediate interest shown by both the Belgian and American Governments in the sightings. A formerly classified document, prepared by the United States Defense Intelligence Agency in March 1990, reveals that the whole of the American intelligence community was kept fully apprised of the developments over Belgium in 1989 and 1990. Captioned 'Belgium and the UFO issue', the document was widely distributed, with copies being sent to the CIA, the Secretaries of State and Defence, the White House, the Headquarters of the US Air Force in Europe, NATO and the Commander in Chief of US naval forces in Europe! Let us now examine the document in question:

Numerous UFO sightings have been made in Belgium since

Nov 89. The credibility of some individuals making the reports is good . . . Investigation by the BAF [*Author's note*: Belgian Air Force] continues.

Source A cites Mr. Leon Brenig, a 43-year-old professor at the Free University of Brussels (prominent) in the field of statistics and physics . . . Mr. Brenig was driving on the Ardennes autoroute in the Beaufays region east of Liege, Sunday, 18 March 1990 at 2030 hours when he observed an airborne object approaching in his direction from the North. It was in the form of a triangle . . . and had a yellow light surrounding it with a reddish center varying in intensity. Altitude appeared to be 500–1000 meters, moving at a slow speed with no sound. It did not move or behave like an aircraft.

Source B . . . discusses a Belgian television interview with Colonel Wil De Brouwer, Chief of Operations for the BAF . . . De Brouwer noted the large number of reported sightings, particularly in NOV 89 in the Liege area and that the BAF and MOD are taking the issue seriously. BAF experts have not been able to explain the phenomena either.

De Brouwer specifically addressed the possibility of the objects being USAF B-2 or F-117 Stealth aircraft which would not appear on Belgian radar, but might be sighted visually if they were operating at low altitude in the Ardennes area. He made it quite clear that no USAF overflight requests had ever been received for this type mission and that the alleged observations did not correspond in any way to the observable characteristics of either U.S. aircraft.

(Deleted) related a similar UFO sighting which apparently happened to a Belgian Air Force officer in the same area near Liege during November 89. The officer and his wife were allegedly blinded by a huge bright flying object as they were driving on the autoroute. They stopped their car, but were so frightened they abandoned the vehicle and ran into the woods.

. . . The BAF is concerned to a point about the UFO issue and is taking action to investigate information they have.

The USAF did confirm to the BAF and Belgian MOD that no USAF Stealth aircraft were operating in the Ardennes area during the periods in question . . .[22]

As well as in Britain and Belgium, similar craft have been sighted over the USA as can be seen from the following account related by American UFO researcher William Hamilton III of California:

'On October 26, 1988 while living in the Antelope Valley, my neighbors Ken and Katy saw a large boomerang-shaped craft between 8.35 p.m. and 8.45 p.m. that was estimated to be 600 feet plus in span, and was apparently traveling only about 20–30 mph. A second and identical large object joined behind the first one . . . Two additional witnesses saw the boomerangs pass over the valley from a side-view to the east. These boomerangs were also sighted in the town of Fresno later the same evening.'[23]

During 1991 and 1992, similar aerial vehicles were seen in Pennsylvania. An investigation undertaken by Samuel Greco PhD revealed that: 'The most prevalent form was the boomerang, also described as a "V" or banana shape . . . Another was triangle-shaped. No beams of lights or searchlights were projected to the ground, except for one witness who stated he had seen a pulsed beam flash to the ground. It appeared to him that the pulsed beam was doing a ground search.'[24]

Does an examination of these reports bring us any nearer to understanding the nature of the phenomenon? The many similarities present in the various accounts lead me to believe that the craft all have a common point of origin. But is that point of origin terrestrial or extra-terrestrial?

It has been suggested in some quarters that the many objects of a triangular design seen over Britain are simply terrestrial craft, albeit of a type not yet acknowledged to exist. That certain branches of both the British and American Governments are currently conducting research into highly advanced aeroforms, I do not dispute. Nor do I dispute that a number of those same aeroforms, such as the B-2 and F-117 'Stealth' aircraft, appear similar in design to some of the objects sighted regularly in British airspace since the late 1980s. However, there are a number of factors which suggest that at least some of the 'triangles' cannot be explained so easily.

If these are terrestrial aircraft, then one presumes that they are still on the 'secret list'. If that is so, then I would strongly question the wisdom of any government which brazenly parades its most prized aircraft over highly populated areas such as Essex, Nottinghamshire and Staffordshire, for all to see. Those handling these vehicles seem totally unconcerned that they are attracting the interest of the general public, the media, the British Ministry of Defence and the Belgian Air Force!

It seems risky to fly these craft over foreign soil, like Belgium, where they could be mistaken for a hostile intrusion. For the Americans (who are usually cited as being responsible for the 'secret aircraft') to test-fly new state-of-the-art vehicles over populated areas of Britain and Belgium makes no sense, particularly when one considers the vast amount of desert area available to US authorities in their own country.[25]

We have seen that the United States Air Force officially confirmed to the Belgian Government that none of their Stealth aircraft were responsible for the many sightings over Belgium. Other questions, such as those raised by Staffordshire MP, Bill Cash, have uncovered nothing to suggest that the British sightings are in any way connected with 'secret aircraft' trials. This brings me back to the theory which I stand by, that these objects are representative of an evolving phenomenon from elsewhere. How that phenomenon continues to evolve, we can only wait and see.

CHAPTER 14

MEETING THE MINISTRY

CURRENTLY, THE ONLY BRANCH OF BRITISH GOVERNMENT PUBLICLY acknowledged to be conducting research into the subject of UFOs is Secretariat (Air Staff) 2a, or Sec (AS) 2a as the department is generally known. Operating out of room 8245 in the Ministry of Defence Main Building at Whitehall, Sec (AS) 2a has been the focal point within the MOD for the receipt of UFO reports submitted by members of the public since early 1985 (following an extensive reorganization of the MOD in late 1984).[1]

Evidence presently available suggests that the role played by Sec (AS) 2a with respect to unidentified aerial objects is relatively minor. Indeed, I have been advised that no staff within the department are appointed to study the subject on a full-time basis.[2] Nick Pope, who was the Desk Officer within Sec (AS) 2a responsible for handling UFO reports between 1991 and 1994, has informed me that for Sec (AS) 2a: 'There is no specific "UFO budget", excepting the staff costs, i.e. around 20% of my salary, together with a tiny percentage of some other salaries, reflecting my line management's supervisory role.'[3]

Bearing this in mind, what is Sec (AS) 2a's policy on the UFO issue? '. . . the main concern . . . is to determine whether or not UFOs present a threat to the security and defence of the United Kingdom,' I was told by Clive Neville of Sec (AS) 2a in 1988. 'Unless we judge that they do, and this is not normally the case, no attempt is made by MOD to investigate or identify the objects.'[4]

In early 1994, having advised the Ministry of Defence that I was writing this book, I was granted permission to conduct a tape-recorded interview with Nick Pope, which subsequently took place in the pleasant surroundings of a London hotel. Over an enjoyable liquid lunch, Pope related to me his responsibilities as Sec (AS) 2a Desk Officer, and openly discussed his department's role in the investigation of UFO reports.

> As I think you already know, our reason for looking at these things, all we're doing is looking for any evidence of a threat to the defence of the UK. Now, what we do depends to a huge extent on the quality of the report we get. Sometimes a lot of reports are very vague, you'll get someone report something and they may not even be sure of the day. They may say, 'One day last week, I was out walking my dog late at night, and I saw something flash across the sky.' Now in that sort of situation, there is very little you can do, (a) because you don't have precise information of when it took place, and (b) because the nature of what has been reported is so vague it could have been anything. It could be an aircraft light, a satellite in low orbit, a meteorite; all sorts of things.
>
> Where we do get more exciting cases, and by that I mean where either the description looks like it's a structured craft seen at fairly low level in some detail or, perhaps, if you've got a multiple-witness event or anything that makes the case stand out and makes it interesting, there, we can do a little more work. We can speak to the Royal Observatory at Greenwich, perhaps. One thing we can do is to check with our own people to see if we had any low-flying activity in the area at the time, whether there was something going on in the area, perhaps a pop concert involving the use of laser lights; those are the sort of checks that we can do. Now in some cases, in the first instances I described, the vague lights in the sky, there's very little we can do other than offer a standard reply and we'll try and be as helpful as possible, saying what we do, why we do it, and what we think.

Is there any evidence to suggest that any of the UFO reports analysed by Sec (AS) 2a have had implications for the defence and safety of the UK?

No. There's no evidence of a threat to the UK that I've come across.

Bearing this in mind, what exactly would constitute a threat? (Pope smiled.)

That's the sixty-four-thousand-dollar question, I suppose. Some sort of hostile action, but because it hasn't happened, my answer is speculative and it's very difficult to say. I would say some sort of definite show of hostile force or intent.

How does Pope respond to the allegations that the Ministry of Defence is actively practising a policy to withhold UFO data from the general public?

When people put to me the allegations about 'Is there a cover-up?', I say, 'Have a look at what we're doing.' Every sighting we get we encourage people to speak to people like Quest and Bufora [two of Britain's largest civilian UFO study groups]. We're pushing into the public domain sightings that otherwise would not come to light at all. And that to me is the last thing that any organization involved in a cover-up would be doing. We actively encourage people to make reports.

What sort of investigations are undertaken by Pope's department with regard to photographic data on UFOs?

It's interesting, we're getting more and more camcorder and video footage with the proliferation of these things throughout society and more and more good video footage is coming forward, which is a good thing. I can't go into the details of our operational capabilities, but, rest assured, we do take a detailed and careful look at footage that is sent to us.

Does Pope retain copies of such material?

> It depends; it's really up to the member of the public. Sometimes
> people will lend you something saying, 'I want this back', and
> you'll have a look at it and, respectful of their views, hand it
> back. Sometimes people will say, 'Oh yes, you can keep this; it's
> a copy'.

I have shown that UFO sightings are frequently reported to the Ministry
of Defence by police personnel throughout the country. What sort of
working relationship exists between Sec (AS) 2a and the British Police
Force when it comes to unidentified flying objects?

> Basically, each police station should have a blank form, where
> UFO sightings can be reported, and then they should . . . fill
> in the details and send them to us. [They are] simply acting as
> a point where data can be recorded direct from the member of
> the public, and then sent direct to us. They're acting, as it were,
> as middlemen; as a post-box.

Pope has confirmed to me that, prior to 1985, the job that Sec (AS) 2a
currently undertakes regarding the UFO phenomenon was handled by
DS8, and prior to that, S4AIR and S6.[5] As we have already seen, in
1967 a decision was made by the Ministry of Defence to preserve the
UFO-related files of those particular departments, thus ensuring their
eventual release under the terms of the Government's 'thirty-year ruling'.
I questioned Pope as to why this action was taken.

> I speculate that it's something that derives from the fact that there
> was a huge wave of sightings in 1967 and that would have, in turn,
> sparked public interest in the subject. I think prior to 1967, there
> were so few reports and it was such a funny subject that didn't
> logically fit anywhere. In 1967, everything changed and it was
> felt that here was something the public would be interested in,
> ask questions on and, therefore, these are not papers we should
> be throwing away. Now that's a guess, but I think it's probably

the correct one. Our position, as far as I'm concerned, is that we were quite happy for these old reports to be made public. I think it's a very good thing, as much as we can make public, I'm eager to do it.

With regard to today's files, what sort of system does Pope operate?

. . . we have two main files; one is a 'Correspondence' file, which is where someone like yourself writes to me and asks me some questions and I reply. And then there's our 'Sightings' file. You've seen the numbers of reports we get; if we got in the business of opening a file for each [report] it would be ridiculous. Bear in mind also, of course, that most of them wouldn't contain much more than the actual report itself.

You only really open a file where you've got a lot of papers on the same subject. If all you've got is a letter from the member of the public, and a response from me, then there's no earthly point in opening a discrete file.

If Sec (AS) 2a received the details of, for example, a wave of UFO sightings over the city of Edinburgh on one particular evening, would this necessitate the opening of a special file?

Not necessarily; it's really a matter of judgement. If the Desk Officer thinks that a particular wave of sightings is going to run and run then they'll open a discrete file. That doesn't mean anything except that the papers are easily accessible. That's why, for example, we've got a file on Rendlesham Forest.

At this point in our meeting, I showed Pope a copy of the document released by the United States Defense Intelligence Agency under the provisions of the American Freedom of Information Act, concerning a proposal orchestrated by the British Government in 1967 suggesting that they liaise with the Soviet Union on the issue of unidentified flying objects. Was Pope aware of any liaison between our Government and other nations?

I suspect that when we first looked at UFO sightings, we must have at least touched base with the Americans, and I'm aware, for example, that we've got one of the old Project Blue Book reports, so the Americans must at least have sent us that.

[*Author's note*: this particular report was forwarded to me by Pope on April 11, 1994. Dating from February 1, 1966, the 11-page document describes Blue Book policy up until the time in question, and is supplemented by a statistical breakdown of recorded UFO sightings as submitted to Blue Book staff.]

Our policy is very similar to what the Americans said after Blue Book, i.e., there is a lot of interesting stuff out there; we think we can explain most of it, not all. A small percentage seems to defy explanation. We keep an open mind on that but, so far, there's no evidence that any of this is extra-terrestrial. Now, as far as I understand it, that's the American position and has been since the end of Blue Book, and that's our position too. Whether those two policies were developed independently, or as I suspect, because there must have been some degree of talking to each other, I don't know. I suspect that after all this blew up in 1947, people at least got in touch with opposite numbers and said, 'What do you think?', but that's guesswork. I don't have any papers and, as far as I'm aware, the PRO don't either.

Nick Pope has been willing to admit that, in the course of their work, Sec (AS) 2a are 'assisted by specialist staffs with responsibilities covering the air defence of the UK. These staffs examine such data routinely, as part of their normal duties. Their task – like ours – is to look for evidence of any threat to the UK. If no such evidence is found, no further action is taken.'[6] Was Nick Pope willing to add anything further to this statement?

What I can tell you is, along with us, reports and data go to those departments in the UK who are concerned with air defence, and what this is really, is a casting of an expert eye over these reports, really mirroring the sort of work that we do, but from a specialist point of view. Now, it's not our practice to name those departments.

Is there any indication, as far as Pope is concerned, that there has been an involvement in UFO investigations on the part of MI5, MI6 or the Government Communications Headquarters at Cheltenham?

It's not our practice to discuss the role of the Security Services, notwithstanding recent 'Citizen's Charter' things. I know that you can, for example, pitch up at Her Majesty's Stationery Office and get a copy of the new Security Services Bill or something like that, but we don't enter into discussion about them at all and you shouldn't read anything into that either way really. It's just that if you asked me about Security Service involvement in any subject I would give you the same answer.

Was Nick Pope, as Sec (AS) 2a Desk Officer, aware of any UFO sightings that had been subjected to the Official Secrets Act?

No ... having said that, I'm bound by the OSA, military personnel are bound by that and Queen's regulations. Now, there's nothing in there that says that you won't report UFOs for whatever reason. If I saw a UFO, I would have to report it. I would be bound by the Official Secrets Act, but that wouldn't have any effect on my reporting it. It sounds a bit convoluted, I know, but I think the basic answer to your question is, no.

Midway through 1987, a sensational document gained worldwide publicity following its publication in Timothy Good's *Above Top Secret*. Allegedly, the document, dated November 18, 1952, was a Top Secret briefing paper intended for the 'eyes-only' of President-elect Dwight D. Eisenhower informing him of the crash and recovery of an extra-terrestrial spacecraft on American soil in July 1947. Furthermore, it was stated that following the crash – which was reported to have taken place near to the town of Roswell, New Mexico – a Top Secret research and development/intelligence operation, the 'Majestic Twelve', was established to deal with the matter. Since both the Majestic Twelve and the Roswell crash are discussed later, at this point I will merely state that the entire

issue has provoked a furious controversy, and intense investigations into
the reported crash at Roswell and the legitimacy, or otherwise, of the
documentation continue.

In January 1994, Nick Pope advised me that, '. . . while we are aware of
the so-called MJ12 documents, and the controversy that surrounds them,
we have no knowledge of the matters they refer to, and have undertaken
no research into their authenticity.'[7]

Was Pope's awareness of Majestic 12 based on an official interest?

> No, that's purely through reading. Again, it's the sort of thing
> we were likely to be asked and we were asked. So I made it my
> business to try and find out what the allegations were and what
> the key players in the UFO lobby thought about it. But there
> was no official involvement in that. It was just me trying to make
> sure that I could speak to people in an informed and expert way.
> As far as I'm concerned, that's a matter for the Americans to say
> whether a document is official or not.
>
> My personal view [on the Roswell crash] is that something
> occurred. Now precisely what, I don't know. I don't think that
> anyone disputes that something crashed to earth on that day
> in 1947. Whether it was a weather balloon or whether it was
> something else, I don't know.

Pope was also sceptical of the possibility that a high-level cover-up existed
within Government circles to contain the fact that a covert extra-terrestrial
presence existed on Planet Earth.

> My argument to that, is that you've only got to look at the
> A-bomb, which must have been the most sensitive secret in
> existence at the time, because it gave the Americans, absolutely,
> the advantage. Yet within a few years of the test of that particular
> weapon, the Soviets had it. Surely that must have been their
> absolute top-priority secret, I would think. I can't see that
> anyone could keep an extra-terrestrial presence on Earth secret
> if it was done with knowledge of Government. Also, I come back
> to the question, why would the secret be kept? People say there

would be worldwide panic. As far as I'm concerned [that's] not
supported by any firm research, just people's personal opinion
based on sci-fi 'B-movies'.

In conclusion, how would you like to see the role of Sec (AS) 2a progress
in the UFO field?

Really down the road that I think we're already taking, where I
would like to see a good working relationship where people can
phone me up, I can phone people up, and we can all be very
open and honest.[8]

What are we to make of Nick Pope's comments? Firstly, I should stress
that I am absolutely convinced that Pope has been entirely honest and
straightforward with me, both in person and in correspondence. Secondly,
the refreshing degree of co-operation that is now afforded both UFO
researchers and witnesses by Sec (AS) 2a is most welcome and Pope is to
be applauded for instigating much of that co-operation. Also, it is to
Pope's credit that he availed himself of much of the literature on the
UFO subject, thereby ensuring that he was able to speak on the matter
with a high degree of authority.

More significantly, there is now a willingness on the part of Sec (AS) 2a
to open up selected papers to interested members of the general public,
as Pope explained to me in 1992: 'With regard to access to our files in
Sec (AS), we have always taken the view that we do not release material
"en bloc" . . . That said, we will always try to be as helpful as possible; if
people ask about a specific sighting, we can search our files and release a
copy of any UFO report we have received that might tie in . . . We will
also help by answering any questions about MOD policy on UFOs.'[9]

Notwithstanding this, there are a number of points which deserve
comment. For example, Pope has advised me that Sec (AS) 2a has no
appreciable 'UFO budget' to support its investigations. Yet, as Timothy
Good has learned, in 1978 no less than £11 million was appropriated by
the MOD to ensure that in-depth studies into the UFO enigma were
undertaken.[10]

Pope also maintains that there is no available evidence to suggest that any of the UFO reports examine by Sec (AS) 2a have had a bearing on the defence of the UK. This is puzzling since, as I have demonstrated, there were numerous close encounters between UFOs and the military in the 1950s – many of which took place in close proximity to sensitive Government installations. And in the Gaydon case of 1957, the pilot of a Gloster Meteor was forced to take avoiding action to prevent a mid-air collision with a UFO over an active RAF 'V-bomber' station.

There is no doubt in my mind that these particular incidents simply must have had a bearing on national security and the defence of the realm. Are we to believe that incidents such as the above simply 'petered out' and are no longer reported? I find this theory totally implausible; sightings of UFOs by military personnel continue to be reported throughout the world. To demonstrate, the last ten years have seen an abundance of such encounters from countries as disparate as Puerto Rico, Belgium and the former Soviet Union. Are we to imagine that UFO phenomena have exclusively avoided contact with the British Isles while continuing to appear throughout the rest of the globe?

How then do we reconcile this situation with Pope's comments that Sec (AS) 2a has never examined any UFO reports which suggest that the defence of the country has been compromised?

We have already seen that on November 14, 1962, the Air Ministry issued new instructions concerning the reporting procedures applying to UFOs. Sightings by civilians would be investigated by S6, and reports filed by military sources would be channelled through to AI (Tech) 5b. Following the establishment of the Ministry of Defence in 1964, the UFO-related duties of S6 were transferred to the newly formed S4AIR and DS8. Air Intelligence, of which AI (Tech) 5b was a part, was combined with the intelligence divisions of both the Army and the Navy to create the Defence Intelligence Staff.

Logic dictates that a specialist division within the DIS would have assumed the investigative role previously held by AI (Tech) 5b. Therefore, is it possible that Sec (AS) 2a fulfils a similar function to that of S6, S4AIR and DS8, and consequently staff assigned to Sec (AS) 2a do not possess the necessary 'need to know' regarding UFO incidents which *do* have a bearing on national security? I think that this is most definitely the case.

This scenario becomes all the more likely when one considers the following statement made to me by Nick Pope: 'I cannot recall having seen a UFO report submitted by military personnel, with the exception of the sightings by personnel from RAF Topcliffe in 1952, and Lt. Col. Halt's report on the UFO sighting near RAF Woodbridge in 1980.'[11] Pope has also informed me that, 'as well as the reference to S6, I am aware that the job I do has previously rested with S4 and DS8'.[12]

Then there is the matter of the Official Secrets Act. Nick Pope is adamant that, as far as Sec (AS) 2a is concerned, the UFO issue is not subject to the constraints of the OSA. Conversely, we have the following testimony of Frederick Wimbledon who was involved in an astonishing UFO incident in 1956: 'Any of us who were involved in these things were sworn to secrecy under the thirty year rule and even then could still be "incurring the displeasure of Air Ministry" with subsequent threat of prosecution under the Official Secrets Act.'[13]

What on earth is going on here? Either Pope or Wimbledon is mistaken – something which I do not for one moment believe – or Sec (AS) 2a is being denied access to the details of 'sensitive' UFO incidents such as those that Wimbledon was involved in – a theory I am strongly inclined to support.

If further proof were needed, I have been advised by Nick Pope that the UFO records held by Sec (AS) 2a are 'unclassified' in nature.[14] As we have seen, however, at various times since 1947 UFOs have been afforded 'Secret' and very possibly 'Top Secret' status. Again, this suggests a degree of compartmentalization of data within the Ministry of Defence.

It is intriguing to note that Nick Pope draws a parallel between Sec (AS) 2a's attitude towards the UFO issue, and that of Project Blue Book – an official UFO study programme co-ordinated by the US Air Force. Established in 1953, Blue Book was borne out of two previous USAF investigative projects pertaining to UFOs, 'Sign' and 'Grudge'. Between 1948 (the year that saw the creation of Project Sign) and 1969 (the year in which Project Blue Book was officially terminated), 12,618 reported UFO sightings were investigated by USAF personnel assigned to the above projects.

According to the American Air Force: 'Of these sightings, 11,917 were found to have been caused by material objects (such as balloons, satellites, and aircraft), immaterial objects (such as lightning, reflections, and other natural phenomena), astronomical objects (such as stars, planets, the sun, and the moon), weather conditions, and hoaxes . . . only 701 reported sightings remained unexplained.[15]

Concerning the sightings which remained unidentified, the USAF was adamant: 'Of the very few that remained unidentified, there was no indication of a technology beyond our own scientific knowledge, or that any sightings could be considered an extra-terrestrial vehicle. More importantly, throughout Project Blue Book, there was never a shred of evidence to indicate a threat to our national security.[16]

This indicates a policy and attitude very close to that of Sec (AS) 2a. Interestingly, convincing evidence has been located to show that investigators assigned to Blue Book, Grudge and Sign, did not possess the necessary clearance which would have allowed them access to UFO reports which *did* suggest that US national security had been compromised. The evidence to which I refer can be found in a now-declassified USAF memorandum prepared in 1969 by Brigadier General C.H. Bolender, the Air Force's Deputy Director of Development: '. . . Moreover, reports of unidentified flying objects which could affect the national security are made in accordance with JANAP 146 or Air Force Manual 55–11, and are not part of the Blue Book system.'[17]

As Stanton Friedman, a nuclear physicist who has worked for General Electric, General Motors and Westinghouse, states: 'From a very practical viewpoint, Blue Book was, for most of its existence, a public relations effort to keep the public off the Air Force's back.'[18]

Is it feasible that the existence of an alien presence on our planet could be successfully withheld from the public? Nick Pope believes not, and cites the fact that within several years of the American Government's successful testing and deployment of the atomic bomb (one of their most highly guarded secrets), detailed knowledge of the workings of the weapon was in the hands of the Soviet Union. If US authorities had been unable to prevent that particular secret leaking to a foreign, and potentially hostile nation, then surely it would be nigh-on impossible for any government to contain so startling a fact that the Earth has extra-terrestrial visitors?

Whilst this argument appears sound, evidence and documentation in my possession suggest otherwise.

Thanks to the ongoing research of Bryan Gresh, Senior Vice President of Altamira Communications Group, and George Knapp of KLAS-TV, Las Vegas, it has now been proven that information relating to the reported UFO crash at Roswell in 1947 quickly fell into the hands of the Soviets. During a research trip to Russia in 1993, Gresh and Knapp were able to secure an interview with Valeriy Burdakov who, in the 1950s, was a scientist at the prestigious Moscow Aviation Institute. According to Burdakov, his interest in UFOs caught the attention of Sergei Korolyov, the founder of the Russian space programme. Korolyov did not admonish Burdakov for his beliefs; rather, he confided in him some astonishing facts.

Burdakov recalls that in 1948 Korolyov was invited to a meeting by Josef Stalin. It was at that meeting that Stalin asked Korolyov to give his opinion on a wealth of material relating to the UFO phenomenon which the Soviets had gathered during a 'Top Secret' study. Burdakov further recalls that some of the information had been gleaned from reports filed by Soviet operatives in place in New Mexico at the time of the affair at Roswell. What conclusions did Korolyov reach?

'Korolyov told Stalin the phenomenon was real,' said Burdakov. 'He told him the UFOs were not dangerous to our country, but they were not manufactured in the United States, or any other country. Stalin thanked him, and told Korolyov his opinion was shared by a number of other specialists.'[19]

Since these particular revelations did not surface until the 1990s, I can only assume that, as with British and US authorities, the Soviets chose to restrict access to their information on UFOs to a small and select group. Contrary to Nick Pope's beliefs, this only adds weight to the theory that governments, on a worldwide scale, can successfully keep UFO data classified with relative ease – for decades.

Although there can be no doubt that the Manhattan Project (the official name of the US operation to build an atomic bomb) was certainly one of America's most closely guarded secrets during, and after, the Second

World War, is it likely that the UFO issue was considered to be of equal, if not greater, importance by the US Government of the time? While the sceptic may scoff, evidence suggests that this is so.

On November 21, 1950, a senior radio engineer with the Canadian Government's Department of Transport, Wilbert Smith, wrote a 'Top Secret' memorandum specifically dealing with UFOs which was designated for the Controller of Communications. Smith recounted that while attending a conference of the National Association of Radio Broadcasting in Washington, he learned that two books had been published concerning UFOs: *Behind the Flying Saucers* by Frank Scully, and *Flying Saucers are Real* by Donald Keyhoe. What did Wilbert Smith have to say about this?

> Both books dealt with the sightings of unidentified objects and both books claim that flying objects were of extra-terrestrial origin and might well be space ships from another planet. Scully claimed that the preliminary studies of one saucer which fell into the hands of the United States Government indicated that they operated on some hitherto unknown magnetic principles. It appeared to me that our own work in geo-magnetics might well be the linkage between our technology and the technology by which the saucers are designed and operated. If it is assumed that our geo-magnetic investigations are in the right direction, the theory of operation of the saucers becomes quite straightforward, with all observed features explained qualitatively and quantitatively.
>
> I made discreet enquiries through the Canadian Embassy staff in Washington who were able to obtain for me the following information:
>
> a. The matter is the most highly classified subject in the United States Government, rating higher even than the H-bomb.
> b. Flying Saucers exist.
> c. Their modus operandi is unknown but concentrated effort is being made by a small group headed by Doctor Vannevar Bush.
> d. The entire matter is considered by the United States authorities to be of tremendous significance.[20]

The importance of the facts uncovered by Smith cannot be understated. Coupled with the disclosures relating to early UFO research undertaken by the Russians, we can now see that a conspiracy of silence to contain the true facts about UFOs existed in both the USA and the USSR. Although there is no evidence to suggest that this situation came about as the result of a joint agreement, I consider it probable that, since the decline of the Cold War, a degree of co-operation on the UFO subject now exists between Russia and the USA.

Taking this into consideration, I believe that I am able to offer a qualified counter-argument to Nick Pope's viewpoint that continued Government secrecy would be impossible to maintain. There is now no doubt that, more than forty years ago, the UFO issue received a classification status higher than that afforded to the H-bomb, thereby ensuring that breaches of security were kept to a minimum. As a number of US intelligence agencies continue to take an active interest in UFOs, I see no reason why this situation should have changed. Paradoxically, the few leaks of information which did occur, such as those involving Soviet agents present at the time of the Roswell incident, were themselves concealed by opposite numbers when it became apparent that the UFO enigma was genuine and appeared to be alien in nature.

In conclusion, what can be said of Sec (AS) 2a and its ongoing role in the UFO field? There is no doubt in my mind that Sec (AS) 2a legitimately investigates UFO reports filed with the MOD by members of the public in much the same way as its predecessors, DS8, S6 and S4AIR, did. In contrast, there is nothing to indicate that Sec (AS) 2a has had a hand in the investigation of any military–UFO encounters of any great significance. The department's woefully inadequate file on the UFO event at Rendlesham Forest in 1980 (see chapter 11) tends to add weight to this theory, as does Nick Pope's assertion that the use of the Official Secrets Act has not been invoked to silence witnesses to UFO encounters – something which clashes acutely with the recollections of Frederick Wimbleon.

In light of this, let us now turn our atention to an entirely separate branch of the British military which appears to have had longstanding involvement in the UFO mystery – the Provost and Security Services.

CHAPTER 15

THE PROVOST AND
SECURITY SERVICES

FOR A NUMBER OF YEARS, RUMOURS HAVE CIRCULATED TO THE effect that highly classified investigations into UFO activity are undertaken by specialist operatives housed at the Royal Air Force facility at Rudloe Manor, Wiltshire. Such claims first gained widespread publicity in Timothy Good's *Above Top Secret*.[1] Should we treat seriously these allegations?

RAF Rudloe Manor is home to the headquarters of the Royal Air Force Provost and Security Services. This body's duties include the investigation of crime and disciplinary matters involving RAF personnel, security vetting of personnel, and the issuing of identity cards, passes and permits.

Far more significant, investigators attached to the P&SS are also trained in the field of counter-intelligence (C/I). Such training is undertaken at the RAF Police School. Prospective candidates for counter-intelligence work are required to take specialized courses in subjects such as computer security and surveillance. Before being considered for C/I work, personnel have to attain the rank of substantive corporal within the RAF Police. After training, successful applicants can expect to be posted to a Royal Air Force station on C/I duties or to a P&SS unit.

C/I investigators are responsible for issues affecting the security of the RAF, which includes the loss of classified documents, matters pertaining to espionage cases, and the protection of royalty and VIPs when visiting RAF stations.[2]

Also situated within the headquarters of the Provost and Security Services is a division known as the Flying Complaints Flight. The FCF primarily investigates low-flying complaints involving military aircraft in the United Kingdom. These investigations can very from establishing how many aircraft were in the area of a complaint, to the formal interview of the aircrew concerned. Within the FCF, there is one Royal Air Force Provost Officer and fifteen RAF Policemen engaged on investigative duties. They are, in turn, supported by three civil servants.[3]

In *Alien Liaison*, Timothy Good relates the account of a former special investigator for the P&SS who claimed specific knowledge of its involvement in the UFO subject: 'I am sure beyond any reasonable shadow of doubt that all initial investigations into UFOs are carried out by investigators of the P&SS who are serving in a small secret unit with the Flying Complaints Flight based at HQ, P&SS, Rudloe Manor.'[4]

Further corroboration has come from a former counter-intelligence investigator, who revealed the following to Good's source: 'I had access to every Top Secret file there was, except Low Flying, because I understand they dealt with UFOs. We could get in anywhere, but not in that department. I remember they used to have an Air Ministry guard in the passage – you couldn't get past them. We could see the Provost Marshal's top secret files but yet I couldn't get into the place dealing with UFOs . . .'[5]

In 1988, the Ministry of Defence, as represented by Sec (AS) 2a, admitted to me that RAF Rudloe Manor did receive unsolicited reports of UFO sightings from members of the public, but specifically denied that any clandestine research into the subject was undertaken there.[6] Similarly, Nick Pope was openly sceptical of the possibility that the Provost and Security Services at Rudloe Manor were covertly investigating UFO sightings under cover of the Flying Complaints Flight.

Commenting on the allegations concerning Rudloe Manor made in both *Above Top Secret* and *Alien Liaison*, Pope advised me:

Members of the public, a lot of them, don't know the procedure for reporting a UFO. Some people will phone the press, some will phone us direct, some people, and this is the key point, will phone their nearest RAF base. I suspect that someone has reported something to Rudloe Manor, as people can and do. Someone at Rudloe Manor has said, 'Yes, I'll take details of that', and from there [the allegations] grew and grew. I know this story from *Above Top Secret* and I don't agree with the conclusions in there. I'm not aware of any secret research that they're doing or anything like that. As far as I'm concerned, they were just doing their job.[7]

Whilst Pope's views are entirely reasonable, I am able to report that important documentation has now surfaced which confirms the involvement of both the RAF Police and the Provost and Security Services in the investigation of reported UFO sightings, and corroborates much of that which Timothy Good's sources have alleged.

The following report was made available to me by the Public Record Office in 1994 where it is now available for inspection. Prepared by Sergeant C.J. Perry of the RAF Police, it provides some invaluable information.

At Aylesbury on 16th February, 1962 at 1530 hrs. I visited the Civil Police and requested information on an alleged 'Flying Saucer' incident. I was afforded every facility by the Civil Police authorities and although no official report had been made, details of the incident were recorded in the Station Occurrence book.

The details are as follows:- Mr. [Ronald] Wildman of [witnesses address], Luton, a car collection driver, was travelling along the Aston Clinton road at about 0330 hrs. on 9th February 1962 when he came upon an object like a hovercraft flying approximately 30 feet above the road surface. As he approached he was travelling at 40 m.p.h. but an unknown force slowed him down to 20 m.p.h. over a distance of 400 yrd., then the object suddenly flew off. He described the object as being about 40 feet wide, oval in shape with a number of small portholes around the bottom edge. It emitted a fluorescent glow but was otherwise not illuminated.

Mr. Wildman reported the incident to a police patrol who notified the Duty Sergeant, Sergeant Schofield. A radio patrol car was dispatched to the area but no further trace of the 'Flying Saucer' was seen. It was the opinion of the local police that the report by Mr. Wildman was perfectly genuine and the experience was not a figment of imagination. They saw that he was obviously shaken.

I spoke to Sergeant Schofield and one of the Constables to whom the incident was reported. Both were convinced that Mr. Wildman was genuinely upset by his experience.[8]

A copy of Sergeant Perry's report was forwarded to the Air Ministry who, in their two-page report on the case, admitted that: '. . . this incident is one for which there can be no indisputable solution.'[9] In response to newspaper enquiries, the Air Ministry ventured the possibility that Mr Wildman had merely viewed a cloud, illuminated by the headlights of his car. This suggestion was not accepted by Mr Wildman, who was convinced that he had seen a solid object of some sort:

It was oval-shaped and white with black marks at regular intervals round it, which could have been portholes or air vents. It was about twenty to thirty feet above the ground and at least forty feet wide across – which in my estimation was fantastic. The object, which was silent, kept ahead of me by approximately twenty feet for 200 yards, then started to come lower. It continued like this till it came to the end of the stretch. Then a white haze appeared round it, like a halo round the moon. It veered off to the right at a terrific speed and vanished; as it did so it brushed particles of frost from the tree tops on to my windscreen. It was definitely a solid object because the reflection of my headlights was thrown back from it.[10]

That the RAF Police (of which the P&SS is a functional element) would take the time to send a representative to the civil police to obtain details of a UFO incident, and subsequently forward all available information to Whitehall, suggests far more than casual involvement on their part in the UFO subject. Indeed, the scenario that this implies is one of routine collaboration between the RAF Police and the Air Ministry. This theory is further bolstered by the fact that approximately six months after the sighting took place, the Provost and Security Services once again became intimately involved in the UFO enigma.

In October 1962 Miss Anne Henson of Taunton, Somerset, forwarded a letter to RAF Chivenor detailing her sighting of an unidentified flying object on the evening of August 30, 1962. Upon receipt of her letter, the staff at Chivenor did something most unusual. Rather than forward Miss Henson's letter directly to Secretariat 6 at the Air Ministry – as should have been the case since the witness was a civilian – a copy was passed on to Wing Commander C.M. Gibbs, OBE, DFC, the Officer in Charge of the Flying Wing at Chivenor. On October 24, Wing Commander Gibbs met with Sergeant J.S. Scott of the Special Investigation Section of the Provost and Security Services and personally handed him a copy of Miss Henson's letter. At that point, the P&SS launched its own investigation. I quote from Sergeant Scott's final report:

MISS ANNE HENSON, aged 16, said . . . that on 30th August, 1962 between 10.30 p.m. and 10.55 p.m. she opened the window of her room which faces N.N.E. and saw a diminishing star-like object with what appeared to be red and green coloured flames coming from it. It was slightly larger than the average star and appeared to be round. After about 2½ minutes it became very small and she could only see it with the aid of binoculars. She was quite sure that it was not the navigation lights of an aircraft because she had seen these many times and could recognise them immediately . . .

. . . She did not look for it again until 17th October 1962, when she saw the object again which was partially obscured by fog. With the aid of binoculars she compared the object with several stars and noticed that the stars were silvery white whereas the object was red and green . . . Near to and above the object she noticed another exactly similar but smaller object . . . She noticed a difference in the colour of the original object which was now emitting green and orange flames in the same way as before . . .

MRS C. HENSON, mother of MISS ANNE HENSON, said that she had seen the object described by her daughter. She could offer no explanation as to the identity of the object but was of the opinion that it was not a star. She declined to make a written statement . . .

[A] visit was made on 1st November, 1962 when the sky was clear and all stars visible. MISS HENSON, however, said that the object was not in view on this particular night . . . Observations were maintained for one hour but nothing was seen.

MISS HENSON was asked to continue her observations and on the next occasion on which she saw the object or objects to compile a diagram showing its position in relation to the stars. This she agreed to do.

On 28th November, 1962, the next available opportunity, [the witnesses address] was again visited. However, although observations were maintained for 2 hours the sky remained obscured and nothing was seen. MISS HENSON was interviewed and said that she had seen the objects again on two occasions and although she had compiled a diagram . . . she had omitted to note the date. She said that she would again watch for the objects noting times and dates and compile another diagram which she will forward by post to this Headquarters.

MISS HENSON reports unidentified aerial phenomena and provides a diagram showing their position in relation to stars. The objects have not been seen by the Investigator who cannot therefore give an opinion as to their identity.

It is considered that MISS HENSON is a reasonable person, although at 16 years of age girls are inclined to be over-imaginative. However, MISS HENSON is supported by her mother, a person of about 50 years of age, who seems quite sincere.

The matter should be brought to the notice of [the] Department at Air Ministry set up to investigate such phenomena.[11]

Prior to being sent to the Air Ministry, a copy of Sergeant Scott's report, which was classified 'STAFF CONFIDENTIAL', was forwarded to his superior, Wing Commander H. Mundy, also of the Provost and Security Services. It was Wing Commander Mundy's recommendation that the report should first be sent in triplicate, to the Provost and Security Services Headquarters at Government Building, Acton for, I quote, 'information and consideration of action'. As the sighting had been reported by a civilian, and there was no evidence to suggest that national security had a bearing on the case, the P&SS finally dispatched a copy of the report to S6 at the Air Ministry.[12]

Baffled by the sighting, S6 duly forwarded the complete file to AI (Tech) 5b for examination. In one of the very few papers currently available for inspection which originated with AI (Tech) 5b, it was concluded that, in all probability, Miss Henson had viewed a celestial object, or objects, under unusual atmospheric conditions. S6 was duly informed of this, and advised Miss Henson of the results of the investigation.[13]

There are a number of issues in this case which cry out for attention. Note that Sergeant Scott of the P&SS was apprised of the details on October 24, 1962. Yet it was not until late December of that year that S6 finally received a briefing of the event. Given that S6 was supposedly the focal point within the Air Ministry for the receipt of UFO reports from members of the public in the early 1960s, it seems odd that the Provost and Security Services would neglect to inform S6 of the details for almost two months – unless, as seems to be the case, the P&SS have a mandate to conduct their own independent enquiries. Note also that Sergeant Scott actually made several visits to Miss Henson's home in an attempt to view the phenomenon for himself and prepared a two-page report on the case which was classified at 'STAFF CONFIDENTIAL' level. This hardly seems consistent with the activities of a branch of the British military which is purported to have no significant involvement in the investigation of UFO sightings.

Upon receipt of the file pertaining to this case, which totals eleven pages, I forwarded a copy to Air Commodore J.L. Uprichard, Director of Security and Provost Marshal (RAF), for comment. His reply, dated May 4, 1994, reads:

> Thankyou for your letter dated 28 April 1994, concerning the investigation of alleged Unidentified Flying Objects (UFOs). The Royal Air Force Provost and Security Services organization is a functional element of the Royal Air Force Police with responsibility for investigating alleged criminal offences and security breaches within the Service. As part of that remit, the Flying Complaints Flight investigates alleged breaches of the United Kingdom Low Flying System.
>
> The 1962 report to which you referred is a rare example of an alleged UFO sighting being treated as a low flying incident and investigated accordingly. Routinely, we neither investigate nor evaluate such reports.[14]

The importance of Air Commodore Uprichard's letter cannot be over-emphasized. Although such investigations are classed as being 'rare', we now have documented proof, from no less a source than the Director of Security and Provost Marshal himself, that UFO encounters have been treated as low-flying incidents by the P&SS and have been 'investigated accordingly'. In an anonymous capacity, this is something which Timothy Good's sources have maintained for years.

Getting people to speak on record about the British Government's role with respect to unidentified flying objects is never easy, particularly when national security rears its head. Fortunately, there are exceptions. One person who has been willing to divulge what he knows about the 'P&SS–UFO link' is Jonathon Turner, a former medic with the Royal Air Force. Having served for ten years with the RAF, Turner retired in 1993 and is now on six years' reserve.

Whilst stationed at RAF Lyneham, Turner learned that reports of UFO sightings by military pilots were never recorded in the flight logs. Instead, details would first be channelled through to the Squadron Commander, who would then advise the Station Commander of the situation. From there, all relevant information would be forwarded to the P&SS for examination. More significantly, if national security was considered an issue, the pilots and crews would be advised to 'keep quiet', and reminded of the fact that they were bound by the the Official Secrets Act.

Between 1985 and 1990, Turner was based at RAF Brawdy, Pembroke-shire, where he served as a medical assistant. Interestingly, during his assignment, Turner was told by a colleague on base that the public relations officer at Brawdy actively monitored local UFO incidents and passed the details of 'many of them' on to a US Navy source. If so, then this may indicate an ongoing international collaboration on matters pertaining to UFOs between the Governments of the USA and the United Kingdom. Tellingly, in 1988, Sergeant Dave Pengilly of RAF Brawdy commented with regard to the UFO issue: 'Each report . . . is always investigated . . . We don't like unidentified things in our airspace.'

One of the most illuminating aspects of Jonathon Turner's revelations regarding the P&SS is that, when national security is considered an issue, the Official Secrets Act is still being used to muzzle Royal Air Force pilots – something strenuously denied by Sec (AS) 2a's spokesman, Nick Pope. As I have stressed, I do not believe that Pope has in any way misled me on this matter, and suspect that Sec (AS) 2a is essentially kept in the dark – as is the general public – at least as far as encounters between UFOs and the military are concerned.[15]

While investigating the activities of the Provost and Security Services, I received several communiques, which can only be termed 'enigmatic', from a source professing past affiliations to the P&SS. The gist of the information was that, in conjunction with the Ministry of Defence, the Flying Complaints Flight at RAF Rudloe Manor has inadvertently tracked unknown objects flying at low level over the United Kingdom with what is known as the 'Skyguard' radar system. Although technical details pertaining to the system are not readily available, the Ministry of Defence has confirmed to me that Skyguard does play a major role in the investigation of low-flying complaints in the United Kingdom:

As part of the MOD's commitment to ensuring that military low flying activity in the UK, defined as below 2000 feet, is conducted as safely as possible, and in accordance with low flying regulations, the Flying Complaints Flight (FCF) of the RAF Police conducts around a dozen surveys of low flying activity per year, each lasting four days, at varied locations around the country. Since 1989, this has included the deployment of a Skyguard radar system, a number of which were captured from Argentinian forces during the Falklands War. The radar is used to monitor the speed and height of aircraft at low level, including fast jets, to ensure that the pilots are adhering to the regulations. In addition to the low flying monitoring task, the radars are also used for electronic warfare training, primarily at RAF Spadeadam where they are based.

Low flying monitoring deployments are made to areas seeing a significant amount of low flying activity. Locations are decided upon by MOD approximately every six months and take account of such factors as the pattern and volume of complaints received or where particular problems have been identified. Since 1989, Skyguard has been deployed on 35 occasions and has observed around 1900 aircraft.[16]

Based on conversations with my source and the above evidence supplied by the MOD, I am of the opinion that the tracking of any unknown objects over the UK by Skyguard would have been viewed as an extremely serious event by both the MOD and the FCF. Moreover, since Skyguard has only been deployed since 1989, it implies that seemingly unknown, structured craft still continue to penetrate British airspace with relative ease.

In much the same way as the P&SS is responsible for the investigation of crime and disciplinary matters involving the British Royal Air Force, the United States' Air Force Office of Special Investigations (AFOSI) fulfils a similar role in the USA. Again like the P&SS, investigators attached to AFOSI receive intensive training in matters pertaining to counter-intelligence, and their involvement in UFO investigations has been well-documented. In the late 1980s for example, AFOSI gave assistance to the FBI who at the time were making enquiries into the so-called 'Majestic 12' documents.[17]

Does a working liaison exist between the P&SS and AFOSI on the issue of unidentified flying objects? It has been confirmed to me by Special Agent Patrick R. Hernst of AFOSI that 'on each military installation where US personnel are assigned, an AFOSI detachment exists. Therefore, we work closely with base Ministry of Defence officials and off installation police departments'.[18] Oddly, when I brought the subject up, AFOSI advised me that they did not know if they had a working relationship with the P&SS at Rudloe Manor, which is decidedly curious. After all, one would expect that AFOSI themselves would know with whom they liaise and on what subjects. Similar enquiries that I have made with Rudloe Manor have been met with a stony silence.[19]

Almost a decade has now passed since Timothy Good first revealed that covert UFO investigations were undertaken by the Provost and Security Services at RAF Rudloe Manor. In that time, we have come a long way. We have the testimony of Jonathon Turner, the Skyguard revelations, the two documented UFO investigations undertaken in 1962, and the comments of no less a source than Air Commodore J.L. Uprichard, Director of Security and Provost Marshal (RAF).

All this evidence relates to the P&SS–FCF link with the UFO issue up until 1995. In the latter part of that year, however, events took an extraordinary turn. On November 19 researcher Chris Fowler wrote to the Ministry of Defence specifically enquiring about the claims in Timothy Good's *Above Top Secret* that research into UFO activity was undertaken from RAF Rudloe Manor. Rather than deny such charges, the MOD made a stunning admission. Spokeswoman Kerry Philpott wrote in her December 14 reply to Fowler: 'Rudloe Manor is the Headquarters of the RAF Police, which does serve as a focal point, amongst other things, for flying complaints. In the past, Rudloe Manor was indeed the RAF co-ordination point for reports of "unexplained" aerial sightings.'

Quite what prompted this complete turnaround on the part of the

MOD remains unclear, but there are a number of issues which need to be addressed. First, Kerry Philpott is Nick Pope's successor in Sec (AS) 2a. As will be recalled, however, when I interviewed him in 1994, Pope had no such awareness that Rudloe Manor played such a role; indeed, he was openly sceptical of the claims made by Timothy Good's sources. I have also shown why, in my opinion, Sec (AS) 2a is specifically kept out of the loop when it comes to the investigation of sensitive UFO incidents. Witness the testimony of RAF medic Jonathon Turner, who has stated to me that as far as 'pilot encounters' with UFOs are concerned: 'All UFO reporting is carried out at the Flying Complaints Flight, which is a smokescreen for UFO investigations.' In view of this, from where did Kerry Philpott learn that Rudloe Manor served as the RAF coordination point for reports of 'unexplained' aerial sightings?

Recognizing that we were on the verge of one of the most important breakthroughs in recent years, both myself and Timothy Good began to make our own enquiries. For his part, in early January 1996, Timothy learned that Kerry Philpott's information came from her speaking to staff at Rudloe Manor, who gave an assurance that their role in coordinating UFO data on behalf of the RAF came to an end in early 1992.[20]

One month later, this was clarified to me by Group Captain John Rose, Officer Commanding, P&SS (UK):

> I can confirm that Flying Complaints Flight was responsible for coordinating reports of unexplained aerial sightings until 1992. I have not been able to determine the date on which Flying Complaints Flight began to fulfil this role. Please note, however, that Flying Complaints Flight only moved to RAF Rudloe Manor (with the rest of HQ P&SS (UK)) in 1977. RAF Rudloe Manor itself would have had no role in the coordination of unexplained aerial sighting reports prior to the arrival of HQ P&SS (UK). Indeed, it is likely, although we are unable to confirm this, that Flying Complaints Flight coordinated such reports whilst at the previous location of HQ P&SS (UK) at Acton.[21]

Perhaps the most intriguing aspect of Group Captain Rose's letter is his comment that it was 'likely' that FCF co-ordinated 'unexplained aerial sighting' reports whilst it was stationed at P&SS HQ (UK) at Acton. Given that the move to Acton occurred in 1950, this implies that FCF have been involved in the coordination of UFO data for decades. Yet, until 1996, no confirmation of this was forthcoming from the MOD. Whilst it could be reasoned that the Ministry was simply choosing to keep the general public ignorant of the facts, the comments made to me by Nick Pope suggest that, as Desk Officer in Sec (AS) 2a, he too was kept in the dark. Moreover, the fact that Kerry Philpott had to consult with staff at Rudloe Manor before being able to answer Timothy Good's questions suggests that her knowledge of the UFO-related functions of the FCF was no more than that of Pope. And the mystery does not end there.

In answer to Chris Fowler's enquiries, Kerry Philpott advised him that on receipt of a UFO report, staff at Rudloe Manor would have simply forwarded it to Sec (AS) 2a for appropriate action. This implies that Rudloe Manor acted as little more than a convenient 'post-box' for reports. Based on conversations with several sources in early 1996, however, I have to question this version.

On March 5, 1996, I had the good fortune to conduct a personal interview with Group Captain Rose and was informed that, whilst today UFO reports are forwarded to the Ministry of Defence, prior to 1992, 'we held the information down here and decided what to do with it'. And as Group Captain Rose also admitted, if a UFO report were seen to be relevant to the work of Flying Complaints Flight there was a distinct possibility that it would still go direct to FCF today: 'If an airbase thought there was a low-flying problem, they would probably report it to us, then, you know, it would be reported up, and it could be that it could fall into the category of the "unexplained".' This despite the fact that Sec (AS) 2a maintain that all UFO reports received at RAF facilities go direct to their office at Whitehall.

There are other problems with the claims that FCF-originated UFO reports have routinely reached Sec (AS) 2a. Throughout March 1996 I had been keeping Nick Pope apprised of my investigations into the whole issue of Flying Complaints Flight involvement with UFOs. As he advised me on March 2, when he was assigned to Sec (AS) 2a, the UFO reports held in his office dated back to approximately 1985; yet, having had the opportunity to examine them, Pope was clear on the fact that he could not recall having seen any UFO reports which might have come to Sec (AS) 2a from FCF in the period 1985–91. And in the post-1992 period?

According to Group Captain Rose: '. . . the lead lies with the Secretariat of the Air Staff, and certainly they are the ones who've issued us with the policy since '92, to forward everything to them'. However, Nick Pope was the only publicly recognized authority on UFOs in the Secretariat of the Air Staff between 1991 and 1994, and he assures me that he issued no such policy to FCF, or to the P&SS as a whole.

Is it therefore possible that the orders for FCF to forward all of their UFO data to the MOD after 1992 came from another office within the Air Staff? Nick Pope feels that this is not the case, and I have to agree with him. The Secretariat of the Air Staff is a relatively small body comprising approximately twenty-five people, of whom around ten are assigned to Sec (AS)1 and fifteen to Sec (AS) 2a. In addition, within the Air Staff there exists what is known as a 'Float File' where, according to Pope, 'every bit of work you do is circulated and everyone knows what everyone else is doing.'[22]

Although I am certain that Pope is 'telling it as he sees it', the fact remains that someone in the MOD set down a policy to ensure that in the post-1992 era, all UFO reports received at Flying Complaints Flight were forwarded to the MOD. By his own admission, Nick Pope was not that person, and he has confirmed to me that, up until he left Sec (AS) 2a in 1994, he did not recall seeing any UFO reports arrive at his office from FCF. I therefore have to assume that those reports went elsewhere.

In fairness to Pope, although he took a keen interest in determining what my enquiries into the FCF-UFO issue uncovered, he still does not subscribe to the theory that, until 1992 at least, Flying Complaints Flight were conducting their own UFO investigations, independently of Sec (AS) 2a. As he advised me in March 1996:

> I think it is reasonably clear that RAF Rudloe Manor only ever received UFO reports by default, as it were, and were drawn into the subject only because Flying Complaints Flight has the capacity to trace unidentified military aircraft that have been the subject of a noise/low flying complaint from a member of the public.
>
> At no time do they seem to have taken any unilateral action with regard to investigating UFO reports. That is not to say that,

over the years, Flying Complaints Flight did not assist Sec(AS) or DS8 with investigations, by attempting to correlate military aircraft activity with times and locations of UFO sightings. Such a move, however, would have been at our instigation.[23]

Whilst I respect Pope's opinion, I beg to differ. For example, Pope contends that Rudloe Manor only received UFO reports 'by default'. However, we now have proof that possibly for decades, Flying Complaints Flight served as the UFO coordination point for Britain's Royal Air Force. Such a precisely defined role suggests that FCF were at the forefront of the British Government's UFO investigations.

I also cannot agree that any investigations in which Flying Complaints Flight did play a role would only have been at the 'instigation' of Sec (AS) 2a. Although it has long been the Ministry of Defence's contention that all of its UFO investigations are conducted, in the first instance, by Sec (AS) 2a, and that the corresponding data is held at Whitehall, I refer the reader back to the statement made to me by Group Captain John Rose of Rudloe Manor, that prior to 1992, 'we held the information down here and decided what to do with it'. Rather than gel with Nick Pope's 'no unilateral action' theory, this comment suggests that prior to 1992, FCF were the people calling the shots, as opposed to Sec (AS) 2a.

Of course, one question has yet to be answered: Why, after years of silence, has there finally been official confirmation of the fact that Flying Complaints Flight was the recipient of UFO data for decades? I strongly suspect that whatever FCF learned about UFOs during the period 1950–1992, that data is no longer stored at Rudloe Manor and has been transferred elsewhere. As Group Captain Rose has informed me, the only paperwork currently held at Rudloe Manor is an inactive file of correspondence between FCF and the Ministry of Defence which relates to the handling of UFO reports.[24] With an admission that FCF ceased in 1992 to have a role of any significance, perhaps there is a desire on the part of Rudloe Manor to distance itself from the rumours of ongoing involvement in the UFO issue. And make no mistake, such claims abound.

*　　*　　*

One of the more intriguing rumours concerning the Provost and Security Services in general, and the RAF Police in particular, is their intense interest in the 'Crop Circle' mystery. As I write, there can be few people in the UK who remain unaware of the phenomenon, largely because, at times, media interest in the mystery has reached epidemic proportions.

Quite what (or indeed, who) is guilty of peppering Britain's landscape with the now-familiar crop circles, and the more elaborate 'pictogram' designs, is an issue which has been hotly debated for years. Numerous theories have been put forward to explain the phenomenal number of designs which have appeared throughout the country (and now, the world) since the late 1980s, but in my opinion we are still no closer to fully understanding the true nature of the mystery.

Of those who have considerably expanded our knowledge of the crop circle issue, one of the most vocal has been George Wingfield. Eton-educated and previously employed at the Royal Greenwich Observatory, Wingfield has learned that in September 1990, the British Government called a secret ministerial briefing to debate the matter. According to Wingfield's information, the meeting was convened essentially to try to determine the nature of the circles, lest the British Government be placed in the embarrassing position of having to admit its ignorance of the phenomenon.[25]

Although Nick Pope has told me that he was not aware of any such meeting having taken place, he does hold firm views with respect to the 'circle puzzle': 'I draw a parallel between the way in which incredibly complex patterns appear in a field, with the way in which we broadcast through radio astronomy. Perhaps it is an attempt at communication. Where that communication comes from, whether it's extra-terrestrial or something to do with the Earth, I don't know.'[26]

That such a statement should come from a serving Ministry of Defence official is, I am convinced, of extreme importance. After all, if Pope has taken the decision to acquaint himself with the facts, then what of other military and RAF divisions? And, indeed, what of the P&SS?

In 1991, RAF medic Jonathon Turner was stationed at Royal Air Force Lyneham. He recalls one particular occasion when, on July 15, a crop circle was discovered on the nearby Hackpen Hill. Shortly afterwards, examples of the more elaborate pictograms began appearing too. His interest piqued, Turner chose an off-duty day to visit the area and to take some photographs of the various patterns and formations which had appeared. As he soon learned, however, Turner was not alone.

Parked near a run-down farm building was a car: an RAF Police car. Turner subsequently had a brief conversation with the police officer, and questioned him about his presence. This provoked a cryptic response from the RAF policeman, who admitted that he was 'probably monitoring the activity on the Downs regarding the crop circles'.[27]

Were it not for the fact that Turner was himself in the military at the time, it is unlikely that the officer would have been so forthcoming. And I have to ask: On whose orders was the officer 'monitoring the activity'? Given that the RAF Police has its base of operations at Rudloe Manor, the possibility of Flying Complaints Flight involvement in the investigation of yet another inexplicable phenomenon cannot be ruled out. Indeed, as we shall now see, it appears that the revelations concerning the pre-1992 activities of Flying Complaints Flight only tell a fraction of the story.

Via a former RAF Police source who left the service in 1992, I have learned that the Provost and Security Services have a covert team of surveillance operatives on constant alert known as 'Sharkwatchers'. With respect to unexplained aerial sightings, it is the function of the Sharkwatchers to: (a) monitor and infiltrate civilian UFO investigative groups; and (b) monitor the activities of military personnel with certain 'off-beat' hobbies, which includes UFOs.

According to the data related to me, the prime motive for carrying out such operations is to ensure that military personnel are not divulging sensitive UFO data to those without official clearance. I am reliably informed that the unauthorized release of such material is termed 'Beadwindow'. If the P&SS Sharkwatchers deem that Beadwindow may be taking place, steps are taken to monitor the activities of those suspected of talking out of turn. If Beadwindow is ultimately confirmed, an intense surveillance operation is put into place, which can include the 'tapping' of domestic telephone lines. In such instances, I am told, detailed transcripts are made of all relevant telephone conversations (on occasion with the assistance of the Government Communications Headquarters at Cheltenham), and all material is duly forwarded to the Ministry of Defence at Whitehall for appropriate action. If considered necessary, that 'appropriate action' can include visiting UFO witnesses and military operatives to request their silence.

With so many people now divulging information pertaining to the UFO-related activities of the Provost and Security Services, I have to ask: Are they following some form of carefully executed agenda? Has a decision been taken to slowly acclimatize us to the true facts surrounding P&SS involvement in this enigma? I can only answer 'Yes' to both questions. Quite what the future will bring we can only wait and see, but it is my firm belief that as far as the Provost and Security Services are concerned, we have barely begun to see the tip of a very large iceberg.

CHAPTER 16

THE DEFENCE
INTELLIGENCE STAFF

AN INTEGRAL PART OF THE MINISTRY OF DEFENCE, THE DEFENCE
Intelligence Staff (DIS) was created on April 1, 1964, out of the amalga-
mation of the pre-1964 service intelligence branches and the Joint Intelligence Bureau, and now serves as a unified body able to serve the MOD,
the Armed forces and a variety of other Government departments.[1]

Broadly speaking, the DIS carries out the same function as that of its
predecessors, Army, Navy and Air Intelligence. That is, to provide the
MOD with a central, unified intelligence organization which can provide
objective assessments of defence intelligence matters in both peacetime
and wartime. Its primary function is to give warning of preparations for
war or attack by a potential enemy.

Much of the work of the DIS is devoted to military issues such as tactics,
orders of battle (generally known as ORBATS), weapons and capabilities.
Other areas are covered to ensure a more complete picture; these include
science and technology, nuclear, chemical and biological capabilities, arms
traffic, control and verification and economic aspects of defence.[2]

The DIS analyses information gathered from a wide variety of sources,
both overt and covert, including military attachés posted to British
missions overseas. In addition, the DIS also studies material provided
by Signals Intelligence (SIGINT) operations, which is supplied by both

the Government Communications Headquarters at Cheltenham, and the United States' National Security Agency.[3] As I will soon show, the NSA has had intimate involvement in the UFO issue for more than four decades.

With the bulk of its activities co-ordinated from within the Ministry of Defence Main Building at Whitehall, the work of the DIS is overseen by the Chief of Defence Intelligence (CDI). Specialized departments within the DIS include the Directorate of Economic and Logistic Intelligence, the Directorate of Management and Support of Intelligence, and the Directorate of Scientific and Technical Intelligence.[4] It should therefore come as no surprise to learn that the DIS takes a keen interest in unidentified flying objects.

As the reader will recall from my interview with Nick Pope, all the UFO reports held by Sec (AS) 2a are considered 'unclassified' in nature and appear to constitute no threat to the defence of the realm. Pope has also admitted that in the course of conducting enquiries into UFO encounters, assistance is given to Sec (AS) 2a by 'specialist staffs' with responsibilities covering the air defence of the United Kingdom.

Despite Sec (AS) 2a's reluctance to publicly discuss the involvement of these specialist staffs, I am now in a position to do so. To fully appreciate the importance of this, it is first necessary to clarify the regulations which apply to the records held by Sec (AS) 2a. Although it has always been the policy of Sec (AS) 2a that UFO documentation generated by the division cannot be released en bloc, in certain circumstances, selective UFO reports may be released to interested parties, as Nick Pope has explained to me:

> With regard to access to our files in Sec (AS), we have always taken the view that we do not . . . open our files for public viewing. This is because we would have to treat all requests the same, and once we had released material to one person or group, we would have to do the same for any subsequent requests, as we could not 'play favourites'. I am afraid that we simply do not have the time or resources to make such an open-ended commitment. That said, we will always try to be as helpful as possible; if people ask us

about a specific sighting, we can search our files and release a copy of any UFO report we have received that might tie in. We would have to delete information pertaining to the witnesses identity though, for obvious reasons of privacy.[5]

An examination of such reports, many of which I possess, shows that Sec (AS) 2a is required to routinely log a variety of data relating to reported UFO sightings. This includes: the date, time and duration of the sighting; the description and angular elevation of the UFO; the position of the observer in relation to the UFO; the meteorological conditions at the time of the encounter; and the movements of the UFO. Witnesses are also asked to make note of any 'Nearby Objects', including telephone lines, high-voltage lines, generating plants, TV or radio masts and factories. What the released papers do not tell us is what consideration is given to these reports by the 'specialist staffs' which lend assistance to Sec (AS) 2a. That is, save for several reports which, with the benefit of hindsight, appear to have been released in error by the MOD.

On a number of occasions in the 1980s, Quest International, one of Britain's most respected UFO organizations, obtained copies of various Ministry of Defence documents which showed that UFO reports forwarded to both DS8 and to Sec (AS) 2a were also circulated to other departments within the British Government. I am obliged to Mark Birdsall, one of the country's leading UFO researchers and a director of Quest International, who supplied me with copies of these particular reports in 1989. What differentiates these papers from any others released by the MOD, is the fact that they display distribution lists, clearly intended for internal use only, showing that as well as to DS8 and Sec (AS) 2a, documentation pertaining to UFOs was also being routinely forwarded to two divisions within the Royal Air Force: the Airborne Early Warning (AEW) department and the Ground Environment (GE) division. Of equal significance, copies of those same reports were distributed to two branches of the Defence Intelligence Staff: DI55 and the Directorate of Scientific and Technical Intelligence (DSTI).

Since the MOD refuses to discuss the role of these departments with respect to the UFO mystery, and no further documentation has surfaced displaying such distribution lists, I suspect that the release of there papers represented a monumental error on the part of the Desk Officer in Sec (AS) 2a at the time, the result of which was a rare glimpse into the MOD's 'inner sanctum'.

By making this information public, am I in violation of the Official Secrets Act? Although not wholly certain, Nick Pope suspects not, since it was, after all, one of his predecessors who had released the documents to Quest International in the first place. However, he qualified this by stating: 'That's really for your publisher, I suppose, to take a decision on.'[6] Given that this information was not 'leaked' by a confidential source, but was made available officially, albeit mistakenly, by the MOD, I remain confident that there is very little that the Ministry can do (aside from quietly rueing the day that the papers entered the public domain).

Upon receipt of the documentation it became apparent to Quest International that this was a matter of some significance. What was DI55? What function did it perform with respect to unidentified flying objects? Answers were needed. Graham Birdsall, editor of Quest's prestigious *UFO Magazine*, recalls their attempts to uncover more details from the Ministry of Defence:

> One of the departments listed was DI55 – so we placed a telephone call to this department, and by pretending we were another department within Whitehall itself, sought particular details about a known UFO case.
>
> Surprise, surprise, we were given details about the case, and witnesses involved.
>
> Further questions inevitably brought on suspicion, and finally we were asked to clarify who we were exactly . . . so we told them. There was a long pause of silence, and then we were told to refer to AS2 for any further comment.
>
> Shortly afterwards, the MOD confirmed they had another department which acted as a 'clearing house' for some UFO reports. This was in stark contrast to their earlier denials that no other official department dealt with UFOs. A cover-up?[7]

Beyond establishing that DI55 receives copies of UFO reports from Sec (AS) 2a, it has proven extremely difficult to obtain pertinent information regarding the full extent of DI55's role in this field. But there are indicators. The Public Record Office has confirmed to me that between 1974 and 1979, DI55 conducted an in-depth study of Soviet capabilities to launch an attack on mainland Britain and its adjacent waters. This is one of a number of files currently retained by the Ministry of Defence which relate to the activities of the Defence Intelligence Staff, and as the Public Record Office has advised me, '. . . these records are retained because they contain information relating to the security and intelligence agencies and are obviously highly sensitive.'[8] Clearly, DI55 has a substantial role to play in the ongoing defence of the British Isles.

One document originating with the Ministry of Defence, also provided by Mark Birdsall, refers to 'DI55 SIG'. 'SIG' is an abbreviation of 'Signals Intelligence' or 'SIGINT'. As previously noted, the DIS liaise closely with both the Government Communication Headquarters at Cheltenham (GCHQ), and the United States' National Security Agency (NSA) on SIGINT matters. On October 9, 1980, Eugene Yeates, the NSA's Chief of Policy went on record as stating that the NSA had located 156 UFO-related documents which were, '. . . based on intercepted communications of foreign governments or SIGINT operations and, thus, remain properly classified.'[9]

Taking this into consideration, are we able to offer any definitive conclusions concerning DI55? I find the fact that DI55 has a SIGINT division to suggest the possibility that its role in UFO matters extends much further than merely examining unclassified UFO reports on behalf of Sec (AS) 2a. Since the DIS is in routine contact with the NSA, which operates on a global scale, then we are faced with a completely new scenario – which may involve a worldwide monitoring of the UFO subject by DI55 and its associated branches within the DIS, including the Directorate of Scientific and Technical Intelligence.

As has already been shown, both the Scientific and Technical divisions of the Air Ministry were implicated in research conducted in the wake of the UFO sighting at RAF Topcliffe in 1952. As this situation continued throughout the early 1960s, when reports of UFO encounters filed by the

2   *A Covert Agenda*

military were dealt with exclusively by AI (Tech) 5b, it is safe to assume
that DSTI fulfils a similar role today.

Secreted within room 3388 of the Ministry of Defence Main Building at
Whitehall is a little-known department: the Defence Intelligence Agency
Liaison office. Variously referred to as DIAL London, or simply DIALL,
the department was established in 1964 under the control of the US
Defense Intelligence Agency (DIA). However, a US Military Intelligence
Liaison office had existed prior to that time. Although a relatively small
operation, the primary function of DIALL is to represent the interests of
the DIA to the British Defence Intelligence Staff.[10]

What is the Defense Intelligence Agency? Created in 1961 by US
Defense Secretary Robert McNamara, the DIA, like the British DIS,
brought together the military intelligence branches of the US Army, Navy
and Air Force into a combined organization. Currently, the DIA satisfies
the foreign intelligence and counter-intelligence requirements of the
Secretary of Defence, the Joint Chiefs of Staff, various components of the
Defense Department, and provides the military intelligence contribution
to national intelligence. It also manages the Defense Attaché System,
which assigns military attachés to American embassies throughout the
world.[11]

As of 1995, the DIA released approximately 200 pages of once-classified
documents dealing with UFOs – including two particularly startling
papers which concern fruitless attempts to intercept and shoot-down
UFOs sighted in the vicinity of military air bases. Also, the DIA has
informed me that a number of UFO reports found within its archives
are, '. . . specifically authorised under certain criteria established by an
Executive Order to be kept secret in the interest of national defense.'[12]
Without a doubt, the DIA views UFOs with some concern.

Is there an ongoing liaison between the DIA and the Ministry of
Defence on matters of mutual concern regarding unidentified flying
objects? If so, one would expect that DIALL would be a prime mover in
co-ordinating the flow of data between both parties. Robert P. Richardson,
Chief of the DIA's Freedom of Information division, told me in 1991 that:
'There is no indication of any liaison involving DIAL London regarding

the subject of unidentified flying objects.'[13] I have, fortunately, uncovered evidence which suggest that the issue is not as clear cut as the DIA would have us believe.

In early 1990, I was informed by a US intelligence source that a substantial amount of photographic evidence concerning UFOs, much of which originated with the DIA, was stored at the Federal Records Center at Suitland, Maryland, USA. Acting on this information, I filed a Freedom of Information request with the DIA in an attempt to procure the release of this material. Despite my initial optimism that something of significance would surface, this did not prove to be the case. During the course of my investigations, I learned that in responding to my FOIA requests on this topic, the DIA was routing its replies through the DIALL office at MOD headquarters in Whitehall![14] What was so important about this matter that it required liaison with the MOD's Defence Intelligence Staff? To this day, I have yet to receive a satisfactory answer.

There is a curious sequel to this affair. In 1994, I attempted to learn more about the above, and resolved to contact DIALL direct. This proved unsuccessful, as DIALL refused to respond to my enquiries in any way whatsoever. Instead, DIALL contacted Mrs Lyn M. Patterson, the Special Executive Assistant with the US Embassy in Grosvenor Square, London, and asked her to respond to my questions. This she did, and advised me to contact a certain branch of the DIA which has its base of operations at Arlington, Virginia. I followed her lead, but was not blessed with a response . . .[15]

There have been other occasions when responses to my Freedom of Information requests were routed through London addresses. For instance, in 1991 I received a number of UFO records which had been recently declassified by the US State Department. Although FOIA requests to the State Department are dealt with by its Washington DC office, in my particular case, matters were dealt with by the State Department's 'Regional Security Office' in London.[16] Is this UK–USA collaboration on UFOs simply coincidental? I rather think not.

On October 8, 1993, following a routine FOIA request submitted to the DIA, I received a copy of a document which conclusively proves that, despite Ministry of Defence denials, departments within the Defence

Intelligence Staff are conducting their own investigations into UFOs –
completely independently of those undertaken by Sec (AS) 2a.

The document concerns a conference on the UFO issue held in China in
1992 and raises a number of interesting points. For example, the entire file
runs for at least forty-two pages, yet the DIA has deemed that only three
pages are releasable, and those that have been declassified are themselves
highly censored. Once again, 'national defence' is cited as a reason for
withholding what could be crucial data. With this in mind, I quote from
the DIA report:

> China Unidentified Flying Object (UFO) Research Organization
> hosts national conference in Beijing on 11 May. The organization
> hopes that China will be selected to host the first world UFO
> conference, which is scheduled for 1993. More than 200 Chinese
> researchers are attending the conference to study reports of flying
> saucers or 'Fei Die' in China. About 5,000 UFO sightings have
> been reported in China in the past 20 years.[17]

Copies of this report were forwarded to a number of departments within
the American Government, including the National Security Agency,
Wright-Patterson Air Force Base (which has had longstanding involvement in the study of the UFO phenomenon), the Central Intelligence
Agency, and the American Embassy in Beijing. Most astonishing of all,
the DIA also flashed a copy of the report, via electronic signal, to the
Ministry of Defence's DIS at Whitehall![18]

Since Clive Neville of the MOD had informed me in 1989 that: '. . .
we are only interested in reported [UFO] sightings which occur in the
airspace of the United Kingdom . . .', this raises an obvious question:
Why is the DIS receiving briefings relating to UFO conferences held on
the other side of the world in China? Not surprisingly, the DIS refuse to
discuss this matter with me.[19]

Having failed to secure an official statement from the DIS, I forwarded
a copy of the entire report to Nick Pope at Sec (AS) 2a for comment. Pope's
response was:

> I am afraid that it is not our policy to discuss the distribution

of UFO data within the Ministry of Defence, beyond saying that Sec (AS) are assisted by specialist staff with responsibilities covering the Air Defence of the UK. These staff examine such data routinely, as part of their normal duties. Their task – like ours – is to look for evidence of any threat to the UK. If no such evidence is found, no further action is taken.[20]

Although not without interest, this does not tell us a great deal. Five months later, during the course of my taped interview with him, Pope gave me a slightly modified response. Having reminded him that I had supplied him with a copy of the DIA report on the UFO conference at Beijing, Pope advised me thus: 'I've not seen this document arrive to us, apart from you sending it, so I don't know what happened with it.'

Does this not then imply that the DIS carried out its own independent assessment of the contents of the document? Pope's response is intriguing: 'I don't know. That's a whole area that I don't want to comment on, and it's not anything to do with the UFO subject per se; one doesn't talk about intelligence divisions or their role in relation to any subject.'[21]

What conclusions can be drawn from the information currently in hand? The MOD is certainly ill at ease about discussing the UFO-related activities of both DI55 and the Directorate of Scientific and Technical Intelliegnce (DSTI) – particularly since it was due to an error on the MOD's part that the ongoing involvement of these two departments in UFO research became public knowledge. And despite official denials, we now know that an exchange of UFO data between the United States' DIA and the MOD's DIS does take place at Whitehall, giving all the indications that the DIS monitors UFO activity on a worldwide scale. We also have the testimony of Nick Pope, confirming that the DIS did not brief Sec (AS) 2a on the contents of the DIA report on the 1992 UFO conference in China.

Bizarrely, had I, a member of the public, chosen not to supply Pope with a copy of the report, he would have remained oblivious to the fact that a sister division within the MOD had received its own copy months before.

So, how many more UFO reports are being withheld from Sec (AS) 2a by the DIS?

On June 21, 1995, with the assistance of both the Ministry of Defence and the Public Record Office, I obtained a 300-page file of UFO reports dating from 1964 which had previously never been seen outside of the confines of Government. Having gone through the file with a fine-tooth comb, I can report that those papers which have been released add a considerable amount to what we know about the DIS and its involvement with UFOs.

The papers to which I have been given access show that, shortly after its creation in 1964, the DIS's Directorate of Scientific and Technical Intelligence (DSTI) was implicated in the investigation of a number of UFO incidents, the vast majority of which were reported to the MOD by members of the public. Moreover, as well as conclusively establishing that the DSTI has been investigating UFO encounters for more than thirty years, the papers show that a number of secret divisions within the DIS also took an active interest in unidentified aerial objects in 1964. Chiefly, those departments were DI10, DI65B and DI61E. Although very little is known with regard to the internal workings of the three departments, all were kept routinely informed of UFO movements over the United Kingdom.

On May 1, 1964, three United States Air Force guards on duty at RAF Brize Norton, Oxfordshire, saw what was described as 'a bright light moving in [a] WNW direction', which suddenly soared 'straight up' for about three seconds, then hovered for a while, and finally departed from the area at a 'drifting' pace. Not only that, on the following evening the strange object reappeared, again acting in a similar fashion. Both DI10 and DI65B were on the distribution list for the official report on the sighting (as was Fighter Command Headquarters), which was stamped: 'PRIORITY. WARNING. NO UNCLASSIFIED REPLY PERMITTED. CONFIDENTIAL'.[22]

Midway through July 1964, a similar 'bright light moving at speed' was seen in the vicinity of RAF North Cotes, near to the River Humber. Two staff from the base, Chief Technician Conrad and Junior Technician King, watched the strange light for eight and a half minutes as it first travelled 'west of east of North Coates (sic)', then, when directly over the

RAF station, 'turned north east and disappeared'. The DIS were quick to respond and, on the orders of the Air Force Operations Room (AFOR) at the Ministry of Defence, Chief Technician Conrad was told to telephone DI61 direct with the relevant details.[23]

Like the DIS, the Air Force Operations Room was created in 1964, having previously been known as the Air Ministry Operations Centre. Five weeks before the Ministry of Defence came into being, there was some concern shown by the Air Ministry that the process by which UFO reports were distributed throughout Whitehall would be compromised as a result of the then-forthcoming reorganization. That concern was shown in a February 24, 1964, memo from Mr T.J. Brack (a Resident Clerk with the Air Ministry), to S4, AI (Tech) 5b and the Air Ministry Operations Centre: 'Reports of Objects in the Sky. The Resident Clerk may receive reports of objects in the sky from members of the public. He should note the description given by the informant and he should pass these details to the Air Ministry Operations Centre. If the caller requests a reply from the Department he should also report the facts to S4f (RAF).'[24]

Mr Brack's memo tells us two important things: that the department within the Air Ministry at that time most responsible for the handling of UFO reports was the Air Ministry Operations Centre (AMOC) and not S4, as has long been assumed; and that, in actuality, the Resident Clerks at Whitehall were only obliged to keep S4 informed of UFO incidents where the 'reporter' desired a response.

That AMOC's successor, the Air Force Operations Room, continued to be the driving force where UFOs were concerned in the post-Air Ministry years is proven, to my satisfaction, by virtue of the July 1964 UFO encounter at RAF North Cotes. As I have detailed, it was on the express orders of the AFOR that DI61 was brought into the investigation of that particular sighting. To this day, it is to the AFOR, and not Sec (AS) 2a, that all UFO reports submitted to the Ministry of Defence by the Civil Aviation Authority are initially forwarded.

To those who say that, as far as UFOs are concerned, a policy of official secrecy on the part of the British Government would be impossible to maintain, I say this: it was not until 1995 that Whitehall chose to reveal that DI65B, DI61E and DI10 were all implicated in UFO research more than thirty years ago. Moreover, had the inclination been there, I am quite sure that this decades-old information could have been successfully concealed almost indefinitely. Are these very welcome disclosures concerning the Defence Intelligence Staff a pointer towards what we can expect to see in future releases of data? One would certainly like to think so.

CHAPTER 17

UNDER SURVEILLANCE

SINCE COMMENCING MY UFO RESEARCH, ONE MATTER HAS CONTINUED to mystify me: why do those piloting the UFOs take no effective counter-measures to ensure that their craft are free from detection by Earth-based radar systems? The alien agenda appears to be covert in nature and one imagines that they would ensure we did not notice their visits. Not so, apparently. 'Radar invisible' aircraft, such as the Northrop B-2 bomber and the Lockheed F-117 fighter, are now a reality and are regularly deployed by the American military to areas of conflict. I find it totally implausible that an advanced visiting civilization would not be in possession of a similar technology. Why they choose not to make use of it is curious indeed.

As far back as 1949, radar proved its worth when, during Operation Bulldog, the movements of a huge UFO were monitored by at least four tracking stations throughout the United Kingdom. Similar encounters took place in 1953 at the Anti-Aircraft Command Centre at Lea Green, at RAF Lakenheath in 1956, and at RAF West Freugh in 1957. Forty years on, there is literally no area of the country that is free from the watching eyes of Britain's ground-based and airborne early-warning systems.

With its headquarters at High Wycombe, Buckinghamshire, RAF Strike

Command directs and administers the 'teeth' of the Royal Air Force
– the air defence fighters, offensive support aircraft, maritime forces,
air transport forces and air-to-air refuelling tankers. The Command is
divided into five groups. No. 1 Group, based at Benson, Oxfordshire,
controls the offensive elements of the Royal Air Force, such as the
Tornado GR1 and GR4, plus the Jaguar and Harrier aircraft. No. 2
Group, which is currently located at Rheindahlen, Germany, has the
responsibility of co-ordinating all RAF forces within that country. The
co-ordination and control of maritime assets, including search-and-rescue
helicopter squadrons, falls under the jurisdiction of No. 18 Group. And
air-to-air refuelling is controlled by No. 38 Group, which has its base of
operations at High Wycombe. Finally, there is No. 11 Group . . .[1]

Operating out of RAF Bentley Priory, Middlesex, No. 11 Group is
responsible for the efficient management of Britian's air defence resources.
These include the Sentry airborne early warning aircraft, ground radar
stations, and the Ballistic Missile Early Warning Station (BMEWS) at
RAF Fylingdales, Yorkshire. For nearly half a century, No. 11 Group
has been implicated in matters relative to UFOs.

The earliest documented evidence of that involvement uncovered so far,
concerns the attempted interception of four UFOs tracked approaching
the United Kingdom near Harwich, Essex, on October 9, 1953. In that particular case, Bentley Priory authorized the scrambling of aircraft from RAF
Waterbeach. Unfortunately, the interception failed and the UFOs exited
British airspace as quickly as they had arrived. Nevertheless, a substantial
file on the encounter was brought to the attention of the Air Ministry.[2]

Two months later, it was Flight Lieutenant C.P.B. Russell, also of
No. 11 Group, who prepared the Air Ministry's 'Reports on Aerial
Phenomena' document. The reader will recall that one of the highlights
of the document was a very clear warning issued to RAF stations
throughout the country: '. . . personnel are to be warned that they are
not to communicate to anyone other than official persons any information
about phenomena they have observed . . .'[3] When that paper was updated
from 'Restricted' to 'Secret' level in 1956, it was once again No. 11 Group
who co-ordinated its distribution throughout the Royal Air Force.[4]

*   *   *

We have just seen how in the 1980s the Ministry of Defence declassified a number of very revealing UFO-related documents which were forwarded to Quest International. It was largely due to this 'gaffe' that DI55's role in the study of UFO encounters became widely known. In addition, the papers also showed that two branches of the Royal Air Force were on the distribution list for such data: 'Airborne Early Warning' (AEW) and 'Ground Environment' (GE), both of which have the responsibility of maintaining a vigilant watch on Britain's airspace.

It so happens that one such GE division is housed at RAF Neatishead, Norfolk, which was implicated in UFO incidents in 1952 and 1956. A second GE division is based at none other than . . . RAF Bentley Priory. In 1994, I resolved to uncover further details concerning the role played by these particular departments with respect to the UFO subject, and made a number of significant discoveries.

Flying Officer J.S. Hathaway, Public Relations Officer at RAF Stanmore Park, has informed me that the activities of the GE division of the Royal Air Force are not open to discussion. Citing the need for security, he was reluctant to comment beyond saying that, '. . . the work carried out . . . covers a variety of aspects . . .'[5] However, when I approached Bentley Priory direct, and confronted the base with the documentation made available to Quest International in the 1980s, it was confirmed to me by Flight Lieutenant M.A. Tunaley that, yes, Bentley Priory did have an ongoing role to play when it came to the MOD's UFO investigations:

> The subject of UFO reporting is dealt with by the Deputy Directorate of Ground Environment and Airborne Early Warning at the Ministry of Defence. However, if the Ministry considers it appropriate, they ask us . . . to comment on air activity at the time of the reported sighting and whether data recordings from radar sources highlight any unusual activity that has not already been investigated. You may already be aware that occasionally our radar stations are informed of UFO activity, but all reported sightings are passed directly to the Ministry; a decision on whether further action is necessary then rests with them.[6]

Flight Lieutenant Tunaley's response to me is most interesting. According to his information, 'UFO reporting' is co-ordinated by the Deputy Directorate of Ground Environment and Airborne Early Warning, yet the MOD's usual stance is that UFOs fall under the jurisdiction of Sec(AS)2a – a department to which Flight Lieutenant Tunaley made absolutely no reference. Here we see yet further proof that Sec (AS) 2a is simply the public face of a vast infrastructure.

Although RAF Bentley Priory has the responsibility of managing the Royal Air Force's Airborne Early Warning aircraft, the AEW division itself is actually housed at RAF Waddington, Lincolnshire. In July 1992, Waddington became the home of No. 8 Squadron, currently equipped with the most expensive aircraft ever procured by the RAF – the Boeing E-3D AWACS, now referred to as the Sentry AEW MK1.

The Sentry routinely cruises at an altitude of 29,000 feet, significantly extending the range of ground-based radars, and giving longer warning time of the approach of potentially hostile targets. Any unidentified objects can be easily detected by the Sentry's AN/APY-2 surveillance radar, and information can be transmitted directly to ground and ship-based units using a variety of digital links.[7]

Has the Sentry been implicated in the tracking of unidentified flying objects over the United Kingdom? This is an area which would be ripe for investigation and comment, were it not for the fact that much of the work of the AEW division is subject to the constraints of the Official Secrets Act. However, Flying Officer S.R. Jones at Waddington, acting on behalf of his commanding officer, admitted to me in 1994 that staff at the base are obliged to 'scrutinize' UFO reports as submitted through official channels.[8]

The Sentry AEW aircraft at Waddington also serve as the E-3D Component of the NATO Airborne Early Warning Force (NAEWF). This means that the potential is there to monitor the movements of any unidentified target that leaves British airspace and intrudes upon the territory of other NAEWF-affiliated countries.[9] Since NATO was briefed on the overflights of the many triangular-shaped UFOs seen over Belgium in 1989 and 1990, the likelihood is that British authorities were also made aware of the situation.

In 1991, an eye-catching advertisement appeared in a variety of British newspapers under the heading 'UFO or VIP?' Ostensibly, the advert was designed to attract people who were keen on making careers for themselves as RAF Fighter Controllers. An examination of pertinent sections of the advert is revealing:

> A blip appears on the radar screen. It is your job to decide whether it is friend or foe. And you've got less than two minutes . . . There is no time to relax; it has to be intercepted immediately. You scramble Quick Reaction Alert Tornado F3s . . . You are responsible for guiding the pilots to their target . . . Whether it is reporting on unidentified objects, guiding fighter pilots, or checking on thousands of man-made objects orbiting the earth – Fighter Controllers are maintaining the defence of their country in one of the most high-pressure environments there is.[10]

If one reads the wording of the advert carefully, the implication which shines through is this: at some point in his or her career, a Fighter Controller with the RAF may be required to deal with sightings of 'unidentified objects' which necessitate the scrambling of Tornado F3 interceptors. Under whose authority does the use of the Tornado F3 fall? RAF Bentley Priory's, whose UFO-related activities are now beyond doubt. Although primarily a defensive aircraft, the F3 is a formidable fighting machine, equipped with four 'SkyFlash' radar-guided missiles and four 'Sidewinder' infra-red air-to-air missiles, not to mention an internally mounted 27-mm cannon. In fact, the ideal vehicle with which to confront a potentially-hostile UFO.

That still further elements of the British military diligently survey UFO activity on a routine basis, is something which has been confirmed to me by Squadron Leader Mark Watson of London Air Traffic Control Centre (Military). Commenting on what are known in military circles as 'unknown radar-returns', Squadron Leader Watson advised me in early 1996 that during a normal working day, 'many' things are observed 'about which civilian and military radar controllers have no knowledge'.[11]

A similar account comes from a source with close connections to RAF Leuchars, Scotland. As researcher Jonathon Dillon has learned (from an informant whose identity I am aware of) staff at the base regularly track unknown objects operating in British airspace, and that while such incidents are 'played down', details of all 'radar irregularities' are logged and investigated accordingly. As Dillon's source states: '. . . it has confirmed for me that the RAF are aware of regular breaches of UK airspace by unknown craft'. Intriguingly, Dillon has also been advised that amongst the personnel at Leuchars, there is considerable interest in the UFO mystery.

It may not be only the UFOs and their occupants that are routinely monitored by the British Government. Evidence exists which suggests that those of us who attempt to elicit information from our Government on this subject are also ripe for investigation. As far as the USA is concerned, this is a proven fact. Since the late 1940s, agencies such as the FBI, the CIA and, in later years, the National Security Agency and Defense Intelligence Agency, have all had a hand in monitoring the activities of those US citizens seen as being potentially 'troublesome' when it comes to UFOs. During the 1950s, Leonard Stringfield was the subject of an official FBI investigation, which specifically related to his interest in unidentified flying objects, as the following FBI memorandum of November 2, 1954, shows:

> Attached for the Bureau's information is the 10/1/54 'Newsletter' of the Civilian Research, Interplanetary Flying Objects, designated Vol. 1, No. 7 . . . which identifies Leonard H. Stringfield . . . as the director of the organization. On the first page of this 'Newsletter' Stringfield reports that he had a private talk with Lt. Colonel John O'Mara, Deputy Commander, Intelligence, U.S. Air Force, on 9/21/54 and that in essence Colonel O'Mara had told Stringfield that flying saucers do exist and that past contradictions were unfortunate.
>
> . . . Stringfield has also stated to [censored] that he believes his home telephone is being monitored, presumably by the Air Force, and that he makes phone calls to Wright-Patterson Air Force Intelligence Officer John O'Mara . . . from his office.[12]

In a similar fashion, Stanton Friedman, the world's leading authority on the UFO incident at Roswell, New Mexico, in 1947, has also been the subject of an FBI investigation. Although the bulk of his file is still classified, Stanton has informed me that 'a very small portion' has now been made available to him.[13]

It is not only UFO researchers themselves who are targeted for surveillance. Various elements within the US intelligence community routinely monitor publications on the UFO subject, and even go to the trouble of sending representatives to 'UFO conferences' – covertly, of course. In 1980, the National Security Agency admitted that it had located records which concerned the account of 'a person assigned to NSA' who had attended a UFO symposium.[14] Oddly enough, when I attempted to obtain a copy of these same records via the Freedom of Information Act in 1988, the NSA's Director of Policy, Richard W. Gronet, explained to me that: 'We have been unable to locate such a document.'[15]

US Government agents were also in attendance at the first European meeting of the Society for Scientific Exploration, which was held on August 7–8, 1992, in Munich, and had the UFO subject on its agenda. A three-page document pertaining to the conference, originally classified at 'Secret' level, was made available to me via the DIA in 1993. Its contents make for interesting reading:

> The expressed aim of the SSE meeting was to promote the exchange of ideas, results and goals among researchers in various fields of anomalies, and inform the public of the discussion among active scientists concerning current controversial issues. Papers and communications were in English, and German language abstracts of the various parapsychology (PS) papers presented were distributed at the beginning of the meeting.
>
> The conference sessions examined PSI and other extraordinary mental phenomena, crop circles, (were they messages or hoaxes), geophysical variables and their influences on human behavior, astro-psychology, the Earth and unidentified flying objects (UFO), and additional highlights, to include near death experiences (NDE).[16]

*   *   *

So much for US authorities, but to what extent does the British Government keep check on those of us who attempt to prise open the doors of UFO secrecy? As the bulk of the Government's research into UFOs is undertaken by a number of departments within the Ministry of Defence, it is to the Ministry that we must first turn in an attempt to answer this question.

During the course of my interview with Nick Pope, I asked him whether or not Sec (AS) 2a had an official policy which required staff to monitor books, magazines, and periodicals that dealt with UFOs.

> That's sort of difficult. Although we do have a core MOD policy which is, as I've explained, looking at things to see if there's a threat, a lot depends on the attitude of the individual desk officer in the job at the time. Now, I took the view that when I took up my post, that if I was to be the Government's expert on UFOs, I owed it to myself and, more importantly, to the public, to be as well informed about that as possible.
>
> To draw a comparison, another part of our division deals with low-flying complaints. They obviously need to know the difference between a Hercules transport aircraft and a Tornado fighter bomber. Now, they need some specialist knowledge so they can talk to the public in an expert way. I took the view that I needed exactly the same thing so I made it my business to read into the subject, to read some of the books, to be as helpful as I could to the ufologists that contacted me, and yes, I've seen some of the magazines, and I've tried to keep myself informed. Now whether you see that as an official policy or something that I've done is, I think, open to debate. I mean, I see it as something that's necessary for me to do my job. Others may take a different view, I don't know.[17]

Was Pope aware of any occasion upon which a serving member of the MOD had attended, in an official capacity, a public conference on the UFO subject? 'I'm aware of one occasion when one of my predecessors actually went to a public meeting which was filmed by the BBC *Man Alive* series back in 1970,' Pope told me. 'In the late 1960s . . . I know that there were some fairly pro-active people in the Ministery . . . but that's all I can suggest on that.'[18]

I have seen no evidence to support the idea that staff from within Sec (AS) 2a regularly monitor UFO conferences on an official basis today. However, as I have shown, in 1992 the MOD's Defence Intelligence Staff, whose work is both compartmentalized and highly sensitive, received a document from the United States Defense Intelligence Agency which detailed a UFO conference held in China in that same year. If the DIS is routinely briefed on overseas UFO conferences, as this document would appear to confirm, then it is all but certain that an interest would be taken in similar British-based events.

By Nick Pope's admission, his department was not briefed by the DIS on the contents of the 'China' document, nor would he enter into discussion on the role that the DIS might have played with regard to the contents of the document. 'That's a whole area that I don't want to comment on . . .' was Pope's response to my questioning. But is there any evidence to suggest that various divisions within the British Government, including the DIS, routinely keep watch on the activities of Britain's UFO researchers?

In the last decade, Quest International has grown from a Leeds-based UFO society to a nationwide organization with connections throughout the world. With a readership of over 100,000, Quest's official publication, *UFO Magazine*, is considered to be one of the leaders in its field. Under the editorship of Graham Birdsall it regularly reports on Government involvement in UFO matters. It is thanks to Quest's diligent probing that the involvement of DI55 in UFO investigations came to light in the 1980s. It is not surprising, therefore, that Quest's activities have attracted a considerable amount of official interest.

In 1977, Graham Birdsall and his brother Mark investigated a major UFO sighting near to Harrogate, North Yorkshire, which involved a number of witnesses who had viewed strange, aerial objects in the vicinity of Menwith Hill – a vast 'listening post' controlled by the US National Security Agency. Graham and Mark duly approached Menwith Hill for comment and, at one point, were actually allowed on-base. This led to a curious series of events. Soon after visiting the base Graham received a telephone call from a Mr Mills, the senior NSA security officer at the base. Mills had just taken up his post at Menwith Hill and was keen to cement good local relations. Graham engaged the NSA man in conversation for approximately one hour – something which few civilians can claim.

Within a short space of time the Birdsall family began to notice an 'awful lot' of interference on the telephone that Graham had used to speak to Mills. This continued for days, then weeks. On one occasion, Graham was speaking with his brother, Mark, when several clicking noises were heard on the line, followed by their voices repeating back the very same words which they had spoken only minutes before . . .[19]

It would appear that official interest in Quest International continues. Since 1989, Anthony Dodd, Quest's Director of Investigations, has conducted a lengthy investigation of a UFO crash which allegedly took place in South Africa in that same year. As a result of this, Dodd's activities have reportedly been brought to the attention of the intelligence agencies of a number of countries, including Britain and France. At the height of his enquiries, Dodd was actually informed by a contact within British intelligence that French operatives were watching his every move and, even more disturbing, that a proposal had been put forward that Dodd be 'taken out'. Fortunately, this idea was rejected when it became apparent that it had the potential to create more problems than it would solve.[20] Since the sceptic may consider this to be somewhat incredible, I should stress that Dodd is a highly reliable source, having served an exemplary twenty-five-year career with the British police force.

At their 1992 conference, one of Quest's featured speakers was Robert Dean, a retired US Army command sergeant major, who has spoken extensively about his knowledge of a major UFO study undertaken by NATO in the early 1960s. 'Do not resent those persons in the audience who work for intelligence, they are basically good people . . . they are only doing their job,' Dean told the capacity crowd, as he remarked that he had yet to attend a UFO conference which was not monitored by the intelligence services.[21]

Two years later, Dean spoke again at Quest's annual conference and made a similar comment. Shortly afterwards, I received a telephone call from Graham Birdsall, informing me that a trusted source within the aerospace industry had advised him that Ministry of Defence personnel were present at the lecture, specifically to monitor the various topics under discussion.[22]

Established in 1946, the Government Communications Headquarters (GCHQ) at Cheltenham provides a variety of Government branches and military commands with Signals Intelligence data. This accords with the requirements of the Joint Intelligence Committee, whose function it is to produce a weekly survey on intelligence for Ministers and officials known as the 'Red Book'. JIC members include personnel from both the Ministry of Defence and the Foreign Office. GCHQ derives its SIGINT data from a variety of sources, including intercepted foreign communications and signals. For this purpose it controls and administers the Composite Signals Organisation which operates from a number of locations both in the UK and overseas.[23]

In 1947 Britain and the USA signed the highly secret 'UKUSA Agreement', which ensured that both countries, plus Canada, New Zealand and Australia, would mutually benefit from the shared use of SIGINT data. As a result of that agreement GCHQ now has a very close working relationship with the US National Security Agency – an organization with a lengthy 'UFO history'.[24]

Although the NSA is mainly concerned with the analysis of intercepted foreign communications, the agency also has a sophisticated surveillance system in place to monitor domestic telephone conversations, something which journalist and author Crispin Aubrey has discussed: 'In the United States the giant National Security Agency (NSA), officially concerned with overseas monitoring, has been discovered intercepting the communications of thousands of private citizens, especially those involved in protest movements. For many years, the entire daily output of three large cable companies was collected by the NSA . . . and the results passed on to the American equivalents of MI6, MI5 and the Special Branch.'[25]

In 1992, Robert Durant, an American researcher and civilian pilot, discussed the theme of an all-encompassing, Government-controlled operation designed to monitor the civilian UFO research community. Durant's comments are largely directed at American investigators, but are of equal relevance to their British counterparts, particularly in light of what we now know about the NSA and its role in domestic surveillance operations:

> You, the reader, are among the approximately 4,000 Americans who subscribe to ufological journals or newsletters, buy UFO books through the mail, attend conferences, or spend time with others who engage in such activities. Not a large group. We are only 3% of the total number of citizens the government admits to watching with intense care. A very easy group to identify and track. Building your file is so much easier than compiling one on a Russian spy or a Mafioso.
>
> There is a file on you at the Internal Revenue Service, the Social Security Administration, the driver's bureau of the state in which you are licensed, the commercial credit companies that do business with your bank and your lenders, your doctor's office, and so forth and so on. Is it really unreasonable to suspect that a UFO file would be created?[26]

Thought-provoking words. If the NSA plays an active role in the sort of surveillance operation that Durant has in mind, then what of its British counterpart, GCHQ? In 1990, GCHQ spokesperson J.C. Turner told me that 'we are not interested in UFOs', and as far as the NSA was concerned, 'cannot comment on any supposed relationship with other agencies'.[27]

It seems odd that Turner refers to the NSA–GCHQ relationship as 'supposed', when it is easily demonstrable that both agencies work side by side on a daily basis. In his book *Spycatcher*, Peter Wright, formerly of MI5 recalled: '. . . all GCHQ product was shared with its American counterpart, the National Security Agency . . .'[28] In addition, the late James Rusbridger, a one-time operative for MI6, went on record as stating that staff at two NSA-controlled listening stations in the United Kingdom (Morwenstow, Cornwall, and Menwith Hill, Yorkshire) intercepted private telephone calls when necessary. 'By getting the Americans to do it,' said Rusbridger in 1993, 'the British Government is able to say truthfully, though misleadingly, that GCHQ does not tap domestic telephone calls.'[29]

In 1993, in a special edition of *UFO Magazine* devoted to the 1989

UFO crash in South Africa, Graham Birdsall published a one-page confidential memorandum which appeared to relate to the incident in question, and implicated the CIA, the NSA and the DIA in the matter. Birdsall admitted that, 'for legal reasons', he was unable to comment in detail regarding Quest's acquisition of the document, but did state that there were certain 'intelligence sources' within the UK who were sympathetic to Quest's activities. Birdsall also added 'there is bound to be strong interest at the British Government's listening station – GCHQ Cheltenham'.[30]

On March 29, 1996, GCHQ was once again dragged into the UFO controversy when two security guards employed there, Ruby Hoare and Ron Jones, watched as a silent, brightly lit craft flew over their heads at 4.30 a.m. while they patrolled the base.

'We just looked at it. We weren't frightened. We were just amazed,' said Hoare, while Jones added: 'I have never seen anything like it before in my life. It was travelling very fast. It definitely was not a plane.'

'No doubt they did see something but I couldn't say what it was,' said a tight-lipped GCHQ spokesman.[31]

What of the future? One of the major stumbling blocks we currently face is this: virtually every aspect of GCHQ's work is imbued with official secrecy, which effectively prevents us from addressing the UFO–GCHQ link any further. In July 1993, for example, it was announced that GCHQ was reviewing, with a view to ultimately declassifying, the wartime daily selection of decrypts prepared for Prime Minister Winston Churchill. If these fifty-year-old papers, which GCHQ inherited from the Government Code and Cypher School, are only just entering into the public domain, then it is most unlikely that contemporary documentation relative to the UFO question will be declassified for many years to come.[32]

There is, however, one thing which we can be sure of: whether it is scanning the skies for unidentified intruders, or keeping a surreptitious watch on civilian UFO researchers, the British Government has its finger on the pulse of all aspects of the UFO enigma.

CHAPTER 18

DEAD ON ARRIVAL

THERE SEEMS TO BE LITTLE DOUBT THAT SINCE THE LATE 1940s THE British Government has acquired a large body of data, directly pertinent to the UFO subject, which it does not choose to share with the populace at large. The official records relating to a whole host of UFO incidents reported by military personnel in the late 1940s and early 1950s are unavailable for examination at the Public Record Office. Likewise, early in 1953, Cyril Townsend-Withers was informed that the Air Ministry had established a project which evaluated UFO reports and was open to the possibility of an extra-terrestrial presence.[1] Details of that project have never surfaced, and the MOD denies that such a project ever existed. Similarly no-one outside of officialdom has ever viewed the gun-camera footage taken by a Royal Air Force pilot as he pursued a UFO over the east coast of England in August 1956.

In the early 1960s UFO reports submitted to the Air Ministry by military personnel were evaluated by AI (Tech) 5b, whose papers are now reported destroyed. In December 1980 a structured UFO was seen on land adjacent to a strategic military base in Suffolk. Fourteen years later I am informed by the Ministry of Defence that the official records generated at the time cannot be located. In 1981 a vast UFO was seen hovering over a military facility on the island of Cyprus. Once again, no public comment from the MOD.

A Covert Agenda

The undoubted unease shown by the Ministry of Defence when it has to issue public statements with regard to UFOs is plain to see. Is the Ministry's policy justified? Taken as a whole, the rich variety of evidence examined by the British Government since 1947 certainly points towards the probability that our planet has played host to otherworldly visitors. Evidence, unfortunately, is not proof. It could be argued that it would be wholly irresponsible for the MOD to announce that, 'Yes, extra-terrestrials are here', without being one-hundred-per-cent certain of the fact. But is the British Government in possession of undeniable evidence of UFO reality, in the form of crash-recovered exhibits of extra-terrestrial technology?

Within weeks of Kenneth Arnold's sighting of nine crescent-shaped UFOs over Washington State in 1947, it was rumoured that an unidentified flying object had crashed in the remote desert of New Mexico and had been recovered by American authorities. Since that time, other crashes have reportedly occurred throughout the world. One such incident, we have seen, may have taken place atop a Welsh mountain on January 23, 1974. Moreover, a handful of other reports exist which suggest that several alien vehicles have come to grief on British soil. If so, does a secure facility exist somewhere in Britain which houses the remains of one or more extra-terrestrial spacecraft? As far-fetched as it may seem, the answer could well be 'Yes'. Prior to examining the evidence, let us return to New Mexico, circa July 1947, and the most exhaustively investigated UFO incident of all time.

'RAAF Captures Flying Saucer On Ranch In Roswell Region' – the headline that leapt from the front page of the July 8, 1947, edition of the *Roswell Daily Record*, a newspaper named after the small New Mexican town whose people it served. Amazingly, this was not some fanciful story concocted by an enterprising hoaxer. Rather, the newspaper caption was based on the following officially sanctioned press release issued by the nearby Roswell Army Air Field:

The many rumors regarding the flying disc became a reality yesterday when the Intelligence office of the 509th Bomb Group of the Eighth Air Force, Roswell Army Air Field, was fortunate enough to gain possession of a disc through the cooperation of one of the local ranchers and the sheriff's office of Chaves County.

The flying object landed on a ranch near Roswell sometime last week. Not having phone facilities, the rancher stored the disc until such time as he was able to contact the sheriff's office, who in turn notified Maj. Jesse A. Marcel of the 509th Bomb Group Intelligence Office.

Action was immediately taken and the disc was picked up at the rancher's home. It was inspected at the Roswell Army Air Field and subsequently loaned by Major Marcel to higher headquarters.[2]

Shortly after this astonishing news had spread around the world, another announcement was made. The whole thing had been a false alarm. What had in fact been recovered was merely the radar reflector from an errant weather balloon. To bolster this explanation, Brigadier General Roger Ramey, of the Eighth Air Force at Fort Worth, Texas, allowed press photographers to take shots of the debris from a stricken balloon, which had been laid out on the floor of a small office at the base.[3]

Why Major Marcel had been unable to differentiate between a flying saucer and a downed weather balloon was conveniently left unsaid . . .

Despite the decidely unimpressive-looking nature of the wreckage on display for the photographers, the media apparently chose not to express its incredulity that anyone could confuse what was obviously balloon-borne debris with a UFO. The official explanation was accepted and, at a stroke, interest in the story dwindled and the entire matter was laid to rest. That situation remained practically unchanged for thirty years.

Stanton T. Friedman obtained his Masters of Science in Physics at the University of Chicago in 1956. For the next fourteen years, he worked as a nuclear physicist for a variety of organizations, including General

Electric, Aerojet General, Westinghouse and General Motors. During that time Friedman developed an intense interest in unidentified flying objects and, in 1970, began to lecture on the subject on a full-time basis. Since then he has spoken at a variety of prestigious establishments such as Alaska Pacific University, the University of North Dakota and General Dynamics. He has also spoken before the United Nations and presented testimony on the UFO issue to a US congressional committee.[4]

On January 20, 1978, Friedman was in Baton Rouge, Louisiana, to give a lecture at the State University. Whilst in the city he agreed to take part in a number of media interviews which had been arranged by an associate. One such interview took place at a local television station. During a break Friedman was introduced to the station manager who, as luck would have it, was a friend of the by-then-retired Jesse Marcel. Acting on this information Friedman wasted no time in contacting Marcel, who had a most interesting story to tell concerning what really happened back in 1947.[5]

'I saw a lot of wreckage but no complete machine,' said Marcel, explaining that whatever the object was, it must have exploded in the air. 'It had disintegrated before it hit the ground. The wreckage was scattered over an area about three quarters of a mile long and several hundred feet wide.

'I was pretty well acquainted with most everything that was in the air at that time, both ours and foreign,' he continued. 'I was also acquainted with virtually every type of weather-observation or radar-tracking device being used by either the civilians or the military.'

Marcel also added that in his opinion the debris was not from a weather-tracking device, nor was it from an aircraft or a missile. 'What it was we didn't know. We just picked up the fragments.' Marcel was certain, however, that the debris was unlike anything he had ever seen before or since, and that 'it certainly wasn't anything built by us'.[6]

During the course of his investigations Friedman hooked up with William Moore, a writer and researcher who expressed an interest in pursuing the case further. As a result of their enquiries Friedman and Moore went on to locate dozens of people with both direct and second-hand involvement in the case. They also confirmed the location where the unusual debris had been found – a remote ranch belonging to one William W. Brazel.

Brazel's ranch was located in an area some seventy-five miles north of the town of Roswell, New Mexico. Regrettably, by the time that Friedman and Moore had begun their investigation, Brazel had long since passed away. Fortunately, Brazel's friends and family, some of whom still lived in the vicinity, recalled well the incident.

Commenting on the strange debris found on the ranch, Brazel's son, Bill, stated that it was: '. . . something on the order of tinfoil except that [it] wouldn't tear . . . You could wrinkle it and lay it back down and it immediately resumed its original shape. [It was] quite pliable, but you couldn't crease or bend it like ordinary metal. Almost like a plastic, but definitely metallic in nature. Dad once said that the Army had once told him it was not anything made by us.'[7]

Jesse Marcel also elaborated on the extraordinary properties present in the material which he recovered. '[It] could not be bent or broken . . . or even dented by a sixteen-pound sledge hammer. Almost weightless . . . like a metal with plastic properties.'[8]

As Friedman and Moore continued to dig for answers, other information surfaced, suggesting that as well as the debris found on the Brazel ranch, a semi-intact UFO, complete with alien bodies, was recovered during the same time-frame – but in a somewhat separate operation. One such lead came from Vern and Jean Maltais, who informed Friedman that a friend of theirs, Grady Barnett, had been a field engineer with the US Soil Conservation Service. He had once confided in them that, whilst working in the New Mexican desert, he had come across a grounded UFO, around which were a number of small, and quite dead, non-human bodies. Needless to say, the military quickly assumed control of the situation.[9]

As the 1970s drew to a close, enough data had been gathered by Friedman and Moore to warrant the publication of a full-length book on the case. *The Roswell Incident*, co-authored by Moore and well-known writer Charles Berlitz, was released in 1980. By 1985, research had uncovered almost a hundred people who had been implicated in the events at Roswell. The official 'balloon' explanation was crumbling fast.

In July 1985, Moore gave a presentation at the annual symposium of the Mutual UFO Network (MUFON) at St Louis, Missouri. During the course of his talk, Moore revealed what had occurred when Friedman brought up the matter of the alien bodies with Bill Rickett, a former Counter Intelligence Corps officer stationed at Roswell at the time of the crash. The following quote is taken from Friedman's own assessment of the interview: 'When I mentioned bodies, Rickett clearly reacted and indicated that this was an area he couldn't talk about. He indicated there were different levels of security about this work – that a directive had come down placing this at a high level. He went on to say that certain subjects were discussed only in rooms that couldn't be bugged.'[10]

During the chapter which details my March 1994 interview with Nick Pope of the MOD, I briefly alluded to the so-called 'Majestic Twelve' document, which surfaced in 1987 and purported to tell the true story behind the UFO crash at Roswell. The first person to present this document to the public was Timothy Good.[11] Although it was not widely known at the time, a copy of that same document had been mailed anonymously to Jaime Shandera, a Hollywood film producer and colleague of William Moore, in December 1984. As a result of Good's decision to publish the document, Moore and Shandera did likewise and the whole controversy surrounding the Majestic Twelve papers burst forth.[12] Not surprising, since the story they tell is, quite literally, out of this world. Several extracts from the papers are related below:

> WARNING! This is a TOP SECRET – EYES ONLY document containing compartmentalized information essential to the national security of the United States. EYES ONLY ACCESS to the material herein is strictly limited to those possessing Majestic Twelve clearance level . . .
>
> . . . a local rancher reported that [a UFO] had crashed in a remote region of New Mexico located approximately seventy-five miles northwest of Roswell Army Air Base . . .
>
> . . . a secret operation was begun to assure recovery of the

wreckage . . . During the course of this operation, aerial reconnaissance discovered that four small human-like beings had
apparently ejected from the craft before it exploded . . .

. . . Implications for the National Security are of continuing
importance in that the motives and ultimate intentions of these
visitors remain completely unknown . . .[13]

Supposedly, the document had been prepared in 1952 by someone
within the American Government as a briefing for incoming president,
Dwight D. Eisenhower. But are the papers really what they seem
to be? Since 1987, the whole issue of Majestic Twelve has been
steeped in controversy. Some claim that the document is genuine,
some that it is a straightforward hoax. Others think that Majestic
Twelve is Government-inspired disinformation, designed to cloud the
truth behind the 1947 incident at Roswell.

Both the United States Air Force and the Federal Bureau of Investigation have stated on record that, in their opinion, the papers are bogus.[14]
I share that opinion, but veer towards the idea that the papers were
created as part of an elaborately orchestrated campaign of disinformation
to discredit, or at the very least steer people away from, the important
work begun in the 1970s by Stanton Friedman. On this same track,
William Moore has written extensively on a US Government-inspired
campaign to spread disinformation amongst a number of American UFO
researchers.[15]

Whatever one's view on the 'Eisenhower Briefing Document', it is
certainly true that, for a while, investigations into the Roswell case
took a back seat as researcher upon researcher delved into the murky
world of Majestic Twelve. Come the 1990s, the focus was once again
on Roswell.

In addition to the ongoing research of Stanton Friedman, William Moore,
and Jaime Shandera, a tremendous amount of new information has been
uncovered in the last few years by Kevin Randle and Don Schmitt, who
have conducted their own in-depth study of the Roswell mystery. Randle,
a Captain in the US Air Force Reserve, and Schmitt have written two

books which detail their findings and, in my opinion, all but prove the extra-terrestrial nature of the wreckage found at Roswell.

According to Randle and Schmitt's information, on the night of July 4, 1947, an extra-terrestrial spacecraft crashed to earth some miles north of the town of Roswell, having already deposited a sizeable amount of debris on the Brazel ranch. Presumably, there had been some form of mid-air explosion prior to the actual crash. In contrast to accepted wisdom, the UFO was not saucer-shaped, but was rather narrow with a bat-like wing and no longer than thirty feet in length.

As far as the question of alien bodies is concerned, Randle and Schmitt's sources have informed them that up to five alien creatures were found in the vicinity of the crash site, one of which, incredibly, may very well have survived the initial impact. Courageously, a number of those implicated in the crash have acknowledged that alien bodies were recovered. These witnesses are Edwin Easley, the Provost Marshal at Roswell; Lieutenant Colonel Albert Lovejoy Duran, a member of the unit assigned to the crash site; and Glenn Dennis, a mortician at the nearby Ballard's Funeral Home, who received a strange telephone call from the mortuary officer at the base. 'He was inquiring about what size, what type of caskets, and how small [were the] caskets that we could furnish that could be hermetically sealed,' said Dennis.[16] Dennis has also signed a sworn affidavit, confirming that a nurse friend at the base had admitted to him that a preliminary autopsy of the alien bodies had been conducted at Roswell Army Air Field.[17]

> . . . she went into this room to get some supplies and saw two doctors in there with a gurney and these small bodies that were in a rubber sheet or a body pouch. Two of the bodies had been very badly mangled, like maybe the predators had been eating on them . . . one of the hands was severed from the body, and when they flipped it over, there were little tiny suction cups on the inside of the fingers . . . The heads were large, eyes were set in. The skulls were soft like a newborn baby's; they were pliable. The ears, instead of one canal, had two canals, no lobes or anything, just a little flap over each canal. The mouths were just very small slits. Their face and nose were concave . . .[18]

Although this book primarily concentrates on the British Government's role in the UFO subject, I make no apology for devoting a sizeable amount of space to a discussion of the Roswell enigma. For several reasons, this incident is probably the most significant on record:

1. More than any other case, Roswell demonstrates that UFOs are a physical reality; they are highly advanced machines piloted by non-human creatures.

2. Those same creatures are not omnipotent supermen; like every organism on Earth, they live and they die; their technology, although far more advanced than our own, is not flawless.

3. Although the wall of secrecy constructed by the US Government at the time is now being eroded, for thirty years the astonishing events at Roswell were successfully concealed from all and sundry; secrets of incredible magnitude can be kept.

4. If one unidentified flying object had crashed then others may have suffered a similar fate. Rumours abound that a UFO crashed at Aztec, New Mexico, in 1948, on the border of Texas and Mexico in 1950, and at Kingman, Arizona, in 1953.[19]

Keeping this last point in mind, let us now examine a number of similar incidents which have reportedly occurred in the United Kingdom.

Throughout the latter part of the Second World War, sightings of strange, luminous flying objects, which came to be known as 'Foo Fighters', were frequently reported through official channels by both Allied and Axis forces alike. Although the phenomenon did not prove to be aggressive in nature, a number of incidents were not without concern. Mark Birdsall, a recognized authority on the issue, has uncovered a copious amount of fascinating information, suggesting that the Foo Fighters were a genuine manifestation of advanced technology.

While conducting investigations which led to the publication of a major paper on the Foo Fighters, Birdsall secured an interview with a former British soldier. He knew of a piece of film footage, held by US

Air Force Intelligence, which actually showed a Foo Fighter in flight as it closed in on an allied aircraft over Germany. According to Birdsall's source, who was described as having a 'substantial background', the Foo Fighter was dark in colour, shaped like a 'circular lens', and seemed to spin in a vertical position as it moved 'furiously' alongside the aircraft.[20]

In the summer of 1977, Leonard Stringfield was asked by a retired US Naval Intelligence officer to present a lecture on the UFO subject at a meeting of the Cincinnati Chapter of the 'World Wings', which was held at Cincinnati's Lunken Airport. During the course of the 'question and answer' session which followed the lecture, one member of the audience, a pilot, arose and brought up the subject of crashed UFOs. Sensing that the individual seemed well-informed, Stringfield asked that he wait for a personal chat after the presentation was concluded.

When the crowd finally dispersed, the pilot led Stringfield to a backroom and said, quite bluntly, 'I have seen the bodies.' The pilot went on to describe how he chanced to see three alien corpses lying in crates in a hangar at Wright-Patterson Air Force Base in 1953, after a UFO crashed somewhere in Arizona.

Over more than a dozen private talks, Stringfield discovered that the pilot had had an extensive military career and was well-informed on matters relating to unidentified flying objects. Of relevance to the issue at hand, Stringfield's informant had heard rumours that a Foo Fighter 'had been retrieved in England' by British military forces during the Second World War.[21]

Stringfield is not alone in having knowledge of this particular crash. John Lear, a pilot who has flown covert missions for the CIA, told me that it was his understanding that the object was later 'strapped to a B-17' and flown to the USA for analysis.[22] Another account comes from the late Dorothy Kilgallen, an American journalist:

> British scientists and airmen, after examining the wreckage of one mysterious flying ship, are convinced these strange aerial objects are not optical illusions or Soviet inventions, but are flying saucers which originate on another planet. The source of my information is a British official of Cabinet rank who prefers to remain unidentified. 'We believe, on the basis of our inquiry

thus far, that the saucers were staffed by small men – probably under four feet tall. It's frightening, but there is no denying the flying saucers come from another planet.[23]

Kilgallen went on to say that the British Government was withholding a report pertaining to the crash, possibly because it did not wish to alarm the general public.[24] Was Kilgallen's account accurate? If so, who was her informant? Retired intelligence officer, Gordon Creighton, had this to say in 1979: 'As regards the identity of the titled Englishman, I had no doubt at the time as to who he was – a great leader and servant of our country who has represented us well both in one of the highest of our military posts in World War Two and in the political sphere during the early post-war era.'[25]

Creighton expanded on this in 1985: 'Our assumption at the time, and in later years, was that the official in question may very likely have been Lord [Louis] Mountbatten. I wrote to Dorothy Kilgallen at once, seeking further information, but never got a reply from her, and she died a few years later. We may take it as certain that she had been effectively silenced.'[26]

In addition, Timothy Good has reported that Creighton believed that the crash had occurred during the Second World War, which may very well tie it to the case referred to by both Leonard Stringfield and John Lear.[27]

Another account which may have a bearing on this incident comes from Dr Olavo T. Fontes of Brazil. In the 1950s, Fontes worked tirelessly to unravel the mysteries of the UFO and, as a direct consequence of his activities, caught the attention of the Brazilian Government. In February 1958, Fontes was visited at his place of work by two gentlemen who identified themselves as officers from Naval Intelligence. 'You know too much about things you weren't entitled to know. We don't like that,' one of the officers told Fontes. Presumably, this was an attempt to unnerve the doctor, and discourage him from probing further. Fortunately, Fontes was having none of it, and called the officers' bluff. This resulted in an astonishing about-face, and Fontes received a detailed briefing on the UFO subject from his mysterious visitors.

As Fontes listened intently, one of the officers confided in him that, by 1958, six UFOs had been recovered throughout the world. Three such objects had crashed in North America; a badly damaged craft had been found in the Sahara Desert; a fifth had crashed somewhere in Scandinavia; and an almost undamaged UFO had been recovered in the British Isles. Fontes elaborated on this in a February 27, 1958, letter to Coral Lorenzen of the Aerial Phenomena Research Organization (APRO): 'All these discs were small craft – 32, 72 or 99 feet in diameter. In all of them were found bodies of members of their crews. They were "little men" and ranged in height from 32 to 46 inches. They were dead in all cases, killed in the disasters. The examination of the bodies showed they were definitely "humanoid" – but obviously not from this planet.'[28]

Did a UFO, complete with crew, crash on British soil during the Second World War? The accounts of Stringfield, Lear, Fontes and Kilgallen lead me to believe that there is some substance to the story. If so, then one can only wonder at the number of similar incidents which may have been successfully concealed over the past fifty years.

Retired US Army Command Sergeant Major Robert Dean – who has divulged an extraordinary amount of information concerning NATO's involvement in the UFO puzzle – has also gone on record as stating that British military personnel were involved in the recovery of a UFO which crashed on German soil in the early 1960s.

Dean claims that, when working with NATO, he had in his hands 'the entire report' pertaining to a flying saucer-type UFO which crashed at Timmensdorfer, near the Baltic Sea, in 1962. The UFO fell on soft soil near to the Russian frontier, and consequently was not totally destroyed, although a third of the craft was buried in the ground. According to Dean, a corps of British military engineers were the first to secure entry to the craft.

Inside were twelve dead bodies of a variety of alien which has become popularly known as the 'Grey' (see chapter 20). Dean added that the British military carried out extensive autopsies and it was discovered that all of the bodies were identical in make-up. The conclusions of the study indicated that the creatures seemed to be 'laboratory products'. As

Dean states: '. . . I saw all the photos taken of the beings and I couldn't believe it.'[29]

During the course of his research, Leonard Stringfield learned that a UFO crashed near to the town of Penkridge, Staffordshire in 1964. Shortly before his untimely death in 1994, Stringfield authorized the publication of the following account concerning the crash:

> Some time in 1964, 'somewhere at sea', between the Caribbean and the Atlantic, a specially rigged LST, a flagship for a naval amphibious force, received a coded radio message in its 'crypto-machine' room, which reported that 'artifacts' had been retrieved with three dead personnel.
>
> According to my informant, former Third Class Petty Officer, S.M. Brannigan, (pseudonym) a specialist trained to translate intercepted Russian transmissions, the decoded report stated that a UFO had crashed in two parts; the main section near Penkridge, in Staffordshire, England, the remains in West Germany. He further stated that the retrievals of the parts and the occupants were conducted by Air Force Intelligence and shipped to Wright-Patterson Air Force Base, adding that US and other NATO interceptors were involved. Brannigan admitted that there was more to the incident, involving coded information, that he preferred to keep confidential.
>
> The Brannigan disclosure, while sketchy, may spotlight only the tip of the iceberg as to the scope of military crash-retrieval operations in foreign lands. Researchers know that reports of crashes are worldwide, from pole to pole, on every continent, and in many countries . . . If such incidents are to be secreted, it is my suspicion that US special retrieval teams have been, and still are, prepared to 'go into action' into any crash location within its sphere of military or economic influence such as was exercised with NATO in the 'artifact' retrievals in England and West Germany.[30]

It should be noted that Stringfield was well-qualified to comment on such matters, since he was a former intelligence operative with the

American Air force. Between 1954 and 1957, he worked alongside the
Air Defense Command division of the USAF, screening and reporting
on UFO activity in the tri-state area of south-western Ohio, northern
Kentucky, and south-eastern Indiana.

Also in 1964, another mystery object fell to earth, this time near
Walthamstow. The date was April 13, and Bob Fall, a bus driver who was
himself from Walthamstow, was driving his 123 bus towards Tottenham
when . . .

> I just glanced into the sky and saw something coming towards
> me very, very fast. It flew straight across the road and, had I
> been a few yards further forward, it would have hit the top deck
> of the bus. I saw it cut through the telephone wires and there
> was a loud crash as it struck the bank [of the River Lea]. There
> was a big splash in the water. I stopped as soon as I could to
> report it. The thing was at least nine feet long, probably more,
> cigar-shaped and silver. If it had been a bird, or birds, I [would
> have] seen the wings. Besides, it was going too fast.

As soon as Mr Fall reported the incident, police quickly arrived and
dragged the river. The object had vanished. I have also learned that Ronald
Caswell, a well-known UFO investigator in the 1960s, told authorities at
the time of a certain Ministry of Defence Wing Commander who had
been apprised of the details of the encounter, which seems to imply that
the Ministry took the initial report seriously. The available MOD files
relative to this case are scant, to say the least, which leads me to believe that
the full story may still lie buried within the bowels of Whitehall.[31]

A decade after the incident at Penkridge, came the still unresolved matter
of the crash of an unusual object on a remote Welsh mountain. What
is particularly striking about that case is the large body of people who
were implicated in the affair to varying degrees. Mrs Annie Williams, of
Llandrillo, saw the object as it passed overhead, and felt the shockwaves
as it hit the ground. Police Constable Gwilym Owen and Police Sergeant
Gwyn Williams also testified that they had felt the object's impact. Mr

Ken Haughton of Betws-y-Coed viewed a huge 'luminous sphere' in the Rhyl area ninety minutes after the crash. David Upton of Gobowen was witness to a 'disc-shaped object divided up into four sections'. Last but far from least, the nurse who actually saw the strange craft at close quarters on the Berwyn Mountains.

And whatever actually took place within Rendlesham Forest, Suffolk, in late December 1980, of two things we can be certain: the case shows no signs of fading away, and new information continues to surface. On July 31, 1994, Charles Halt spoke at a pre-arranged lecture in Leeds, and divulged his recollections of what had occurred fourteen years previously. During the course of his talk Halt astounded the audience by revealing something which had been hitherto unknown: just hours after the encounter, an unscheduled C141 transporter aircraft arrived at Woodbridge, and a group of 'special individuals' departed from the aircraft, headed straight out of Woodbridge's 'east gate' and disappeared into the forest.[32] This leads me to believe that the UFO was very possibly still in the forest, perhaps even disabled.

Were these 'special individuals' part of a rapid-deployment team dispatched to recover the craft? Project Moondust, do not forget, which was created by the American government to respond to sensitive incidents involving UFOs, has now been in existence for decades. Personnel attached to just such a project would have been well prepared to recover the UFO if it had malfunctioned deep within Rendlesham Forest.

Recall that in Charles Halt's memorandum to the Ministry of Defence, the UFO was described as being 'two to three meters across the base and approximately two meters high' – a relatively small object. In contrast, the C141 is a huge aircraft, fully equipped to carry freight, vehicle payloads or, alternatively, up to 200 troops.[33] Secreting a 'mini-UFO' inside a C141 would have presented few problems for experienced operatives.

It may also be relevant to note that during its life as an active military station, RAF Woodbridge was home to a squadron with an intriguing history, as Captain John E. Boyle of the US Air Force told me in 1988:

> In the late 1960s and early 1970s, the 67th Aerospace Rescue and Recovery Squadron stationed at RAF Woodbridge [provided]

standby rescue coverage for the American space flights. Of course, they were never needed to provide emergency rescue actions, but at the time, the unit was trained and available to rescue astronauts with their HH-53 and HC-130 aircraft. In early 1988, the 67th ARRS was redesignated as part of the 39th Special Operations Wing, their primary mission changing from that of rescue to supporting US Special Operations forces. Their secondary mission remains that of search and rescue and they would provide any assistance necessary in future space missions.[34]

Although the 67th's rescue and recovery skills were not needed during NASA's space missions, one wonders if they were implicated in the recovery of 'something' which originated with somebody else's space programme in December 1980 . . .

On July 19, 1991, 'Mr M.L.' of Cheadle, Staffordshire, was visiting friends in the area of Churnet Valley, east of Stoke-on-Trent. At 10.00 p.m., M.L. saw an object fall from the sky near to Ipstones. The object was described as being metallic, rather like aluminium, and was 'ten feet long, cigar-shaped and very bright'. The witness wasted no time in contacting Cheadle police.

The following day, a search of the woodland was undertaken by police, and a helicopter was even drafted in to lend assistance. No object was located, but an area of newly broken branches was found which gave the impression that something had crashed through the trees from above. The search was finally abandoned.[35]

It may be entirely coincidental, but only four days prior to the encounter at Ipstones, a Boeing 737 aircraft almost collided with an equally small, unidentified 'lozenge-shaped' object as it approached Gatwick Airport.

At about 11.00 p.m. on September 26, 1994, a small, twin-tailed aircraft crash-landed onto the runway at RAF Boscombe Down which is situated on Salisbury Plain. At around the time of the crash several aviation enthusiasts had been listening in on 'airband' radios, and were aware that something untoward had taken place. The following day, several of those enthusiasts drove to the airbase (which is near to the

A303 road, four miles from Stonehenge), and were apprehended by local police who had set up road-blocks to keep away prying eyes. Before being ushered away, a number of people succeeeded in catching sight of a disabled craft, which was situated at the end of the runway and, aside from its twin-tail fins, was completely covered over by tarpaulins. Thanks to information uncovered by *Air Force Monthly* magazine, we know that an elaborate retrieval operation was put into place: 'Shortly after the crash an unmarked, civilian registered (CIA operated?) Boeing 737 and a similarly anonymous DC-8 visited and two days later the wreck was loaded onto a C-5 Galaxy and flown to Air Force plant 42 at Palmdale, California. The secrecy surrounding the incident has led to speculation that the aircraft involved was a TR-3A, the existence of which the U.S. Government has yet to officially acknowledge.'

On August 23, 1994, one month before the incident at Boscombe Down, the following report appeared in the *Salisbury Times*:

> A green flying saucer hovered beside the A303 at Deptford last week – according to a lorry driver who rushed to Salisbury police station in the early hours of the morning. The man banged on the station door in Wilton Road at 1.30 a.m. on Thursday after spotting the saucer suspended in mid-air. 'He was 100 per cent convinced it was a UFO,' said Inspector Andy Shearing. The man said it was bright green and shaped like a triangle with rounded edges. It also had green and white flashing lights. Other drivers had seen it and were flashing their car lights at him. A patrol car took the lorry driver back to the spot but there was no trace of the flying saucer. Inspector Shearing said police had been alerted about similar sightings in the same area in the past.

Since the TR-3A is rumoured to be a roughly triangular-shaped craft, this would appear to strongly suggest that the lorry driver had viewed just such a vehicle, particularly since, as I have noted, the A303 road runs very close to RAF Boscombe Down. However, the case is not as cut and dried as it would first appear.

George Wingfield – who was educated at Eton College, and has worked for the Royal Greenwich Observatory, and IBM UK – had the following to say in the *Cerealogist*, a magazine he edits which is devoted to the study of the 'crop circle' mystery: 'If what the lorry driver saw in August was a Black Manta [*Author's note*: 'Black Manta' is the nickname allegedly given to the TR-3A in military circles] it must have a vertical hovering capability similar to the Harrier and also be able to operate silently. Despite much speculation, no one has ever suggested such capabilities for the TR-3A, and at present we can only regard what was seen at Deptford as an "unidentified flying object".'

If the vehicle seen by the lorry driver on the A303 road was something other than the TR-3A, and this has to be seriously considered, then what of the very similar craft which crashed at RAF Boscombe Down? Was it an unidentified flying object or an identified flying object? The immediate veil of secrecy which enveloped all aspects of the case effectively prevents us from making a qualified assessment, but the incident does serve to demonstrate one thing: highly unusual aerial craft do crash on British soil, and the military response is immediate.[36]

On October 31, 1994, residents of both Church Lench and Norton reported seeing a 'barrel-like object' fall into an isolated field at Hepton Hill, north of the Cotswolds in Worcestershire. According to reports, the field was sealed off and people were warned to keep their distance. Soon after, the object was loaded aboard a Royal Navy lorry and taken elsewhere. Questions were put to the Royal Air Force and the Fleet Air Arm, both of whom denied any knowledge of the mystery. However, Paul Brooke, of Norton, confirmed that many people had seen an object resembling a 40-gallon drum or container which it was presumed had plummeted from the sky.

It was not only the military who were keeping a low profile: Inspector Mike Rowlands of Eversham police said, 'I can't categorically say that it did not happen, but my investigations have revealed that it was a bale of straw that was on fire and which was put out by the fire brigade. The reports of something falling from the sky may either be hoaxes or somebody may have seen something and come to the wrong conclusion.' To which Paul Brooke responded: 'Do they think we are mad around here?'[37]

*   *   *

In conclusion, if elements of both the British military and the intelligence community do have in their possession the remains of a number of extra-terrestrial vehicles, then why do they simply not say so? Have they learned something from studying such craft and their alien pilots that is so shocking, so alarming, that we cannot be told the truth? Or is it precisely the opposite? Is the alien technology so advanced that, even today, it defies comprehension? At this stage, I am unable to judge accurately which scenario may be correct, but I submit that if we are ever entrusted with the full facts, we will need to brace ourselves for some startling revelations.

C H A P T E R 19

AROUND THE WORLD

TURNING AWAY FROM THE BRITISH GOVERNMENT'S INVOLVEMENT IN the still-unfolding UFO situation, let us now focus our attention on the rest of the planet. As will be seen from the following accounts, sightings of unidentified flying objects are routinely filed by military sources from numerous countries, and are treated with the utmost seriousness.

One of the earliest UFO encounters ever reported by a member of the American military took place at Muroc Airfield, California, on August 12, 1947. Although US officials have seen fit to withhold the name of the witness from the released file on the sighting, his affidavit, witnessed by Counter Intelligence Corps agent Thomas A. McMillan, is detailed below:

> At 11.50 hours, 8 July 1947, while the undersigned was sitting in an observation truck in Area #3, Rogers Dry Lake, for the purpose of observing a P-82 ejection seat experiment, the following unfamiliarity was observed.
>
> The undersigned was gazing upward toward a formation of two (2) P-82's and an A-26 aircraft flying at 20,000 feet, preparing to carry out a seat ejection experiment, when I observed a rounded object, white aluminum in color, which at first resembled a parachute canopy. The first impression was that a premature

ejection of the seat and dummy had occurred. This body was ejected at a determined height lower than 20,000 feet, and was falling at three (3) times the rate observed for the parachute which was ejected thirty minutes later. As it fell it drifted slightly north of due west against the prevailing wind, toward Mount Wilson . . .

As this object descended through a low enough level to permit observation of its lateral silhouette, it presented a distinct ovular outline, with two (2) projections on the upper surface which might have been thick fins or knobs. These crossed each other at intervals, suggesting either rotation or oscillation of slow type.

No smoke, flames, propeller arks, engine noises or visible means of propulsion were noted. The color was silvery, resembling aluminum painted fabric, and did not appear as dense as a parachute canopy. When the object dropped to a level such that comes into line of vision of the mountain tops, it was lost to the vision of the observer.

It is estimated that the object was in line of vision about 90 seconds. Of the five (5) people sitting in the observation truck, four (4) observed this object and made remarks about it. The following is my own personal opinions about this object:

1. I think it was a man-made object, as evidenced by the outline and functional appearance.

2. Its size was not far from 25 feet with a parachute canopy.

3. The path followed by this object appeared as though it might have been dropped from a great height.

Seeing this was not a hallucination or other fancies of a sense. This statement was given freely and voluntarily without any threats or promises under duress. This statement consists of two (2) pages, and is the truth to the best of my knowledge and belief.[1]

What is particularly noteworthy about this report is the quite amazing parallels it has with the account of Flight Lieutenant John Kilburn who, along with five colleagues, viewed a UFO over RAF Topcliffe in September 1952. In both instances, the UFO was viewed near to an airfield, was described as being silver in colour, and was initially mistaken for a parachute canopy. Perhaps the similarities were not coincidental; perhaps the UFO seen over California in 1947 and over Yorkshire in 1952 were one and the same.

On the evening of March 9, 1958, the men and women of Fort Clayton, a US military base on the Panama Canal, were going about their routine business, blissfully unaware of the strange events that were soon to unfold. Just before 8.00 p.m., the Anti-Aircraft Operations Centre (AAOC) at Fort Clayton reported that an unidentified flying object was being tracked on radar and was flying in a somewhat erratic fashion in the Canal Zone. Within five minutes, a call was put through to the private residence of the Deputy Defence Controller for Anti-Aircraft Defences, who was apprised of the situation. He was to arrive at AAOC at 8.08 p.m.

The UFO continued to be tracked until 8.45 p.m., when two additional 'blips' appeared on the radar screen. A civilian aircraft was directed into the area and attempted to seek out the mysterious objects. This proved unsuccessful, despite the aircraft being vectored to within a hundred yards of the UFOs.

Meanwhile, the Track Radar Unit located at Fort Amador, Flamenco Island, successfully locked on to the UFOs and determined that there were definitely two unknown objects present, flying a roughly circular path over Fort Kobbe (a nearby base), at a height varying from 2,000 to 10,000 feet. This was confirmed by the staff of a second Track Radar Unit situated on Taboga Island.

Although the civilian aircraft recorded no visual sighting of the UFOs, the same cannot be said for the ground crew. Personnel from both Flamenco and Taboga reported seeing red and green aerial lights, yet absolutely no sound emanated from the craft.

The UFOs continued to be tracked until 11.45 p.m., when a decision was taken by staff at Fort Amador to attempt a viewing of the objects with the aid of searchlights. This was duly accomplished on the stroke of midnight. The outcome of this action was far from expected: suddenly, and without warning, the UFOs climbed from a height of 2,000 feet to 10,000 feet in little more than five seconds.

According to the official records, '. . . this was such a rapid movement that the Track Radar, which was locked on target, broke the Track Lock and was unable to keep up with ascent of the objects. As Track Radar can only be locked on a solid object, which was done in the case of the two unidentified flying objects, it was assumed that the objects were solid.'

Further encounters were reported until 2.10 a.m. on 10 March, when the UFOs finally vanished. Shortly afterwards one of the objects, or at least a very similar one, returned. The Search Radar at Taboga Island locked on to an object flying a triangular-shaped flight pattern. Although the altitude of the craft was not determined, it displayed a number of curious characteristics, not the least of which was its fantastic manoeuvrability, allowing it to both hover and accelerate to speeds estimated to be in the order of 1,000 mph – much to the consternation of the US Air Force.

At 11.20 a.m., a USAF jet from the nearby Howard Field was ordered to intercept the UFO in an attempt to determine what was violating military airspace with such apparent ease. The Track Radar indicated that as soon as the aircraft approached the UFO it accelerated rapidly, and thereafter continued to maintain a distance of several miles between itself and the jet. At midday the aircraft returned to base having failed to intercept the UFO. Oddly, the pilot maintained that, like the civilian pilot on the previous evening, he had been unable to make a visual identification of the UFO. Yet clearly the radar screens of at least three military bases were registering the presence of tangible objects carrying out seemingly intelligently controlled movements.

At 4.00 a.m. on the following day the Operations Officer at Fort Clayton received a report of a UFO sighting from the pilot of an inbound Pan American Airlines DC-6. Details of this particular encounter are not as in-depth as one would prefer. However, the pilot reported that the UFO was larger than the DC-6, and appeared to be flying in a south-east direction. This was also confirmed by ground-based radar at 5.08 a.m., and a continuous watch was maintained until 5.36 a.m., when the UFO vanished as quickly as it had appeared.

Although there is some evidence from reading the official records that a similar occurrence took place on March 13, 1958, the relevant documentation has not come to light, which may be significant in itself.

What was the outcome of these events? We may never know. A report on the activities of March 9–13, 1958, was forwarded to a higher authority where, presumably, some form of analysis would have taken place. It is unlikely that anything further would have been learned, particularly given the elusiveness of the craft.

In 1988, I learned that the US Government's report on the case was held in the files of the National Security Agency at Fort Meade, Maryland. After filing a Freedom of Information request with the NSA in an attempt to obtain a copy of the records, I was advised that all the available paperwork was being transferred to the American Air Force. From then, the USAF assumed control. Despite the incident having occurred thirty years previously, the Air force initially refused to release any documentation relative to the encounters over the Panama Canal, stating that the paperwork was 'classified'. After I appealed the Air Force's decision, it was eventually determined that the report could be released, albeit not without a few strategic deletions.[2]

As with the sighting at Muroc Air Field, California, in 1947, the encounter on the Panama Canal has its British counterpart: the incident at RAF Church Lawford on March 26, 1957, where a UFO was tracked travelling at 1,400 mph, having accelerated to that speed from a stationary position. By the Air Ministry's own admission, no explanation was ever found for this mystery. It is impossible to know whether the UFO tracked by Church Lawford and those observed over the Panama Canal originated with the same source. However, the fantastic manoeuvres exhibited by the objects in both incidents inclines me to believe that they did.

The April 24, 1964, UFO episode involving Sergeant Lonnie Zamora of the New Mexico Police Department has often been reported in UFO literature, and has been the subject of a full-length book.[3] Notwithstanding this, I have chosen to make mention of the encounter, since it caught the attention of a whole host of US Government agencies, including the Central Intelligence Agency, whose seldom-seen report follows:

Shortly after 5.30 p.m. on Friday, 24 April 1964 Sgt. Lonnie Zamora of the Socorro Police Department was chasing a speeding auto North on US 65 in the line of duty. While in pursuit he heard a roar and saw flames in an area where a dynamite shack was known to be located. He abandoned chase of the auto and proceeded to where he thought an explosion had occurred. In order to reach this spot he had to travel a little used road over several hills and gullies. After two or three efforts to drive his car up a gravel-covered incline he reached a crest where the object was visible. At this point, 800 feet from the object, he observed what he thought to be a car overturned and standing on its end. There were one or two objects described as coveralls which he assumed to be occupants of the vehicle. He radioed in to police headquarters that he was proceeding up the road to a point about 150 feet from the gully where the object was, he stopped the car, got out, and headed towards the object. The object was on girder-like legs, white (not chrome) and egg-shaped or oval. As he approached the object there were some noises and flame and smoke began to come from the bottom of the vehicle. The noise increased from low pitch to high pitch, was different from that of a jet or helo and not like anything Sgt. Zamora had ever heard. The flame was blue like a welders torch, turning to orange or yellow at the ends. Thinking that the object was going to explode he became frightened. The time was approximately 1745 (1½ hours before sunset), the sun was to his back, slightly to the right. He turned, ran back to get behind the police car, bumping his leg and losing his glasses on the way. He crouched down, shielding his eyes with his arm while the noise continued for another 10 seconds. At this time the noise stopped and he looked up. The object had risen to a point about 15–20 feet above the ground and the flame and smoke had ceased to come from the object. The object had a red marking about 1 foot or maybe 16 inches in height, shaped like a crescent with a vertical arrow and horizontal line underneath. The object hovered in this spot for several seconds and then flew off in a SW direction following the contour of the gully. It cleared the dynamite shack by not more than three feet. He watched the object disappear in the distance over a point on Highway 85 about 6 miles from where he was standing. Disappearance was by fading in the distance and at no time did he observe the object to rise more than 20 feet off the ground. While proceeding to the location when the object was assumed to be an auto Sgt. Zamora was in radio contact with police headquarters. The State Police use the same network and his call was monitored by Sgt. Chavez of the New Mexico State Police. Sgt. Zamora attempted to direct Sgt. Chavez to the location while he was driving toward the object. Sgt. Chavez took the wrong road, and was, in fact heading in the opposite direction for part of the time and would not have been in a position to see the object. He arrived at the point where Sgt. Zamora was parked about three minutes after the object had disappeared. Sgt. Zamora was pale and upset at what he had witnessed. Sgt. Chavez was skeptical of the situation and proceeded to where Zamora had observed the object. Here he found the marks and burns. Smoke appeared to be coming from a bush which was burned but no flame or coals were visible. Sgt. Chavez broke a limb from the bush and it was cold to the touch. The marks were fresh and no other marks were in the area. Diagonals of the four impressions intersect in a perpendicular and the major distance seems to be approximately 13 feet. Sgt. Chavez secured the area and contacted local military authorities. This resulted in the investigation of the sighting.[4]

Whatever Sergeant Zamora saw, it obviously troubled him. I find it particularly interesting that the egg-shaped UFO reported by Zamora was flying at a relatively low level. This is somewhat similar to the account of Ronald Wildman, who viewed an oval-shaped UFO flying at low level over a British road in 1962.

Those who argue against the existence of a genuinely anomalous UFO phenomenon would do well to take note of the astounding events which took place in the skies of Iran in September 1976. These encounters, perhaps more than any other, amply serve to show the concern which is afforded the UFO issue by authorities throughout the world. Shortly after the encounters, the United States Defense Intelligence Agency circulated a report detailing what had taken place to a variety of agencies, including the

CIA, the National Security Agency, the Secretaries of State and Defense, and even the White House.[5] For my part, I have elected to cite the little-known account of Captain Henry S. Shields of the US Air Force, whose report, titled 'Now you see it, now you don't!', was first published in a 'Secret' document prepared by the US Air Force Security Service. Captain Shields' report reads thus:

> Sometime in his career, each pilot can expect to encounter strange, unusual happenings which will never be adequately or entirely explained by logic or subsequent investigation. The following article recounts just such an episode as reported by two F-4 Phantom crews of the Imperial Iranian Air Force during late 1976. No additional information or explanation of the strange events has been forthcoming; the story will be filed away and probably forgotten, but it makes interesting, and possibly disturbing reading.
>
> Until 0030 on a clear autumn morning, it had been an entirely routine night watch for the Imperial Iranian Air Force's command post in the Tehran area. In quick succession, four calls arrived from one of the city's suburbs reporting a series of strange airborne objects. These Unidentified Flying Objects (UFOs) were described as 'bird-like', or as brightly lit helicopters (although none were airborne at the time). Unable to convince the callers that they were only seeing stars, a senior officer went outside to see for himself. Observing an object to the north like a star, only larger and brighter, he immediately scrambled an IIAF F-4 to investigate.
>
> Approaching the city, the F-4 pilot reported that the brilliant object was easily visible 70 miles away. When approximately 25 NM distant, the interceptor lost all instrumentation and UHF/Intercom communications. Upon breaking off the intercept and turning towards his home base, all systems returned to normal, as if the strange object no longer regarded the aircraft as a threat.
>
> A second F-4 was scrambled ten minutes after the first. The backseater reported radar-lock on the UFO at 27 NM/12 o'clock

high position, and a rate of closure of 150 knots. Upon reaching the 25 NM point, the object began rapidly moving away to maintain a constant separation distance while still visible on the radar scope. While the size of the radar return was comparable to that of a KC-135, its intense brilliance made estimation of actual size impossible. Visually, it resembled flashing strobe lights arranged in a rectangular pattern and alternating blue, green, red, and orange. Their sequence was so fast that all colors could be seen at once.

As the F-4 continued pursuit south of Tehran, a second brightly lit object (about one-half to one-third the size of the moon) detached from the original UFO and headed straight for the F-4 at a high rate of speed. The pilot promptly initiated a turn and negative-G dive to escape, but the object fell in behind the F-4 at 3-4 NM distance. Continuing the turn, the pilot observed the second object turn inside of him and then away, subsequently returning to the primary UFO for a perfect rendezvous.

The two UFOs had hardly rejoined when a second object detached and headed straight down toward the ground at high speed. Having regained weapons and communications systems, the aircrew watched the third object, anticipating a large explosion when it struck the ground. However, it landed gently and cast a bright light over a two–three kilometer area. The pilot flew as low over the area as possible, fixing the object's exact location.

Upon returning to home base, both crewmen had difficulty in adjusting their night vision devices for landing. The landing was further complicated by excessive interference on UHF and a further complete loss of all communications when passing through a 150 degree magnetic bearing from the home base. The inertial navigation system simultaneously fluctuated from 30 to 50 degrees. A civil airliner approaching the area also experienced a similar communications failure, but reported no unusual sightings.

While on a long final approach, the F-4 crew noticed a further UFO. This was descibed as a cylinder-shaped object (about the size of a T-33 trainer) with bright steady lights on each end and a flasher in the middle. It quickly approached and passed directly over the F-4. In answer to the pilot's query, the control tower reported no other air traffic in the area, although they subsequently obtained a visual sighting of the object when specifically directed where to look.

The following day, the F-4 crew was flown by helicopter to the location where they believed the object had landed. This turned out to be a dry lake bed, but nothing unusual was noticed. As the helicopter circled off to the west, however, a very noticeable beeper signal was received, and eventually traced to a nearby house. They immediately landed and asked the inhabitants if anything strange or unusual had occurred the previous night. Yes, they replied, there had been loud noises and a very bright light, like lightning. The helicopter returned to base and arrangements were made to conduct various tests, such as radiation checks, in the vicinity of the house. Unfortunately, the results of such tests have not been reported.[6]

There ended Captain Shields' remarkable report. It may be coincidental, but only ten days prior to the Iranian episode, an equally brilliant UFO was seen by the crew of a British European Airways flight en route to Moscow from London. In addition, the highly risky practice of confronting military aircraft 'head-on', as exhibited by the UFO over Iran, is very reminiscent of the incident involving Flying Officer D.W. Sweeney in 1957. It should be stressed, however, that no direct harm came to Sweeney.

Almost a decade after the UFO sightings over Iran, it was the turn of Brazil to feel the full brunt of a UFO invasion force, as the following DIA report demonstrates:

According to sources, at least 20 unidentified objects were observed by several aircrews and on radar the night of 19 May 86. The objects were first seen by the pilot of a Xingu aircraft, transporting Ozires Silva, former President of Embraer, between Sao Paulo and Rio De Janeiro. Fighters were launched from Santa

Cruz AB at approximately 2100 hours. Although all three made radar contact, only one of the three pilots managed to see what he described as red, white and green lights. Shortly afterward, radar contact was made with similar objects near Brasilia and three Mirages were launched from Anapolis AB. All made radar and visual contact at 20,000 feet. They reported that they were escorted by thirteen of these discs with red, green and white lights at a distance of one to three miles. The objects then rapidly disappeared from both ground and airborne radars.

The Air Minister is quoted by the press as saying there were three groups of targets on the ground radar and that the scopes of the airborne radars were saturated.

Comment: While RO does not believe in UFOs or all the hoopla that surrounds previous reporting, there is too much here to be ignored. Three visual sightings and positive radar contact from three different types of radar systems, leads one to believe that something arrived over Brazil on the night of 19 May.[7]

Whatever truth lies behind the five UFO encounters described above, they certainly point towards the fact that Governments all over the globe are keeping a watchful, not to mention concerned, eye on this unearthly enigma. In the USA, for example, literally tens of thousands of pages of official UFO-related documents have now been declassified in accordance with the terms of the US Freedom of Information Act. A similar situation has unfolded in both Canada and Australia and, as I write these words, new revelations are surfacing which concern the former Soviet Union's near-half-century involvement in the UFO puzzle. Beyond any shadow of doubt, this is truly a phenomenon of global proportions.

CHAPTER 20

A COVERT AGENDA

IF EXTRA-TERRESTRIALS THERE BE, THEN WHY ARE THEY HERE? UNLESS one adheres to the view that all of the many UFO encounters reported since 1947 are entirely random events, which I do not, then, presumably, our mysterious visitors are following some form of pre-determined agenda. If so, then what is that agenda? A number of possibilities spring to mind: the enslavement or destruction of the human species; the desire to offer spiritual guidance to the human race; or an unobtrusive monitoring of our society and the way in which it operates. Alternatively, the UFO presence on our planet may be entirely self-serving and we are seen as little more than an annoyance to our cosmic cousins. Let us examine in more detail these possibilities.

GLOBAL DOMINATION

The scenario of an advanced, extra-terrestrial species waging war on the human race is one which has been put to good use in the pursuit of entertainment. One has only to look at films such as *Alien, Predator* and *Independence Day* to see that there is a huge market hungry for such escapism. But what of the real world? How would the average man or woman respond to the arrival of a hostile alien presence on our planet? A good indication can be gauged from the reaction that followed the broadcasting of Orson Welles' 1938 radio production of H.G. Wells' book, *War of the Worlds.* It plunged thousands, if not millions, of Americans into turmoil when it was erroneously believed that a Martian assault on the Earth had begun.[1]

What proponents of the 'UFOs are hostile' theory forget, however, is that in H.G. Wells' classic book, the aliens were marauding creatures, armed with death rays and bent on world domination. There is no evidence, currently available, to suggest that world domination or the extinction of mankind are part of the alien agenda.

There have been a number of incidents recorded where UFOs have acted aggressively, but outright hostility is very seldom displayed. In the 1956 encounter at RAF Lakenheath, for example, the intercepting pilots were primed and ready for an aerial dogfight with the UFO – which could surely have destroyed the aircraft had it been deemed necessary – yet such belligerence failed to materialize.

I am not personally aware of a Royal Air Force pilot actually 'downing' a UFO, nor would I recommend that anyone pursues such a potentially hazardous course! Several such attempts have been made elsewhere, notably over Iran in 1976, as we saw in the previous chapter. Yet even in those cases the UFOs took no direct offensive action against the aircraft involved. Therefore can we consider those piloting the UFOs to be wholly benign? Possibly . . . possibly not.

One of the key factors which have been instrumental in moulding the British Government's somewhat guarded approach to the UFO subject is, I suspect, the unnerving number of UFO encounters which have taken place near to military installations. Regardless of the intent of the visitors, this cannot be without significance. I hypothesize two scenarios:

(a) The intelligences behind the UFOs are conducting a systematic study of our defence capabilities to determine whether or not we are in a position to withstand an all-out attack, should they decide on such a course of action.

(b) The intelligences behind the UFOs are concerned by our preoccupation with global warfare and, by studying our military arsenals, are attempting to gauge how much of a threat we pose to each other.

I would urge the reader to consider the implications that both possibilities present. Unfortunately, the British Ministry of Defence cannot afford to muse over such possibilities, hence its concern every time that a UFO is sighted near to a military complex. I should qualify the above by saying that, since the modern age of UFOs has now been with us for nearly half a century, the threat of outright invasion becomes less and less as time goes by.

GUIDANCE

If 'they' discover you, it is an old but hardly invalid rule of thumb, 'they' are your technological superiors. Human history has shown us time and again the tragic results of a confrontation between a technologically superior civilisation and a technologically inferior people. The 'inferior' is usually subject to physical conquest.[2]

This highly perceptive statement is taken from a previously classified document, titled 'UFO Hypothesis and Survival Questions', which was found in the files of the United States' National Security Agency.

Very possibly, the extra-terrestrials do have our best interests at heart and are attempting to lend some form of spiritual guidance to the human race. It may very well be that they are actuely aware of the 'culture shock' that can follow the meeting of two vastly different civilizations and are shying away from open contact until we are deemed ready to accept them on equal terms. One has only to look at the loss of cultural identity suffered by the Native Americans and the Australian Aborigines when faced with the presence of an outside people. Perhaps now that the Cold War has come to an end and a degree of co-operation now exists between the once-warring factions on our planet, there is a greater chance of being welcomed into some form of cosmic brotherhood. Of course, this pre-supposes that the alien agenda warrants such action.

COSMIC SCAVENGERS

Thanks to films such as *E.T.* and *Close Encounters of the Third Kind*, an image has been established in the minds of many that any visiting alien species is going to be benevolent in nature, and full of worldly (or universal!) wisdom. Maybe. But it would be wise to err on the side of caution. Given the physical similarities between ourselves and many of the entities seen in the vicinity of UFOs – not to mention those believed autopsied following the UFO crash at Roswell in July 1947 – it may be the case that, although more advanced scientifically, the aliens also have a sense of purpose in life somewhat akin to our own. If so, they may also be afflicted by many of the negative attributes that go towards making up the human character, namely greed, self-centredness and bigotry.

Hence, in much the same way as man exploits the Earth's resources, perhaps our alien visitors are doing likewise. The cattle mutilations which have been widely reported throughout the United States of America are perfect demonstrations of such 'scavenger' activity. Linda Howe, who has conducted some sterling research into this very disturbing issue, has presented a large body of evidence which leads me to believe that the mutilations are the work of a visiting alien species. The following New Mexico Police report, declassified by the FBI, gives some indication of the nature of the mutilations. It also makes for macabre reading:

> On 06-13-76 at approximately 8.00 p.m. Mr Manuel Gomez, Dulce, New Mexico contacted writer by public service stating that he had found a three year old cow on his ranch which appeared to have been mutilated and that he would like for writer to check into it.
>
> Writer contacted Mr Paul Riley of the New Mexico Cattle Sanitary Board and proceeded to the Gomez ranch . . . At the scene, writer examined the carcass of a 3 yr. old black White-Faced cow which was lying on its right side. The left ear, the tongue, the udder, and the rectum had been removed with what appeared to be a sharp precise instrument . . .
>
> Investigation continued around the area and revealed that a suspected aircraft of some type had landed twice, leaving three

pod marks positioned in a triangular shape. The diameter of each pod was 14". The perimeter around the three pods was 16½". Emanating from the two landings were smaller triangular shaped tripods 25" and 4" in diameter. Investigation at the scene showed that these small tripods had followed the cow for approximately 600'. Tracks of the cow showed where she had struggled and fallen. The small tripod tracks were all around the cow. Other evidence showed that grass around the tripods, as they followed the cow, had been scorched . . .

There was also evidence that the tripod marks had returned and removed the left ear. Tripod marks were found over Mr Gomez's tire tracks of his original visit. The left ear was intact when Mr Gomez first found the cow. The cow had a three month old calf which has not been located since the incident. This appears strange since a small calf normally stays around the mother cow even though the cow is dead.

. . . Investigation has also revealed that on all cattle mutilations which have occurred in New Mexico and surrounding states, that the object of the mutilations has been the lymph node system.[3]

This particularly grisly and distressing account speaks for itself. However, the mention of triangular-positioned pod-marks is highly reminiscent of the 1980 incident at Rendlesham Forest, where similar pod-marks were found shortly after the landing of a UFO near to RAF Woodbridge. Lest we forget, Colonel Charles Halt's report to the Ministry of Defence on the Rendlesham encounter includes the following statement: '. . . the animals on a nearby farm went into a frenzy'.[4]

John Lear, the only pilot in the world to have obtained every airman certificate issued by the American Aviation Authority, has cultivated a number of sources within the American intelligence community, and had the following to say about the cattle mutilations in a 1987 'statement':

The EBE's [*Author's note*: EBE is an abbreviation of 'Extra-terrestrial Biological Entity', a term reportedly used in Government circles to describe alien creatures] have a genetic disorder in that their digestive system is atrophied and not functional.

In order to sustain themselves they use an enzyme or hormo-
nal secretion obtained from the tissue that they extract from
humans and animals . . . The cattle mutilations that were prevalent throughout the period from 1973 to 1983 and publicly
noted through newspaper and magazine stories and included a
documentary produced by Linda Howe for the Denver CBS
affiliate KMGH-TV, were for the collection of these tissues by
the aliens.[5]

If Lear's information proves to be correct, then I would suggest
that a truly nightmarish situation is unfolding, particularly since cattle
mutilations are still regularly reported throughout the USA today. But is
it just cattle that are mutilated?

Although such reports are, thankfully, few and far between, the late
Leonard Stringfield was given details of a worrying incident which
allegedly took place in Cambodia in 1972, at the height of the Vietnam
War. According to Stringfield's source (a high-ranking army officer), a
US Army Special Operations team out on patrol came across a group
of alien creatures loading various human 'body parts' into large bins and
sealing them. A pitched battle ensued, which resulted in fatalities on both
sides. As the soldiers pulled back, the aliens quickly retreated to their craft,
taking with them the body parts. Needless to say, a major cover-up was
quickly enforced.[6]

Rogue cases such as these do little to inspire the feeling that the visitors
are essentially benevolent. Yet, examined logically, this may simply be the
cosmic equivalent of a visit to the local butchers! Horrific from our point
of view, but who is to say what code of ethics an extra-terrestrial species
adheres to?

It may not only be the indigenous life-forms of Earth which are
attracting the aliens. There is one element without which no living
organism can survive – water. By all accounts, a relatively rare commodity
throughout the rest of the solar system, yet something which abounds on
our planet. Does the Earth represent little more than an interplanetary
oasis to the UFO intelligences?

As anyone who has ever reported the sighting of a UFO to the Ministry
of Defence will know, the MOD has a standard reporting form which is

used to log details of anomalous sightings. One question which is routinely asked of witnesses is whether or not there were any lakes, dams, rivers or reservoirs in the vicinity of the UFO. This question suggests to me that there is an awareness on the Ministry's part of certain behavioural patterns that the UFOs appear to follow.

This theory receives a degree of support from the account of Herbert Schirmer, a police patrolman of Ashland, Nebraska, who was taken aboard a UFO in the early hours of December 3, 1967. Schirmer – who was later to become the youngest ever chief of police in the Midwest, viewed the UFO at 2.30 a.m. as he drove towards the intersection of Highway 63 on the outskirts of town. Upon his return to the police station Schirmer duly wrote up the details of his sighting in the station log book. To his dismay he later found that there were approximately twenty minutes of his night patrol which could not be accounted for.

Shortly afterwards Schirmer was hypnotically regressed. It was revealed that during the period of missing time, he had been taken on board the craft and given certain details of the alien mission on Earth. Still under the influence of the hypnotic regression, Schirmer recalled the following from his memory: 'They asked about the Lincoln City Water Reservoir, which is just down the hill. In some way which I do not understand, they draw a type of power from water. This is why we see them over rivers, lakes and large bodies of water.'[7]

SPACE BROTHERS

No study of the alien intent would be complete without making mention of the highly controversial issues of 'Contactees' and 'Space Brothers'. During the 1950s and 1960s in particular, numerous people throughout the world claimed face-to-face contact with eerily human-like extra-terrestrials. In many of the accounts on record, the aliens were described as being tall, with refined features and flowing blond hair. An example of just such a case can be found in Gavin Gibbons' 1956 book, *The Coming of the Spaceships*:

... they looked very like Earth men, with white skins and long hair down to their shoulders. Their foreheads seemed immensely high, with the features almost entirely in the bottom half of their faces. Their heads were enclosed in what appeared to be some sort of transparent helmets and they were dressed in clothes of turquoise blue that resembled ski suits . . . But what appeared strangest of all . . . was the unsmiling expression on the faces of the men from the sky. Sternly they gazed down . . . not in an unkindly fashion, but almost sadly, compassionately.[8]

As if in response to the Cold War paranoia which gripped the planet in the post-World War Two era, the aliens routinely expressed their concern about the ever-escalating arms race, and advocated that we all live in peace and harmony with one another. These are certainly laudable sentiments, but how much faith can we place in those making claims of such alien interaction with the human race?

Two of the most well-known of the contactees were George Adamski and George W. Van Tassel, both of whom alleged contact with human-like aliens. In retrospect it can be seen that some of their assertions were somewhat naive. Adamski, for example, maintained that he had met with visitors from a variety of planets within our own solar system. Based on current astronomical knowledge, the idea that our solar system is teeming with life seems somewhat unlikely to say the least. Similarly, George Van Tassel also made claims concerning the origin of the aliens which seem equally unlikely.

Several years ago I immersed myself in much of the literature concerning the contactees and found a great deal of it to be wanting. However, I am also convinced that some of the accounts most definitely have a basis in fact. I cannot help but wonder if the aliens themselves, by promoting such incredulous tales concerning their point of origin, were attempting to 'test the waters' in gauging our reaction to their presence on our planet.

In any case, it is a proven fact that both Adamski and Van Tassel were the subject of investigations on the part of the Federal Bureau of Investigation. Since both men are now dead, the FBI has declassified its files pertaining to the two. In the case of Adamski, his lectures were routinely monitored by the intelligence services, as a 1959 report prepared by Leon Crutcher, First Secretary of the US Embassy in New Zealand, demonstrates:

1. Mr George ADAMSKI, the Californian 'flying saucer expert' and author of the book Flying Saucers Have Landed and others, has been visiting New Zealand for the last two weeks. He has given well-attended public lectures in Auckland and Wellington as well as meeting with smaller groups of 'saucer' enthusiasts. In Wellington his lecture filled the 2200 seats in the Town Hall . . .

2. Adamski's lectures appear to cover the usual mass of sighting reports, pseudo-scientific arguments in support of his theories and his previously well-publicized 'contacts' with saucers and men from Venus . . . He is also making references to security restrictions and saying that the US authorities know a lot more than they will tell.

3. The report of Adamski's lecture in Wellington in The Dominion was flanked by an article by Dr I.L. Thomsen, Director of the Carter Observatory, vigorously refuting Adamski on a number of scientific points . . .

4. Interest in flying saucers in New Zealand seems to be roughly comparable to that in the United States. There is a small but active organization which enthusiasts have supported for some years . . .[9]

Aside from the FBI, copies of this document were forwarded to the CIA, the US Army and the US Navy. As far as George Van Tassel is concerned, his writings and lectures were of equal interest to the FBI. A 1965 document shows that the Bureau was keenly aware of the man and his activities:

Van Tassel has been known to the Los Angeles FBI Office since 1954. He is reported to be owner and operator of the Giant Rock Airport, which is located approximately 18 miles from

Yucca Valley, California. He has also been reported to be a
director of the College of Universal Wisdom, Yucca Valley,
California. Numerous complaints have been received by the
Los Angeles Office concerning Van Tassel and his activities
surrounding 'flying saucers', 'spacemen' and 'spacecraft'.

. . . Van Tassel advised that in August 1954 he had been
awakened by a man from space. The spaceman had allegedly
invited Van Tassel to inspect a spacecraft, or flying saucer,
which was manned by three other male individuals who were
identical in every respect with earth people. Van Tassel furnished
detailed descriptions of an unarmed, bell-shaped flying saucer
and claimed the spacemen were mutes who conversed with him
through thought transfers.

Van Tassel stated that he advocates and follows a metaphysical
religion and research which is based on thought transfers, and that
through the thought transfer media he has ascertained that there
will be a third world war with a destructive atomic explosion.
He further stated the above facts could be verified through the
Bible, and that the peace-loving space people would not enter or
provoke a war.

. . . During 1960 Van Tassel gave a lecture before the Denver Unidentified Flying Objects Investigative Societies, Denver,
Colorado. This lecture was described by a Special Agent of the FBI
as more of a religious-economics lecture rather than concerning
unidentified flying objects. A summation of Van Tassel's speech
was furnished as follows:

1. Space people in relationship to occurrences in the Bible.

2. Atom Bomb detrimental to earth and universe.

3. Economy is poor and would collapse under ideas brought
by space people.[10]

Regardless of how much stock we place in the ideas and accounts of
Adamski and Van Tassel, there is no doubt that their claims of extra-
terrestrial contact were well-known to the US intelligence community.
In the case of Adamski, his FBI file runs to nearly ninety pages, while
Van Tassel's totals 173 pages.

In the United Kingdom, claims similar to those made by both Adamski and Van Tassel have been issued by the Aetherius Society, founded by George King. During a conversation with Adamski in London in 1959, King maintained that he had established contact with aliens very similar to those seen by Adamski.[11] Although I do not personally endorse the teachings and ideas of the Aetherius Society, there is reason to believe that, in the early 1960s at least, George King and his followers were of interest to certain parties within the British Air Ministry.

In the course of my investigations, I have uncovered various references to the Aetherius Society contained within now-declassified Air Ministry documents dating from 1962–3. During that time-frame, Secretariat 6 obtained a variety of papers originating with George King's group which were kept under wraps until the end of 1993, when they were made available for study at the Public Record Office. This strongly suggests that the 'contactee' issue was one which the British Government was well-acquainted with.[12]

Is there any actual evidence to support the idea that, in the 1950s and 1960s, one alien race in particular covertly contacted people such as Adamski and Van Tassel? The short answer has to be: No. Unfortunately, much of the contactee literature is so littered with absurdities that it is almost impossible to examine the matter objectively. But, as I have suggested, perhaps those very absurdities were promoted by the aliens themselves to test our reactions to their presence.

The 'golden age' of the contactee has now largely passed into obscurity, and many researchers within the UFO field have little time for such reports. In my opinion, it would be wrong to completely write off this particular aspect of the UFO mystery – if just one contactee account proves to be genuine, then the purpose behind the alien agenda may become much clearer to us.

ABDUCTIONS

An anxious, thirty-two-year-old married woman approached a hypnotherapist to find a logical solution to the 90 minutes she and her mother lost on a familiar route some 20 years earlier.

When their shared amnesia had ended simultaneously, they and
their car were lost on a different route that they had not seen
before. Under hypnosis she is terrified and stunned to recall an
abduction of her mother and herself by little gray men aboard
a silver disk. Mother had absolutely no interest in any session
until she heard that her daughter had 'learned something'. The
63-year-old woman tearfully remembered twice as much detail
in her regression, matching her daughter's abduction scenario
perfectly. Both were amazed – neither had expected nor wanted
these results, but the matching correlations were comforting and
a form of verification for each of their unexpected but matching
accounts.[13]

Thus wrote researcher John Carpenter in a September 1995 article for
the journal of the Mutual UFO Network. Determining when the first
'abduction' of a human being by what appear to be alien creatures took
place is no easy task. Most scholars in the field would probably agree that
the phenomenon was relatively unknown until September 19, 1961. On
that night, Betty and Barney Hill, a married couple from New Hampshire,
USA, were driving home from Canada when they were subjected to a
terrifying experience.

Until their arrival home there was little to indicate that anything
untoward had occurred during the journey. It later transpired that
approximately two hours of the time which it took Betty and Barney
to complete their journey could not be accounted for.

After some months of emotional distress, the Hills sought assistance
from Dr Benjamin Simon, a Boston-based psychiatrist and neurologist.
Having been subjected to time-regression hypnosis, both Betty and
Barney recalled what had taken place during that missing two hours.
Astonishingly, they gave almost identical accounts of encounters with
alien beings, who had taken the couple on board their craft and subjected
them to a variety of physical examinations.[14]

Since that day more than thirty years ago, literally hundreds of similar
accounts have appeared throughout the world. A turning point came
in 1981 with the publication of Budd Hopkins' book, *Missing Time*.
Detailing a number of accounts, Hopkins put forward a strong case

suggesting that at least one extra-terrestrial species was involved in the routine abduction of human beings.[15] Hopkins' later work revealed a more sinister possibility too: the abductions were potentially part of some genetic operation, the goal of which was the production of a half-alien, half-human species – a hybrid race.[16]

By far the most commonly reported creature present during abduction cases is one which has become popularly known as the 'Grey'. I have had the opportunity to speak with more than a dozen people who have had the abduction experience, and in each account the similarities are striking. Typically, the Grey is reported as being short in stature, around three and a half to four feet in height; it has grey-white skin, hence the name, and the body is usually described as being thin, if not emaciated. Certainly the most striking feature of the Grey is its head. In the majority of reports, the head is hairless and overly large in proportion to its body; the eyes are black and huge, and almond-like in shape; and most witnesses report that the ears, nose and mouth appear to be almost non-existent. Interestingly, a number of abductees have postulated that their captors appeared to be almost insect-like in appearance.

With minor differences, all of the abductees to whom I have spoken report an initial contact with one of the little grey creatures. Typically, the experience begins at the home of the witness during the dead of night. Following the initial contact the person involved is then transferred to some form of craft where they are subjected to a variety of distressing physical examinations and procedures.

In a number of instances, and I concede that this is highly controversial, abductees report that they have seen what appear to be half-human/half-alien creatures aboard these craft, which they are led to believe are the results of this extra-terrestrial 'gene tinkering' process.[17]

Three separate British abductees have informed me, totally independently of each other, that the Grey creatures now seen with increasing frequency on our planet are the last vestiges of an ancient and dying race, attempting to rejuvenate its waning species with the addition of new blood – namely, us. This idea was expanded upon by writer Martin Kottmeyer in 1994: '[The Greys] skirt virtually every characteristic of life beyond movement; they don't feel, breathe, eat, defecate or copulate. In their need to revitalize their decrepit constitutions and monochrome lifestyles by stealing the essences of humankind, they are fundamentally no different than the undead of literature and film like vampires. Appropriately, we are told they come from a dying world.'[18]

The following case, investigated by Mark Moravec, and detailed by Keith Basterfield, Research Director of UFO Research Australia, took place at Jindabyne, New South Wales, in September 1979:

Two young men, out hunting, reported seeing a bright white, spherical, light on the ground some little distance away. Next night it was seen again. In 1983 one of the men began recalling memories of a two-hour time lapse on one of those nights.

He consciously recalled that they were both surrounded by a blue light as they went near the object. They were floated through a hatch into a grey-coloured, rectangular room in the UFO. After being put on two 'benches' they were examined by several tall beings. The beings were hairless, grey, and had grey bulges where we have eyes. Slit-like mouths and flat noses, with no ears were described. During the examination, and without tearing their clothes, the beings connected 'wires' to the men.

The reporting man felt 'used,' as if a specimen. They were then returned to the original spot where they had been.[19]

As John Carpenter, a trained psychiatric social worker, has pointed out, encounters with the Greys can have devastating consequences for one's well-being:

One experiencer related how her daughter had been phobic at a young age of certain pictures which had hung in her room – cartoon drawings from the 1960s in which gangs of dogs wearing big dark sunglasses are playing cards, shooting pool, or gambling at tables. The reaction was so intense that the pictures had to be removed from her room. It was those 'big dark sunglasses' which reminded her of the visitors who came at night – as learned in a hypnosis session almost twenty years later. Budd Hopkins tells of a lampshade which caused fear in one of his subjects because the light created a triangular design reminiscent of the triangular-shaped head of the little gray beings. But the subject did not make this connection at a conscious level – only at an emotional and subconscious level of awareness initially.[20]

Although it would have been unthinkable a decade ago, the British Ministry of Defence is now willing to enter into debate on the alien abduction phenomenon. Is this due to an awareness on the Ministry's part that the number of people reporting such encounters is increasing rapidly? I do not know, but spokesman Nick Pope has left me in no doubt that MOD staff have made it their business to become acquainted with the abduction mystery. Admitting to me that he had read into the subject 'quite a bit', Pope revealed that: 'We've got a few letters [within Sec(AS)2a] that mention aliens . . . It (sic) does show some of the signs like missing time that people point to . . . we don't know what, if anything, physical or psychological lies behind these claims.'[21]

Although guarded in his response to me, Pope is to be applauded for his brief statement. As far as I am aware, prior to Pope, no serving member of the Ministry of Defence has been willing to go on record with such a statement on this highly emotive topic. If the wealth of abduction accounts in hand is indicative of some form of alien breeding programme, and the MOD suspect this, I see no easy way in which a Government-sanctioned statement confirming that this is so could be issued to the population at large. Indeed, I doubt that any responsible governing body would ever contemplate such a risky move, fraught as it would be with the possibility of public over-reaction.

Which, if any, of the theories I have outlined go some way towards adequately explaining the extra-terrestrial presence on the Earth? It is entirely feasible that the alien may be part-abductor, part-scavenger, part-teacher and potential-warlord all rolled into one. If so, when and if we finally learn the truth, let us hope that we will be fully prepared to accept it.

Where do we go from here? Given their well-documented reluctance to indulge in face-to-face contact with the human race, I suspect that it may be some time before the alien presence on our planet fully reveals itself to us. Therefore, let us look to our Government for answers. There can be no doubt that to those within officialdom, UFOs are looked on as being a matter of great concern. Consider the evidence obtained by British authorities since the late 1940s:

1947 – A UFO is seen at close quarters near RAF Bentwaters, Suffolk, and a large unidentified flying object is monitored on radar near the London area.

1949 – The movements of a huge UFO are tracked by radar from Kent to Yorkshire. Official log books are removed, and those involved are reminded of their obligations to the British Government.

1952 – Numerous sightings of UFOs are reported throughout NATO's 'Mainbrace' exercise in the North Sea.

1953 – The Air Ministry issues warnings to RAF personnel not to discuss UFO sightings outside of official channels. Flight Lieutenant Cyril Townsend-Withers is informed that the Air Ministry has established a project to study UFOs from the point of view that they may be extra-terrestrial.

1956 – A Royal Air Force pilot succeeds in filming a UFO in flight over the United Kingdom, and Flight Controller Frederick Wimbledon is 'sworn to secrecy' regarding his involvement in the encounter.

1957 – Pressure is brought to bear on a British newspaper for publicizing one particular UFO sighting. Multiple UFO intrusions are reported by personnel at the following RAF stations: Lakenheath, West Freugh, Church Lawford, Bempton, Odiham, Ventnor, and Gaydon.

1959 – A UFO appears over London (now Heathrow) Airport.

1963 – The Air Ministry declines an invitation to take part in a television documentary on the subject of UFOs, but refers to the need to 'mitigate the effects of the programme'.

1964 – At least four departments within the newly created Defence Intelligence Staff are kept appraised of the UFO situation, namely: DSTI, DI10, DI61E and DI65B.

1967 – The Ministry of Defence is flooded with hundreds of reports of unidentified aerial objects. London directs the British Embassy in Moscow to approach Russian authorities; a joint observation programme is mooted.

1970 – 400 UFO reports are submitted to the MOD, a figure not surpassed until 1977.

1973/4 – Numerous people report sightings of unidentified helicopters and strange aerial lights over the British Isles. An unidentified object impacts atop a Welsh mountain.

1975/6 – The MOD is implicated in UFO sightings in the Atlantic Ocean and on the Isle of Wight.

1977 – A 'stingray'-shaped UFO is seen over Cumbria by more than ten police officers.

1980 – Radar operators at Birmingham Airport track a slow-moving UFO across England. A UFO is tracked on radar at RAF Neatishead, Norfolk. A triangular-shaped UFO is seen in Rendlesham Forest, Suffolk; witnesses include high-ranking USAF personnel.

1981 – A huge UFO is seen over a military facility on the island of Cyprus.

1983 – An unidentified flying object hovers over the village of Hollesley, Suffolk. Villagers demand a meeting with the US Air Force.

1984 – An aircraft collides with a UFO over Rendlesham Forest.

1987 – A UFO is seen during a military exercise on the Yorkshire Moors; an interception is attempted by the military.

1988 – In a situation which mirrors that of 1967, the MOD is inundated with UFO reports.

1989 – A radar-visual UFO encounter occurs at Mow Cop, North Staffordshire.

1991 – Unidentified aerial vehicles are seen in close proximity to civilian airliners.

1995 – A triangular-shaped UFO almost collides with a British airliner over the Pennines.

Faced with the evidence, it is quite easy to understand the British Government's reluctance to come clean on the UFO issue. While not overtly hostile, our cosmic visitors are not exactly on speaking terms with us either. I am firmly convinced that the British Ministry of Defence came to the conclusion many years ago that UFOs are real. But, unless we are faced with an all-out planetary assault, or the aliens choose to land in true 'take me to your leader' style, there is very little that the MOD can do, other than to keep a concerned eye on how the phenomenon develops. Given this, would it not be to the MOD's advantage to inform the populace at large that something extraordinary is taking place in the skies over Britain? If matters should escalate, do we not have the right to know?

As I mentioned in my Introduction, I earnestly believe that our elected leaders do not know how to break the news to us, in a non-alarming manner, that the Earth has extra-terrestrial visitors. However, in the last few years, I have carefully watched the unfolding of what I suspect may be a cautiously crafted programme to educate the population and to admit at least some of the truth. Consider the following.

In 1991 the Royal Air Force places advertisements within national newspapers, subtly informing prospective RAF candidates that they might, just might, be required to deal with reports of unidentified flying objects. In late 1992 the United States Defense Intelligence Agency releases three pages of documentation, confirming that it has forwarded briefings on the UFO subject to the MOD's Defence Intelligence Staff at Whitehall. In the following year the MOD announces that 1994 will see the release of two previously classified files of UFO data. In January 1994 those papers are released to me and total an amazing 611 pages. Two months later I am granted permission to conduct an extensive, tape-recorded interview with a serving member of the Ministry of Defence to discuss the UFO subject. In that same year official papers surface which, for the first time, affirm the involvement of the Provost and Security Services in the investigation of UFO reports, something later confirmed to me by the Director of Security and Provost Marshal (RAF).

Later in 1994 both the Airborne Early Warning and Ground Environment divisions of the Royal Air Force admit to me that they too are implicated in the study of UFO sightings. In 1995 a further file of once-classified Government UFO records is released, totalling 300 pages, and revealing hitherto unknown details about the past involvement of the Defence Intelligence Staff in the subject.

In 1996 the Ministry of Defence makes a stunning admission: for decades, the Flying Complaints Flight division of the Provost and Security

Services acted as the RAF's coordination point for UFO data. And still further revelations surface when the MOD declassifies a bulky file of UFO reports covering the period 1964–5.

Whilst others may disagree, I submit that this astonishing volte-face is truly representative of an attempt, officially orchestrated, to acclimatize us to the true nature of the UFO mystery. No doubt, any such education programme will be slow and careful. We can hardly be expected to run before we can walk, after all. But let us hope that we are now deemed fit and ready to learn the facts.

By chronicling the history of the British Government's role in the UFO enigma, I hope that my book has gone some way towards convincing people that the matter is both genuine and deserving of study. If it also convinces those in power to be more forthright with the general public on the subject of unidentified flying objects, then my effort will have exceeded its expectation.

APPENDICES

MINISTRY OF DEFENCE
Main Building, Whitehall, London SW1A 2HB
Telephone (Direct Dialling) 071-21-83998
(Switchboard) 071-21-89000

From: Air Commodore J L Uprichard RAF
Director of Security and Provost Marshal (RAF)

D/DSy&PM(RAF)/222/2

N Redfern Esq
20 Paradise Lane
Pelsall
Walsall
West Midlands WS3 4NH   4 May 1994

Dear Mr Redfern

INVESTIGATION OF ALLEGED UNIDENTIFIED FLYING OBJECTS

Thank you for your letter dated 28 April 1994, concerning the
investigation of alleged Unidentified Flying Objects (UFOs). The
Royal Air Force Provost and Security Services organization is a
functional element of the Royal Air Force Police with
responsibility for investigating alleged criminal offences and
security breaches within the Service. As part of that remit, the
Flying Complaints Flight investigates alleged breaches of the
United Kingdom Low Flying System.

The 1962 report to which you referred is a rare example of an
alleged UFO sighting being treated as a low flying incident and
investigated accordingly. Routinely, we neither investigate nor
evaluate such reports. As you state, the desk within the
Department that records such sightings is the Secretariat to the
Air Staff.

Thank you for your enquiry and I hope that the above details
answer your questions.

Yours sincerely

J L Uprichard

● Air Commodore J.L. Uprichard, Director of Security and Provost Marshal (RAF),
confirms to the author the involvement of the Provost and Security Services in a
1962 UFO encounter.

INQUIRE=DOC18D
ITEM NO=00451920
ENVELOPE
CDSN = LGX031   MCN = 92202/01149   TOR = 922020247
RTTUZYUW RUEKJCS7059 2020251-UUUU--RUEALGX.
ZNR UUUUU
HEADER
R 200251Z JUL 92
FM JOINT STAFF WASHINGTON DC
INFO RUEADWD/OCSA WASHINGTON DC
RUENAAA/CNO WASHINGTON DC
RUEAHQA/CSAF WASHINGTON DC
RUEACMC/CMC WASHINGTON DC
RUETIAQ/MPCFTGEORGEGMEADEMD
RHHMMCY/JICPAC HONOLULU HI
RUWSMXI/AMC INTEL CEN SCOTT AFB IL//IN//
RUCQVAB/USCINCSOC INTEL OPS CEN MACDILL AFB FL
RUEHC /SECSTATE WASHINGTON DC
RUEAIIA/CIA WASHINGTON DC
RULKQAN/MARCORINTCEN QUANTICO VA
RUEALGX/SAFE
R 200224Z JUL 92
███████████████████████
TO RUEKJCS/DIA WASHDC
INFO RUETIAA/DIRNSA FT MEADE MD//T5232/B25//
RAYWDA/DIO CANBERRA AS//INFO CTR//
RBDWC/MODUK LONDON//DIS//
RHHMMCR/PACFAST PEARL HARBOR HI//PF//
RCCPDMA/NDHQ CIS OTTAWA
RUEHBJ/AMEMBASSY BEIJING
RUESLE/AMCONSUL SHANGHAI
RUEOAYA/FSTC CHARLOTTESVILLE VA
RUDMMIC/NAVMARINTCEN WASHDC//DC-30//
RUADJNA/CDRUSASTCFEO YOKOTA AB JA
RUADJNA/DET 1 696IG YOKOTA AB JA
RUADJNA/DET 1 692IW YOKOTA AB JA
RUEHSH/AMCONSUL SHENYANG
RUEHIN/AIT TAIPEI
RUCIAEA/HQFASTC WPAFB OH//IM//
RUADJHA/500MIBDE CP ZAMA JA
RHHMMCY/JICPAC HONOLULU HI
███████████████████████
RUHQHQB/USCINCPAC HONOLULU HI//J233//
BT
CONTROLS
UNCLAS SECTION 01 OF 09 ████████████████

UNCLASSIFIED

PART I OF II

UNCLASSIFIED

● A three-page document which originated with the U.S. Defense Intelligence Agency
and details a 1992 UFO conference in China. Note the distribution list, which
includes 'MODUK LONDON/DIS'. Why are the Ministry of Defence's Defence
Intelligence Staff receiving briefings on overseas UFO conferences?

C. CHINA UNIDENTIFIED FLYING OBJECT (UFO) RESEARCH
ORGANIZATION HOSTS NATIONAL CONFERENCE IN BEIJING ON 11
MAY (LAD, 14 MAY). THE ORGANIZATION HOPES THAT CHINA
WILL BE SELECTED TO HOST THE FIRST WORLD UFO
CONFERENCE, WHICH IS SCHEDULED FOR 1993. MORE THAN 200
CHINESE RESEARCHERS ARE ATTENDING THE CONFERENCE TO

STUDY REPORTS OF FLYING SAUCERS OR "FEI DIE" (STC
7378/4308) IN CHINA. ABOUT 5,000 UFO SIGHTINGS HAVE
BEEN REPORTED IN CHINA IN THE PAST 20 YEARS.

SUFFOLK CONSTABULARY

Telephone No. 282178

FELIXSTOWE _____ Police Station

32 High Road West
Felixstowe
Suffolk IP11 9JE

Our Ref: 18(2)F/88

27th October 1988

Dear Mr. Redfern,

I refer to your letter to Woodbridge Police Station dated 18th October 1988.

I can inform you that, at shortly after 4 a.m. on 26th December 1980, the police did receive a call reporting unusual lights being seen in the sky near R.A.F. Woodbridge. The police responded to this call, but there was no evidence to substantiate or indicate the presence of an unidentified flying object.

You may already be aware that three local residents also pursue your interest in U.F.O's and have written a book on this incident called 'Skycrash', namely, Brenda BUTLER, Dot STREET and Jenny RANDLES. Unfortunately, I do not know the name of the publishers, nor if it is still available for purchase.

I hope this helps you in your research.

Yours sincerely,

S. M. PEARCE
Superintendent - Felixstowe Sub Division

MR N REDFERN
20 PARADISE LANE
PELSALL
WALSALL
WEST MIDLANDS WS3 4NH

● Police records relating to the UFO landing near RAF Woodbridge, Suffolk in December 1980.

From Squadron Leader E E Webster RAF

ROYAL AIR FORCE
Eastern Radar Watton Thetford Norfolk

Telephone Watton 881691   Ext 223

Mr N Redfern
20 Paradise Lane
Pelsall
WALSALL
West Midlands
WS3 4NH

Please reply to The Officer Commanding
Your reference

Our reference   ERD/205/1/Org

Date   16 January 1989

Dear Mr Redfern

Thank you for your letter requesting further information about the UFO report
on 28 December 1980.

I am afraid that we are not able to provide you with copies of our log books.
However, I can offer you a verbatim statement of the only entry regarding the
subject incident in the log for that period. The entry is timed at 0325 on
28 December 1980 and states:

     "Bentwaters Command Post contacted Eastern Radar and requested information
     of aircraft in the area – UA37 traffic southbound FL370 – UFO sightings
     at Bentwaters. They are taking reporting action."

"UA37" means the Upper Air Route Upper Amber 37 which runs approximately
North/South some 40 miles east of Bentwaters and is used by civilian airliners.
FL370 means 37,000 feet in altitude.

As I said in my previous letter, all tape recordings from the period – both
sound and radar – have been routinely disposed of. You now have as much
information as we have.

Eric Webster
for Officer Commanding

● RAF Watton, Norfolk admits that records relating to the Woodbridge landing
are on file.

30 September 1988

Mr. Nicholas Redfern
20 Paradise Lane
Pelsall
Walsall
West Midlands WS3 4NH

Dear Mr. Redfern,

I am writing in response to your letter of 30 August in which you ask
about the involvement in the Apollo space program by one of our base
organizations. In the late 1960s and early 1970s, the 67th Aerospace
Rescue and Recovery Squadron stationed at RAF Woodbridge did indeed
provide standby rescue coverage for the American space flights. Of
course, they were never needed to provide emergency rescue actions, but
at the time, the unit was trained and available to rescue astronauts
with their HH-53 and HC-130 aircraft.

In early 1988, the 67 ARRS was redesignated as part of the 39th Special
Operations Wing, their primary mission changing from that of rescue
to supporting U.S. Special Operations forces. Their secondary mission
remains that of search and rescue and they would provide any assistance
necessary in future space missions. However, I have no details on their
plans to do so.

Thank you very much for your interest in the United States Air Force.

Sincerely,

JOHN E. BOYLE, Capt, USAF
Chief, Public Affairs Office

● RAF Bentwaters discloses details of the space-related activities of the 67th Aerospace
Rescue and Recovery Squadron.

From: Flight Lieutenant M A Tunaley RAF

**Headquarters No 11 Group
Royal Air Force
Bentley Priory
Stanmore Middlesex HA7 3HH**

Tel: 0181-950 4000	Ext 7338
(RAFTN: 97271)	
Facsimile:	Ext 7456

Mr Nicholas Redfern
20 Paradise Lane
Pelsall
Walsall
West Midlands
WS3 4NH

*Please reply to The Air Officer Commanding
(Attn: GE Weapons)*
Your reference

Our reference
11G/300/20/GE
Date
16 September 1994

Dear Mr Redfern,

UNIDENTIFIED FLYING OBJECTS

Thank you for your letter of 7 September 1994, enquiring about the processes by which we receive Unidentified Flying Object (UFO) reports.

The subject of UFO reporting is dealt with by the Deputy Directorate of Ground Environment and Airborne Early Warning at the Ministry of Defence. However, if the Ministry considers it appropriate, they ask us, much as they do Royal Air Force Waddington, to comment on air activity at the time of the reported sighting and whether data recordings from radar sources highlight any unusual activity that has not already been investigated. You may already be aware that occasionally our radar stations are informed of UFO activity, but all reported sightings are passed directly to the Ministry; a decision on whether further action is necessary then rests with them.

We hope that this information is in some way of assistance to you but have in any case passed a copy of your letter to the Ministry for their comments and action as they deem appropriate.

Yours sincerely

Matt Tunaley.

● The Ground Environment division of the Royal Air Force at RAF Bentley Priory admits its involvement in the investigation of UFO reports.

From: **Flying Officer J S Hathaway**

ROYAL AIR FORCE

Stanmore Park Stanmore Middlesex HA7 3LR

Telephone: 081-950 4000 ext
GPTN: 97271 ext   **6216**

Mr N Redfern
20 Paradise Lane
Pelsall
Walsall
West Midlands
WS3 4NH

Your reference

Our reference
SP/5030/4/CR

Date
19 October 1994

Dear Mr Redfern

INFORMATION CONCERNING THE GE DIVISION OF THE RAF

1.   Thank you for your letter dated 20 September requesting details of the work that is carried out by the GE Division in other fields.

2.   The work carried out by the GE Division covers a variety of aspects but I am sure you can appreciate that the work that is carried out is not open to discussion.

3.   I apologise for not being able to give you any firm details but I am sure you realise the need for security.

4.   If this unit can be of any further assistance please do not hesitate to contact me.

Yours Sincerely

Public Relations Officer.

● The work undertaken by the RAF's Ground Environment division is highly-sensitive, as this letter from RAF Stanmore Park shows.

(·4)

NEAR COLLISION - AIR TRAFFIC INCIDENT REPORT FORM

NOTE 1°) To be filled in printed characters and in english language.
2°) Shaded boxes contain items to be included in an initial report by radio.
3°) Items marked thus @ must be deleted as appropriate.

SECTION 1 - GENERAL INFORMATION

TYPE OF INCIDENT	A	INCIDENT NEAR COLLISION PROCEDURAL FACILITY @
NAME OF PILOT-IN-COMMAND	B	ZAGHETTI ALITALIA
OPERATOR	C	
IDENTIFICATION MARKINGS OF AIRCRAFT	D	I - DAWC
AIRCRAFT TYPE	E	MD 80
RADIO CALL SIGN-IN COMMUNICATION WITH - FREQUENCY AT TIME OF INCIDENT	F	AZ 284 - LON 124.1 - AT ~ 2000/z
AERODROME OF DEPARTURE	G	MILAN - LINATE
AERODROME OF FIRST INTENDED LANDING AND RE-STIMATION, IF DIFFERENT	H	LONDON - HEATHROW
TYPE OF FLIGHT PLAN	I	IFR
POSITION AT TIME OF INCIDENT - HEADING OR ROUTE TRUE AIRSPEED	J	~ 30 NM SOUTH BIGGIN VOR - HEADING 320° TAS 380
FL, ALTITUDE OR HEIGHT ALTIMETER SETTING ATTITUDE	K	LEVEL FLIGHT CLIMBING (DESCENDING) TURNING @ FL 222 - ALT 1013 - RATE 1050/1/4
FLIGHT WEATHER CONDITIONS AT TIME OF INCIDENT		IMC VMC VMC 30 K= (FM) Distance above 'below cloud 'fog 'haze'
	L	Distance horizontally from cloud
		Between cloud layers
		In cloud 'rain 'snow' cloud 'fog 'haze'
		Flying into 'out of' sun
		Reported 'estimated' flight visibility 30 K= (FM)
DATE AND TIME OF INCIDENT IN GMT	M	REPORTED BY RADIO TO LON 127.) AFIS TWR APP (ACC) FIC @ AT 04/21/91 ~ 2000/z

SECTION 2 - DETAILED INFORMATION

DESCRIPTION OF OTHER AIRCRAFT, IF RELEVANT Type high/low wing, N. of engines Radio call sign, registration Markings, colour, lighting Other available details	N	OBJECT SIMILAR MISSILE - WITHOUT EXHAUST FLAME - UNKNOWN LIGHT BROWN - SIMILAR DESERT COLOUR ABOUT 3 METERS LENGTH - ROUND SHAPE -
DESCRIPTION OF INCIDENT If desired add comment or suggestion, including your opinion on the probable cause of the incident (In case of near-collision give information on respective flight paths, estimated vertical and horizontal sighting and miss distances between aircrafts and evading action taken by either a/c)	O	DURING DESCENT, AT FL 222 I SAW FOR ABOUT 3-4 SECONDS A FLYING OBJECT, VERY SIMILAR TO A MISSILE, LIGHT BRAWN COLOURED, WITH A TRACK OPPOSITE THEN MINE WHICH WAS 320° - IT WAS HIGHER THAN US ABOUT 1000 ft.

AT ONCE I SAID « LOOK AT OUT. LOOK OUT» TO MY COPILOT WHO LOOKED OUT AND SAW WHAT I HAD SEEN - AS SOON AS THE OBJECT CROSSED US I ASKED TO THE ACC/OPERATOR IF HE SAW SOMETHING. ON HIS SCREEN AND HE ANSWERED " I SEE AN UNKNOWN TARGET 10 N.M.

DATE 04/22/91 TIME 8 P.M.	FUNCTION AND SIGNATURE CPT ZAGHETTI OF PERSON SUBMITTING REPORT	FUNCTION AND SIGNATURE OF PERSON RECEIVING REPORT
PLACE LONDON		
OF COMPLETION OF FORM		

SECTION 3 - SUPPLEMENTARY INFORMATION
by ATS unit concerned (not for pilot's use)

HOW REPORT RECEIVED	P	RADIO, TELEPHONE / TELEPRINTER/ VAT ARO AFIS - TWR/ APP ACC/ FIC @
DETAILS OF ATS ACTION Clearance, incident observed on radar, missing given, result of local enquiry, etc.	Q	

@ Delete as appropriate

SIGNATURE OF ATS OFFICER   DATE TIME GMT

ICAO Paris PAC 1000 4011-RAC 501-10

● An Air Traffic Incident Report Form concerning the sighting of a missile-shaped UFO over the United Kingdom in 1991.

Chapter 4

3 UNIDENTIFIED FLYING OBJECTS

A controller receiving a report about an unidentified flying object must obtain as much as possible of the information required to complete a report in the format shown below.

Report of Unidentified Flying Object

A. Date, Time and Duration of Sighting
Local times to be quoted.

B. Description of Object
Number of objects, size, shape, colours, brightness, sound, smell, etc.

C. Exact Position of Observer
Geographical location, indoors or outdoors, stationary or moving.

D. How Observed
Naked eye, binoculars, other optical device, still or movie camera.

E. Direction in which Object was First Seen
A landmark may be more useful than a badly estimated bearing.

F. Angular Elevation of Object
Estimated heights are unreliable.

G. Distance of Object from Observer
By reference to a known landmark wherever possible.

H. Movements of Object
Changes in E, F and G may be of more use than estimates of course and speed.

J. Meteorological Conditions During Observations
Moving clouds, haze, mist, etc.

K. Nearby Objects
Telephone or high-voltage lines; reservoir, lake or dam; swamp or marsh; river; high buildings, tall chimneys, steeples, spires, TV or radio masts; airfields, generating plant; factories; pits or other sites with floodlights or other lighting.

L. To Whom Reported
Police, military organisations, the press, etc.

M. Name and Address of Informant

N. Any Background Information on the Informant that may be Volunteered

O. Other Witnesses

P. Date and Time of Receipt of Report

The details are to be telephoned immediately to AIS (Military), LATCC.

The completed report is to be sent by the originating air traffic service unit to the Ministry of Defence (AFOR).

A LIST OF TELEPHONE NUMBERS AND LOCATIONS IS SHOWN IN THE
DIRECTORY AT APPENDIX H

● All Air Traffic controllers who operate under the jurisdiction of the Civil Aviation Authority (CAA) are obliged to log details of incoming UFO reports.

```
********************************************************************
 Date:       Aircraft:       Location:       Phase of Flight:   CAA Ref:
 -----       ---------       ---------       ----------------   --------
 24 AUG 84  TRISLANDER      IPSWICH         CRUISE             8402680D
```

CAA Narrative:

UK REPORTABLE ACCIDENT : A/C STRUCK OBJECT IN CRUISE. PROPELLER, FUSELAGE,
COWLING & CONTROL RUNS DAMAGED.
THE A/C WAS FLYING IN SLIGHT TURBULENCE WHEN A BUMP WAS FELT. JUST BEFORE
DESCENT THE RIGHT ENGINE CONTROL WAS FOUND TO BE SEIZED SO AN ASYMMETRIC
APPROACH & LANDING WAS EXECUTED. ON INSPECTION IT WAS APPARENT THAT THE LEFT
PROPELLER HAD STRUCK AN UNIDENTIFIED OBJECT, PROPELLING IT THROUGH THE CABIN
ROOF, WITH A PIECE EXITING THROUGH A WINDOW. THERE WERE SEVERAL HOLES IN THE
FUSELAGE & DAMAGE TO THE ENGINE, AILERON & RUDDER TRIM CABLES. THREE PIECES
OF FOREIGN METALLIC OBJECT WERE FOUND, INCLUDING A SMALL CYLINDRICAL MAGNET.
THE UFO HAS NOT BEEN IDENTIFIED. (AIB BULLETIN 10/84). SEE DIGEST 84/D/43.
CAA CLOSURE: NO INFORMATION RECEIVED CONCERNING NATURE OR ORIGIN OF UFO.

```
********************************************************************
 Date:       Aircraft:       Location:       Phase of Flight:   CAA Ref:
 -----       ---------       ---------       ----------------   --------
 26 OCT 84  NOT APP         READING         NOT APP            8404325C
```

CAA Narrative:

UNIDENTIFIED FLYING OBJECT : BRIGHT LIGHT 65DEG ELEV. 200DEG T. DURATION 7
MINUTES.

```
********************************************************************
 Date:       Aircraft:       Location:       Phase of Flight:   CAA Ref:
 -----       ---------       ---------       ----------------   --------
 20 DEC 84  HERALD          AIRWAY W17      CRUISE             8404256G
```

CAA Narrative:

BRIGHT WHITE LIGHTS ARCED ACROSS A/C TRACK. NO RANGE ACTIVITY IN CHANNEL.
LIGHTS ALSO SEEN BY ANOTHER A/C.

```
********************************************************************
 Date:       Aircraft:       Location:       Phase of Flight:   CAA Ref:
 -----       ---------       ---------       ----------------   --------
 24 JAN 85  B707                            CRUISE             8500208J
```

CAA Narrative:

FLASH OF LIGHT APPROX SIZE OF FOOTBALL SEEN AT FL330 STRAIGHT AHEAD
SOUND OF DEBRIS HITTING A/C APPROX 3MIN LATER.NO DAMAGE TO A/C DISCOVERED.

```
********************************************************************
 Date:       Aircraft:       Location:       Phase of Flight:   CAA Ref:
 -----       ---------       ---------       ----------------   --------
 5 FEB 86   PIPER PA31      5427N 0530W     DESCENT            8600373J
```

CAA Narrative:

BRIGHT LIGHT PASSED UPWARDS IN FRONT OF A/C
A/C WAS CROSSING EAST COAST OF IRELAND ON DESCENT.LIGHT TRAVELLED TOWARDS A/C
FROM A 2.30 POSITION RANGE APPROX 1 1/2 MILES AND PASSED 1000FT ABOVE
TRAVELLING RIGHT TO LEFT 1 MILE AHEAD. BURST OF GREEN LIGHT OBSERVED AT PEAK
OF ITS BALLISTIC FLIGHT.A/C HT 1450FT. CAA CLOSURE-POSSIBLY FLARE FIRED AT
ABOUT TIME OF OCC BY ALDERGROVE.PILOT CONSIDERED THIS UNLIKELY BUT NO OTHER
EXPLANATION HAS EMERGED.NIL HAZARD-NFA.

● Various Civil Aviation Authority UFO records 1984–1986.

L.	To whom reported (Police, military, press etc)	Not seriously reported.
M.	Name & Address of Informant	▓▓▓▓▓▓▓▓▓▓▓▓▓▓▓▓
N.	Background of informant that may be volunteered	—
O.	Other Witnesses	None known.
P.	Date, Time of Receipt	1245 15 July 1987
Q.	Any Unusual Meteorological Conditions	None
R.	Remarks	Seemed a sober gentleman.

Date. 15 July 1987.....   ~~~

Squadron Leader
Duty Operations Officer
AF Ops

Copies to: Sec(AS) 2
Sec(AS)2
AEW/GE
DI 55
File AF Ops/1/11

> Sec (AS) 2 distribution:
> AEW/GE
> DI/55
> File 12/2

● A 1987 Ministry of Defence UFO report. Note the distribution list, which shows that copies of such reports are regularly channelled to 'AEW/GE' (Airborne Early Warning/Ground Environment) and to at least one division in the Defence Intelligence Staff – DI55.

● On several occasions in the early 1990s documentation declassified by the U.S. Defense Intelligence Agency was forwarded to the author via the DIA's liaison office (DIALL) at Whitehall. No explanation for this action was ever forthcoming.

REFERENCES

CHAPTER 1 – IN THE BEGINNING

1 Documentation made available to the author by the FBI.
2 Counter Intelligence Corps memorandum from Agent Leslie L. Hubbard, September 9, 1947.
3 Headquarters, Air Defense Command memorandum, September 12, 1947.
4 Memorandum from Lt. Col. Donald L. Springer, USAF, to the FBI, August 27, 1947.
5 USAF Air Intelligence Requirements Division document, October 28, 1947.

CHAPTER 2 – THE EARLY YEARS

1 Air Ministry memorandum, August 8, 1947. Donald Keyhoe, *Aliens from Space* (Panther, London, 1973), p.27. Edward J. Ruppelt, *The Report on Unidentified Flying Objects* (Ace Books, New York, 1956), p. 59.
2 Interview with Jenny Randles, September 3, 1996. Jenny Randles, *From Out of the Blue* (Global Communications [Box 753, New Brunswick, New Jersey 08903, USA], 1991), p. 108.
3 For an in-depth look at the work of the Tizard Committee, see R.V. Jones, *Most Secret War* (Hamish Hamilton, London, 1978).

4 Letters from Ronald Anstee to the Air Ministry, January 30, March 7 and March 21, 1963. Copies of Anstee's letters are contained within Public Record Office file: AIR 2/16918. Crown copyright exists.
5 *UFO Magazine*, May/June 1996.
6 Letter to the author from Nick Pope, Secretariat (Air Staff) 2a, Ministry of Defence, September 24, 1992.
7 Letter from J.R. Oliver to Timothy Good, October 26, 1991. Letter to the author from Timothy Good, December 4, 1991. Letter to the author from Mrs J.D. Oliver, March 23, 1994.
8 Public Record Office file: AIR 20/7390. Crown copyright exists.
9 Public Record Office file: PREM 11/855. Crown copyright exists.
10 USAF Intelligence files, declassified 1985/6.
11 David Clarke and Andy Roberts, *Phantoms of the Sky* (Robert Hale, London, 1990), pp. 115–116.
12 Information related to the author by Ministry of Defence spokesman, Nick Pope, in a March 29, 1994, interview.
13 Report from Pepperell Air Force Base to CSAF, Washington DC, February 10, 1951.
14 FBI teletype of September 20, 1951.
15 David Clarke and Andy Roberts, op. cit., p. 115.
16 *Flying Saucer Review*, Vol. 28, No. 3, 1983.
17 *Flying Saucer Review*, Vol. 36, No. 3, 1991.

CHAPTER 3 – MAINBRACE

1 US Navy records pertaining to Mainbrace made available to the author by Bernard F. Cavalcante, Head Operational Archives Branch, Naval Historical Centre, Washington DC 20374–0571. *Daily Telegraph*, September 20 and September 22, 1952.
2 Letters to the author from Victor Kean, March 27 and April 7, 1995. Project Blue Book Report 2087.
3 Letter to Timothy Good from Leslie Banks, December 23, 1991.
4 Public Record Office file: AIR 16/1199. Crown copyright exists.
5 Ibid.
6 Ibid.
7 Public Record Office file: AIR 20/7390. Crown copyright exists.
8 Ibid.
9 Letter to the author from Leslie Banks, January 11, 1992. Letter to Timothy Good from Leslie Banks, December 23, 1991.
10 US Navy, Second Fleet Historical Record. Aime Michel, *The Truth about Flying Saucers* (Corgi, London, 1958), pp. 136–137. Edward J. Ruppelt,

The Report on Unidentified Flying Objects (Ace Books, New York, 1956), pp. 256–257.

11 Letter to the author from Chester Grusinski, March 14, 1993.

12 Edward Ruppelt, op. cit., p. 257.

13 Lawrence Fawcett and Barry Greenwood, *Clear Intent* (Prentice-Hall Press, New Jersey, 1984).

14 Central Intelligence Agency report, November 13, 1952.

15 *UFO*, Vol. 8, No. 5, 1993.

16 Aime Michel, op. cit., p. 139.

17 Letter to the author from A.H. Lawes, Public Record Office, July 5, 1990.

18 *Sunday Dispatch*, December 7, 1952.

19 Edward Ruppelt, op. cit., p. 256.

20 Letter to the author from Bruno Pappalardo, Search Department, Public Record Office, September 21, 1990.

21 Letter to the author from Derek Barlow, Public Record Office Inspecting Officer to the Ministry of Defence, December 18, 1990.

22 Letter to the author from J. Oliver, Departmental Record Officer, Ministry of Defence, January 8, 1991.

23 Public Record Office file: DEFE 40. Crown copyright exists.

24 Ibid.

25 Desmond Leslie and George Adamski, *Flying Saucers Have Landed* (T. Werner Laurie Ltd, London, 1953), pp. 17–18.

CHAPTER 4 – UNUSUAL AERIAL PHENOMENA

1 Public Record Office file: AIR 20/9994. Crown copyright exists.

2 *The Unopened Files*, No. 1, 1996, p. 64. Jenny Randles, *The UFO Conspiracy* (Blandford Press, Poole, 1987), p. 42.

3 *Loughborough Mail*, September 28, 1995.

4 Letters to the author from John Smith, June 11 and October 28, 1994.

5 *Eastern Evening News*, October 8, 1953.

6 Ibid.

7 *Eastern Evening News*, October 10, 1953.

8 Public Record Office file: AIR 20/7390. Crown copyright exists.

9 Brinsley Le Poer Trench, *The Flying Saucer Story* (Universal Tandem, 1974), p. 31–32. Waverney Girvan, *Flying Saucers and Common Sense* (Frederick Muller, London, 1955), pp. 106–114.

10 *Kent Messenger*, April 18, 1996.

11 Public Record Office file: AIR 20/9994. Crown copyright exists.

12 *Daily Telegraph*, August 3, 1954.

13 Timothy Good, *Above Top Secret* (Sidgwick and Jackson, London, 1987), pp. 34–36.
14 Donald Keyhoe, *The Flying Saucer Conspiracy* (Henry Holt and Company, New York, 1955), p. 217.
15 Public Record Office file: AIR 20/9321. Crown copyright exists.
16 *Flying Saucer Review*, Vol. 1, No. 2, 1955.
17 *Flying Saucer News*, Summer 1955.
18 *Flying Saucer Review*, Vol. 1, No. 4, 1955.
19 Peter Paget, *UFO – UK* (New English Library, 1980), p. 78.
20 Public Record Office file: AIR 22/93. Crown copyright exists.
21 Public Record Office file: PREM 11/855. Crown copyright exists.
22 Public Record Office file: AIR 22/93. Crown copyright exists.
23 Secret Air Force Intelligence UFO Report, Quest Publications International Ltd, 1988.
24 *Encounters*, Issue 3, January 1996.

CHAPTER 5 – 'WE BELIEVE THESE THINGS EXIST'

1 *Uranus*, Vol. 2, No. 6, 1956.
2 *Uranus*, Vol. 3, No. 3, 1956.
3 US Air Force report, declassified 1976.
4 Letters to the author from F.H.C. Wimbledon, June 20 and July 5, 1994. *Sunday Times*, April 9, 1978.
5 Timothy Good, *Above Top Secret* (Sidgwick and Jackson, London, 1987), p. 45.
6 Interview with Nick Pope, Secretariat (Air Staff) 2a, Ministry of Defence, March 29, 1994.
7 Letter to the author from F.H.C. Wimbledon, July 5, 1994.
8 Ibid.
9 Interview with W. Wright conducted by Paul Fuller, May 23, 1992. (Copy in my possession.)
10 *Daily Herald*, September 23, 1956.
11 Public Record Office file: AIR 20/9994. Crown copyright exists.
12 Public Record Office file: AIR 20/9321. Crown copyright exists.

CHAPTER 6 – CLOSE ENCOUNTERS

1 *Flying Saucer Review*, Vol. 3, No. 3, 1957.
2 *Heywood Advertiser*, June 1, 1989.
3 *Heywood Advertiser*, June 8, 1989.

4 Public Record Office file: AIR 20/9320. Crown copyright exists.
5 USAF Intelligence report, March 18, 1958.
6 Public Record Office file: AIR 20/9320. Crown copyright exists.
7 Ibid.
8 Ibid.
9 Public Record Office file: AIR 20/9994. Crown copyright exists.
10 Ibid.
11 *Western Mail*, May 1, 1957.
12 Public Record Office file: AIR 20/9322. Crown copyright exists.
13 Public Record Office file: AIR 20/9994. Crown copyright exists.
14 *Sunday Express*, October 27, 1957.
15 *People*, May 4, 1958.
16 Charles Bowen, *The Humanoids* (Neville Spearman, C.W. Daniel Company Ltd [1 Church Path, Saffron Walden, Essex, CB10 1JP], 1969).
17 *Daily Telegraph*, March 6, 1959. *Times*, February 26, 1959. Frank Edwards, *Flying Saucers – Serious Business* (Lyle Stuart, New York, 1966), pp. 117–118.
18 Frank Edwards, op. cit., p. 118.
19 *News Chronicle*, July 27, 1959.
20 *News of the World*, September 6, 1959.
21 Information related to the author, August 4, 1995.
22 *Newcastle Evening Chronicle*, September 9, 1960.

CHAPTER 7 – OFFICIAL INVESTIGATIONS: 1961–1966

1 Letter to the author from Nick Pope, Secretariat (Air Staff) 2a, Ministry of Defence, September 24, 1992.
2 Letter to the author from Nick Pope, Secretariat (Air Staff) 2a, Ministry of Defence, July 5, 1993.
3 Public Record Office file: AIR 2/16918. Crown copyright exists.
4 *Flying Saucer Review*, Vol. 26, No. 1, 1980.
5 Letter to the author from Nick Pope, Secretariat (Air Staff) 2a, Ministry of Defence, May 4, 1994.
6 Letter to the author from I.D. Goode, Deputy Departmental Record Officer, Ministry of Defence, May 3, 1994.
7 Letter to the author from I.D. Goode, Deputy Departmental Record Officer, Ministry of Defence, July 5, 1994.
8 Public Record Office file: AIR 2/17318. Crown copyright exists.
9 Ibid.
10 Ibid.
11 *Daily Herald*, August 2, 1963.

12 *Daily Express*, August 1, 1963.
13 Public Record Office file: AIR 2/17318. Crown copyright exists.
14 Letter to the author from Timothy Good, June 23, 1994.
15 Timothy Good, *Above Top Secret* (Sidgwick and Jackson, London, 1987), pp. 145–146.
16 Public Record Office file: AIR 2/17318. Crown copyright exists.
17 Ibid.
18 Ibid.
19 Interview with Paul Greensill, July 24, 1995.
20 Public Record Office file: AIR 2/17318. Crown copyright exists.
21 Ibid.
22 *Northern Echo*, November 22, 1963.
23 *Fortean Times*, No. 50, 1988. Letter to the author from Ralph Noyes, August 22, 1994.
24 *Central Intelligence Machinery*, HMSO, 1993, pp. 21–22. Crown copyright. Reproduced with the permission of the Controller of Her Majesty's Stationery Office.
25 Interview with Jenny Randles, September 3, 1996.
26 Arthur Shuttlewood, *UFO Magic in Motion* (Sphere Books, London, 1979), p. 246.
27 Interview with Nick Pope, Secretariat (Air Staff) 2a, Ministry of Defence, March 29, 1994.
28 *Evening News*, March 2, 1966. *Daily Sketch*, March 3, 1966.
29 *Daily Sketch*, March 3, 1966. *Daily Mirror*, March 3, 1966.
30 *Evening News*, March 2, 1966.

CHAPTER 8 – INVASION!

1 Letter to the author from Nick Pope, Secretariat (Air Staff) 2a, Ministry of Defence, December 3, 1992.
2 *Daily Mail*, October 26, 1967.
3 *Times*, October 25, 1967. *Daily Telegraph*, October 25, 1967.
4 *Daily Telegraph*, October 26, 1967.
5 *Guardian*, October 26, 1967.
6 *Daily Mail*, October 27, 1967.
7 *Evening Standard*, October 26, 1967. *Daily Mail*, October 27, 1967.
8 *Daily Telegraph*, October 28, 1967.
9 See Chapter Three.
10 *Daily Telegraph*, October 28, 1967. Robert Chapman, *Unidentified Flying Objects*, Mayflower, 1970, p. 15.
11 *Times*, October 26, 1967.

12 *Daily Telegraph*, October 28, 1967.
13 *Sunday Express*, October 29, 1967.
14 *Sun*, October 31, 1967.
15 *Daily Telegraph*, October 30, 1967.
16 *Guardian*, November 14, 1967.
17 Defense Intelligence Agency report, 19 January, 1968.
18 Letter to the author from Kerry Palmer, Secretariat (Air Staff) 2a, Ministry of Defence, March 22, 1991.
19 Interview with Nick Pope, Secretariat (Air Staff) 2a, Ministry of Defence, March 29, 1994.
20 *Daily Sketch*, May 17, 1968.
21 *Northern UFO News*, No. 162, 1993.
22 Letter to the author from Nick Pope, Secretariat (Air Staff) 2a, Ministry of Defence, September 24, 1992.
23 *Plymouth Western Evening Herald*, March 19, 1994.
24 *Bufora Journal*, Vol. 3, No. 6, 1972.
25 Ibid.
26 Ibid.
27 Arthur Shuttlewood, *The Flying Saucerers* (Sphere Books, London, 1976), pp. 10–11.
28 Counter Intelligence Corps – Army Air Force report prepared by Special Agent Lynn C. Aldrich, July 7, 1947.
29 Leonard Stringfield, *UFO Crash/Retrievals: Search for Proof in a Hall of Mirrors* (1994), pp. 34–37.
30 Arthur Shuttlewood, op. cit., p. 121.
31 *UFO Magazine*, May June 1995.

CHAPTER 9 – THE 'COPTER AND THE CRASH

1 Tom Adams, *The Choppers – and the Choppers* (revised ed., Project Stigma, P.O. Box 1094, Paris, Texas, 75461, USA, 1991).
2 *Aviation Week and Space Technology*, Vol. 142, No. 6, 1995, pp. 18–20.
3 Ibid.
4 Tom Adams, op. cit., p. 39.
5 Leonard Stringfield, *Situation Red: The UFO Siege* (Sphere Books Ltd, London, 1978), pp. 82–83.
6 FBI report, February 16, 1979.
7 Linda Moulton Howe, *An Alien Harvest* (Linda Moulton Howe Productions [P.O. Box 538, Huntingdon Valley, PA 19006–0538, USA], 1989).
8 Tom Adams, *Animal Mutilations: A Decade of Mystery* (MUFON Symposium Proceedings, Mutual UFO Network, 1984), p. 57.
9 *Albuquerque Tribune*, April 15, 1993.

10 *Albuquerque Tribune*, April 16, 1993.
11 *Parade*, December 10, 1978.
12 Jenny Randles, *The Pennine UFO Mystery* (Granada Publishing Ltd, St Albans, 1983), p. 28.
13 *Buxton Advertiser*, September 21, 1973.
14 *Guardian*, January 15, 1974.
15 Ibid.
16 *Birmingham Evening Mail*, January 16, 1974.
17 Ibid.
18 *Birmingham Post*, January 16, 1974.
19 *Guardian*, January 18, 1974.
20 *Guardian*, January 19, 1974.
21 *Times*, January 18, 1974.
22 Ibid.
23 *Guardian*, January 19, 1974.
24 Ibid.
25 *Birmingham Evening Mail*, January 24, 1974.
26 *Guardian*, January 25, 1974.
27 Ibid.
28 Ibid.
29 *Times*, January 24, 1974.
30 *Times*, January 25, 1974.
31 Ibid.
32 *North Wales Weekly News*, January 31, 1974.
33 *Times*, January 25, 1974.
34 *Border Counties Advertiser*, January 30, 1974.
35 *Guardian*, January 25, 1974.
36 David Clarke and Andy Roberts, *Phantoms of the Sky* (Robert Hale, London, 1990), p. 143.
37 Information supplied to the author by Margaret Fry, March 19, 1994.
38 *Wrexham Leader*, January 25, 1974.
39 *Wrexham Leader*, February 1, 1974.
40 *Times*, October 3, 1983.
41 AFCIN Intelligence Team Personnel document, November 3, 1961.
42 Leonard Stringfield, *UFO Crash/Retrievals: Amassing the Evidence* (1982), p. 24. Published privately.
43 Jenny Randles, *UFO Reality* (Robert Hale Ltd, London, 1983), p. 152.

CHAPTER 10 – UNIDENTIFIED VISITORS

1 Peter Bottomley and Gordon Clegg, 'MOD Tracks UFO on Radar', *Bufora Journal*, Vol. 4, No. 12, 1976.

2 Richard Nash, 'Isle of Wight Low Level Sighting', *Bufora Journal*, op. cit.

3 CIA Domestic Collection Division document, November 18, 1976.

4 Norman Oliver, 'Report – Extra!', *Bufora Journal*, Vol. 7, No. 3, 1978. *Bufora Journal*, Vol. 6, No. 6, 1978.

5 Nigel Blundell and Roger Boar, *The World's Greatest UFO Mysteries* (Octopus Books Ltd, London, 1984), p. 27.

6 Timothy Good, *Alien Liaison* (Random Century Ltd, London, 1991), p. 18.

7 Letter to the author from Nick Pope, Secretariat (Air Staff) 2a, Ministry of Defence, December 3, 1992.

8 *Northern UFO News*, No. 72.

9 Letter to the author from Flight Lieutenant J. Bosworth, RAF West Drayton, April 12, 1988.

10 *Northern UFO News*, No. 72.

11 *UFO Magazine*, May/June, 1995.

12 *Flying Saucer Review*, Vol. 27, No. 2, 1981. Letter to the author from Paul Sieveking, March 24, 1995.

13 Department of State record 1981.

CHAPTER 11 – THE RENDLESHAM AFFAIR

1 Brenda Butler, Dot Street and Jenny Randles, *Sky Crash* (Neville Spearman, Sudbury, Suffolk, 1984). *Flying Saucer Review*, Vol. 26, No. 6, 1980.

2 *Guardian*, October 2, 1993.

3 Ibid.

4 *Ufologist*, Vol. 2, No. 3, 1993.

5 Letter to the author from Graham Stanley, Government Services Department, Public Record Office, September 20, 1994.

6 Letter to the author from Clive Neville, Secretariat (Air Staff) 2a, Ministry of Defence, October 7, 1988.

7 *News of the World*, October 2, 1983.

8 Brenda Butler, Dot Street and Jenny Randles, *Sky Crash* (Grafton Books, London, 1986), pp. 133–134.

9 Lawrence Fawcett and Barry Greenwood, *Clear Intent* (Prentice-Hall Inc, New Jersey, 1984), pp. 217–218.

10 Butler, Street and Randles, op. cit., p. 194.

11 Memorandum from Lieutenant Colonel Charles Halt, USAF, January 13, 1981.

12 Those wishing to obtain a copy of the eighteen-minute audio recording can do so c/o Quest Publications International Ltd.

13 Letter to the author from Jenny Randles, July 15, 1993.

14 Ibid.
15 *People*, December 4, 1994.
16 *Flying Saucer Review*, Vol. 27, No. 6, 1982.
17 Letter to the author from Squadron Leader E.E. Webster, RAF Watton, October 25, 1988.
18 Letter to the author from Squadron Leader E.E. Webster, RAF Watton, January 16, 1989.
19 Ibid.
20 *UFO Magazine*, January/February 1995.
21 *UFO Magazine*, Vol. 11, No. 3, 1992.
22 Letters to the author from Suffolk Constabulary, 25 and 27 October 1988.
23 *East Anglian Daily Times*, December 7, 1984.
24 Jenny Randles, *UFO Retrievals* (Blandford Press, London, 1995), pp. 133–134.
25 *News of the World*, October 2, 1983.
26 A.J.S. Rayl, 'Inside the Military Underground', *OMNI* magazine, April 1994.
27 *UFO Magazine*, March/April 1996.
28 Jenny Randles, *From out of the Blue* (Global Communications [Box 753, New Brunswick, NJ, 08903, USA], 1991), pp. 55–56.
29 Jenny Randles, op. cit., p. 56.
30 Interview with Nick Pope, Secretariat (Air Staff) 2a, Ministry of Defence, March 29, 1994.
31 Ibid.
32 Letter to the author from Jenny Randles, (undated) 1993.
33 *News of the World*, October 2, 1983.
34 Ralph Noyes, 'UFO lands in Suffolk – and that's Official!', *The UFO Report 1990*, edited by Timothy Good (Sidgwick and Jackson Ltd, London, 1989), p. 54.

CHAPTER 12 – THE 1980s AND BEYOND

1 Interview with the author, January 12, 1993.
2 Statistical information made available to the author by the Ministry of Defence on September 24, 1992.
3 *Sun*, March 25, 1982.
4 *Flying Saucer Review*, Vol. 28, No. 2, 1982.
5 *News of the World*, October 23, 1983.
6 Civil Aviation Authority records made available to the author in 1995.
7 'Britain's Civil Aviation Authority', Public Relations Department of the CAA, December 1986, p. 13.

8 Civil Aviation Authority records made available to the author in 1995.

9 'Unidentified Flying Objects', Chapter 4, Part 3, Amendment 40, Manual of Air Traffic Services (Part 1), April 14, 1987.

10 *Northern UFO News*, No. 157, October, 1992.

11 *Walsall Observer*, February 19, 1988.

12 *Western Mail*, Cardiff, October 28, 1988. *Daily Star*, October 23, 1988.

13 *Kent and Sussex Courier*, November 4, 1988.

14 Civil Aviation Authority records made available to the author in 1995.

15 *Stoke-on-Trent Evening Sentinel*, December 7, 1989. Letter to the author from Kerry Palmer, Secretariat (Air Staff) 2a, Ministry of Defence, March 5, 1990.

16 *Westmoreland Gazette*, October 19, 1990.

17 *Thanet Times*, November 6, 1990.

18 *Sunday Mail*, Glasgow, November 11, 1990.

19 *Flying Saucer Review*, Vol. 36, No. 2, 1991.

20 Timothy Good, *The UFO Report 1992* (Sidgwick and Jackson Ltd, London, 1991), p. 136.

21 Letter to the author from Squadron leader P.A. Kiver, RAF West Drayton, May 9, 1991, and accompanying CAA press release.

22 *Daily Star*, May 6, 1991.

23 *Independent*, May 6, 1991.

24 *Sunday Times*, May 5, 1991.

25 Ibid.

26 *Independent*, May 6, 1991.

27 *Sunday Times*, May 5, 1991.

28 Letter to the author from O.W. Hartop, Secretariat (Air Staff) 2a, Ministry of Defence, July 2, 1991.

29 *UFO Magazine*, Vol. 10, No. 6, 1992.

30 *International UFO Reporter*, Vol. 19, No. 4, July/August 1994.

31 *Daily Telegraph*, April 29, 1992. *Times*, April 28, 1992. *Guardian*, April 28, 1992.

32 Civil Aviation Authority records made available to the author in 1995.

33 *Times*, February 2, 1995. *Today*, January 28, 1995. *Daily Express*, January 28, 1995. Letter to the author from Kerry Philpott, Secretariat Air Staff 2a, Ministry of Defence, March 24, 1995.

34 *West Sussex Gazette*, August 3, 1995.

35 *Southend Evening Echo*, August 7, 1995. *Southern Standard*, August 10, 1995.

36 *Shropshire Star*, August 24, 1995. *Birmingham Post*, August 25, 1995.

37 *UFO Magazine*, January/February 1996.

38 Public Record Office file: AIR 2/17527. Crown copyright exists.

CHAPTER 13 – FLYING TRIANGLES

1 *Southend Evening Echo*, September 23, 1988.
2 *Southend Evening Echo*, September 26, 1988. *Southend Standard*, September 30, 1988.
3 *Stafford Newsletter*, June 24, 1988.
4 *Birmingham Evening Mail*, October 8, 1988. *Stafford Newsletter*, October 14, 1988.
5 *North Devon Journal*, December 1, 1988.
6 *Essex Chronicle*, February 17, 1989.
7 *Southend Evening Echo*, September 18, 1989.
8 *Hull Daily Mail*, July 14, 1990.
9 *Nottingham Evening Post*, May 24, 1991.
10 *Nottingham Evening Post*, June 5, 1991.
11 *Stroud News and Journal*, October 16, 1991.
12 *Lothian Courier*, October 24, 1991.
13 *Ashbourne News Telegraph*, January 21, 1993.
14 Civil Aviation Authority records made available to the author in 1995.
15 *Maldon & Burnham Standard*, December 15, 1994.
16 *Kingsbridge Gazette*, January 6, 1995.
17 *Matlock Mercury*, March 10, 1995.
18 *Derby Express*, April 6, 1995.
19 *Scunthorpe Evening Telegraph*, August 5, 1995.
20 *UFO Magazine*, November/December 1995 and January/February 1996.
21 Bob Pratt, 'The Belgium UFO Flap', *Mufon UFO Journal*, No. 267, July 1990. Copyright 1990 by the Mutual UFO Network, 103 Oldtowne Road, Seguin, Texas, 78155, USA.
22 Defense Intelligence Agency report 1990.
23 William F. Hamilton III, 'Flying Wings and Deep Desert Secrets', *Mufon UFO Journal*, No. 271, November 1990. Copyright 1990 by the Mutual UFO Network.
24 Samuel Greco, Ph.D., 'Williamsport Wave', *Mufon UFO Journal*, No. 290, June 1992. Copyright 1992 by the Mutual UFO Network.
25 *Jane's Defence Weekly*, December 12, 1992.

CHAPTER 14 – MEETING THE MINISTRY

1 Letter to the author from Nick Pope, Secretariat (Air Staff) 2a, Ministry of Defence, May 10, 1994.
2 Interview with Nick Pope, March 29, 1994.
3 Letter to the author from Nick Pope, May 10, 1994.

4 Letter to the author from Clive Neville, Secretariat (Air Staff) 2a, Ministry of Defence, March 23, 1988.
5 Letter to the author from Nick Pope, May 4, 1994.
6 Letter to the author from Nick Pope, October 11, 1994.
7 Letter to the author from Nick Pope, January 13, 1994.
8 Interview with Nick Pope, March 29, 1994.
9 Letter to the author from Nick Pope, July 1, 1992.
10 Timothy Good, *Alien Liaison* (Random Century Ltd, London, 1991), p. 18.
11 Letter to the author from Nick Pope, October 1, 1992.
12 Letter to the author from Nick Pope, May 4, 1994.
13 Letter to the author from F.H.C. Wimbledon, June 20, 1994.
14 Interview with Nick Pope, 29 March, 1994.
15 USAF Office of Public Affairs Fact Sheet.
16 Ibid.
17 USAF memorandum signed by Brigadier General C.H. Bolender, Air Force Deputy Director of Development, October 20, 1969.
18 Stanton Friedman and William Moore, 'The Roswell Incident: Beginning of the Cosmic Watergate', *MUFON Symposium Proceedings*, 1981, p. 150.
19 Bryan Gresh, 'Soviet UFO Secrets', *Mufon UFO Journal*, No. 306, October 1993. Copyright 1993 by the Mutual UFO Network.
20 Canadian Government Department of Transport memorandum, November 21, 1950.

CHAPTER 15 – THE PROVOST AND SECURITY SERVICES

1 Timothy Good, *Above Top Secret* (Sidgwick and Jackson, London, 1987), pp. 120–124.
2 RAF Provost and Security Services brochure. Copy made available to the author by Flight Lieutenant A.F. Woodruff, RAF Rudloe Manor, June 1994.
3 Ibid.
4 Timothy Good, *Alien Liaison* (Random Century Ltd, London, 1991), p. 14.
5 Timothy Good, *Alien Liaison* (Random Century Ltd, London, 1991), pp. 13–14.
6 Letter to the author from Clive Neville, Secretariat Air Staff 2a, Ministry of Defence, January 10, 1989.
7 Interview with Nick Pope, March 29, 1994.
8 Public Record Office file: AIR 2/16918. Crown copyright exists.
9 Ibid.

10 'The Luton Incident', *The Kensington News and West London Times*, April 30, 1964.
11 Public Record Office file: AIR 2/16918. Crown copyright exists.
12 Ibid.
13 Ibid.
14 Letter to the author from Air Commodore J.L. Uprichard, RAF, Director of Security and Provost Marshal (RAF), May 4, 1994.
15 Letters to the author from Jonathon Turner, September 17 and 21, 1994.
16 Letter to the author from Flight Lieutenant A.F. Woodruff, RAF Rudloe Manor, July 25, 1994. Letter to the author from Richard Worn, Secretariat Air Staff 2b, Ministry of Defence, August 26, 1994. Telephone interviews with source, August 10 and 14, 1994.
17 Documentation made available to the author by the Federal Bureau of Investigation on March 16, 1993.
18 Letter to the author from Patrick R. Ernst, Special Agent, USAF, Federal Liaison Officer, May 23, 1994.
19 Letter to RAF Rudloe Manor, September 20, 1994.
20 Letter to Timothy Good from Kerry Philpott, January 11, 1996.
21 Letter to the author from Group Captain J. Rose, RAF Rudloe Manor, February 28, 1996.
22 Interview with Nick Pope, March 10, 1996.
23 Letter to the author from Nick Pope, March 19, 1996.
24 Interview with Group Captain John Rose, March 5, 1996.
25 George Wingfield, 'The Evolving Crop Circles', *The UFO Report 1992*, edited by Timothy Good (Sidgwick & Jackson Ltd, London, 1991), p.13.
26 Interview with Nick Pope, March 10, 1996.
27 Letter to the author from Jonathon Turner, September 21, 1994.

CHAPTER 16 – THE DEFENCE INTELLIGENCE STAFF

1 Central Intelligence Machinery, HMSO, 1993, pp. 21–22. Crown copyright. Reproduced with the permission of the Controller of Her Majesty's Stationery Office.
2 Information supplied to the author by Graham Stanley, Government Services Department, Public Record Office, September 20, 1994.
3 Richard Norton-Taylor, *In Defence of the Realm?* (The Civil Liberties Trust, 1990), p. 58.
4 Ibid.
5 Letter to the author from Nick Pope, July 1, 1992.
6 Interview with Nick Pope, March 29, 1994.
7 *UFO Magazine*, Vol. 12, No. 3, July/August 1993.

8 Letter to the author from Graham Stanley, Government Services Department, Public Record Office, September 20, 1994.
9 In camera affidavit of Eugene Yeates of the National Security Agency, US District Court of the District of Columbia, October 9, 1980.
10 Letter to the author from Robert P. Richardson, Defense Intelligence Agency, November 19, 1991.
11 John Ranelagh, *The Agency – The Rise and Decline of the CIA* (Sceptre, Sevenoaks, 1988), p. 744.
12 Letter to the author from Robert C. Hardzog, Chief, Freedom of Information and Privacy Act Staff, Defense Intelligence Agency, April 26, 1988.
13 Letter to the author from Robert P. Richardson, Chief Freedom of Information Act Branch, Defense Intelligence Agency, November 19, 1991.
14 Letters to the author from Robert C. Hardzog, May 2 and June 21, 1990.
15 Letter to the author from Mrs Lyn M. Patterson, Special Executive Assistant, Embassy of the United States of America, Grosvenor Square, London, August 18, 1994.
16 Letter to the author from Frank Machak, US State Department, July 29, 1991.
17 Documentation made available to the author by Robert P. Richardson, September 29, 1993.
18 Letter to the author from Robert P. Richardson, December 3, 1993.
19 Letter to the author from Clive Neville, Secretariat Air Staff 2a, Ministry of Defence, May 10, 1989.
20 Letter to the author from Nick Pope, October 11, 1993.
21 Interview with Nick Pope, March 29, 1994.
22 Public Record Office file: AIR 2/17526. Crown copyright exists.
23 Ibid.
24 Ibid.

CHAPTER 17 – UNDER SURVEILLANCE

1 Royal Air Force Briefing Book, produced for the Press Secretary and Chief of Information, Ministry of Defence (Staples Printers Kettering Ltd, 1994), p. 14. Crown copyright exists.
2 Public Record Office file: AIR 20/7390. Crown copyright exists.
3 Public Record Office file: AIR 20/9994. Crown copyright exists.
4 Ibid.
5 Letter to the author from Flying Officer J.S. Hathaway, RAF Stanmore Park, October 19, 1994.

6 Letter to the author from Flight Lieutenant M.A. Tunaley, RAF Bentley Priory, September 16, 1994.

7 Royal Air Force Briefing Book, op. cit., p. 14. *The Royal Air Force Public Relations Magazine*, No. 6, pp. 7–8.

8 Letter to the author from Flying Officer S.R. Jones, RAF Waddington, May 23, 1994.

9 *The Royal Air Force Public Relations Magazine*, No. 6, p.7.

10 *Daily Express*, July 25, 1991.

11 Letter to the author from LATCC, January 24, 1996.

12 FBI memorandum, November 2, 1954.

13 Letter to the author from Stanton Friedman, January 18, 1994.

14 In camera affidavit of Eugene Yeates of the National Security Agency, US District Court of the District of Columbia, October 9, 1980.

15 Letter to the author from Richard W. Gronet, Director of Policy, National Security Agency, December 14, 1988.

16 Letter and accompanying three-page documentation from Jane B. Sealock, Director, Central Security Facility, US Army Intelligence and Security Command, October 20, 1993.

17 Interview with Nick Pope, March 29, 1994.

18 Ibid.

19 *Quest International* (now *UFO magazine*), Vol. 8, No. 3, 1988. Contact UK report, August 20, 1978.

20 *Quest International* (now *UFO magazine*), Vol. 9, No. 2, 1989. *UFO Magazine*, Vol. 12, No. 2, 1993.

21 Quest International's 12th International UFO Conference, September 25, 1993.

22 Information related to the author by Graham Birdsall, October 21, 1994.

23 *Central Intelligence Machinery* (HMSO, 1993), p. 21. Crown Copyright. Reproduced with the permission of the Controller of Her Majesty's Stationery Office.

24 Ernest Volkman and Blaine Baggett, *Secret Intelligence* (W.H. Allen and Co, London, 1989), p. 73. Chapman Pincher, *Too Secret Too Long* (Sidgwick and Jackson Ltd, London, 1985), p. 591.

25 Crispin Aubrey, *Who's Watching You?* (Penguin Books Ltd, West Drayton, Middlesex, 1981), p. 133.

26 Robert Durant, 'Have You Checked Your File Lately?' (Privately published and circulated paper).

27 Letter to the author from J.C. Turner, Government Communications Headquarters, July 10, 1990.

28 Peter Wright with Paul Greengrass, *Spycatcher* (Heinemann Publishers Australia, 1987), p. 85.

29 *Daily Express*, March 3, 1993.

30 *UFO Magazine*, Vol. 12, No. 2 (Quest Publications International Ltd, May/June 1993).

31 *North Western Evening Mail*, Barrow-in-Furness, March 30, 1996.

32 *Open Government* (HMSO, 1993), p. 91. Crown copyright. Reproduced with the permission of the Controller of Her Majesty's Stationery Office.

CHAPTER 18 – DEAD ON ARRIVAL

1 Jenny Randles, *The UFO Conspiracy* (Blandford Press, Poole, 1987), p. 42.

2 Roswell Army Air Force press release, July 8, 1947.

3 Stanton T. Friedman and Don Berliner, *Crash at Corona* (Paragon House, New York, 1992), p. xiv.

4 Information related to the author by Stanton Friedman, December 19, 1993.

5 Stanton T. Friedman and William Moore, 'The Roswell Incident: Beginning of the Cosmic Watergate' (MUFON Symposium Proceedings, 1981), p. 133.

6 Charles Berlitz and William Moore, *The Roswell Incident* (Granada Publishing Ltd, St Albans, 1980), pp. 64–67.

7 William Moore, *The Roswell Investigation, New Evidence, New Conclusions* (1981/2), pp. 9–10.

8 Ibid., p. 9.

9 Friedman and Berliner, op. cit., pp. 13–14, 87.

10 William Moore, 'Crashed Saucers: Evidence in the Search for Proof', *MUFON Symposium Proceedings*, 1985, p. 173.

11 Timothy Good, *Above Top Secret* (Sidgwick and Jackson, London, 1987), pp. 250–253.

12 William L. Moore and Jaime H. Shandera, 'The MJ-12 Documents: An Analytical Report', 1990 (The Fair Witness Project, 4219 W. Olive Avenue, 247, Burbank, California, 91505, USA), pp. 45–46.

13 Copies of the Majestic Twelve papers can be obtained from Quest Publications International Ltd.

14 Documentation released to the author by J. Kevin O'Brien, Chief, Freedom of Information-Privacy Acts Section, Information Management Division, March 16, 1993.

15 Moore and Shandera, op. cit.

16 Kevin D. Randle and Donald R. Schmitt, *The Truth About the UFO Crash at Roswell* (M. Evans and Company Inc, New York, 1994) pp. 8, 10, 11, and 142.

17 Karl Pflock, *Roswell in Perspective* (Fund for UFO Research, 1994), pp. 149–152.

18 Anne MacFie, 'Return to Roswell', *Mufon UFO Journal*, No. 288, April 1992. Copyright 1992 by the Mutual UFO Network.

19 William S. Steinman, 'UFO Crash at Aztec' (UFO Photo Archives, P.O. Box 17206, Tuscon, Arizona, 85710, USA, 1987).

20 Mark Birdsall, *Ghost Rockets and Foo Fighters* (Quest Publications International Ltd, 1988), p. 9.

21 Leonard Stringfield, 'The UFO Crash/Retrieval Syndrome' (Mutual UFO Network, Seguin, Texas, 1980), pp. 2–3.

22 Letter to the author from John Lear, May 6, 1991.

23 *Los Angeles Examiner*, May 23, 1955.

24 Ibid.

25 *Flying Saucer Review*, Vol. 25, No. 4, 1979.

26 *Flying Saucer Review*, Vol. 31, No. 1, 1985.

27 Timothy Good, op. cit., p. 43.

28 Letter from Olavo Fontes to Coral Lorenzen, February 27, 1958.

29 *Flying Saucer Review*, Vol. 39, No. 3.

30 Leonard Stringfield, *UFO Crash/Retrievals: The Inner Sanctum* (1991), p. 72. Letter to the author from Leonard Stringfield, March 29, 1994.

31 *Walthamstow Guardian*, April 17, 1964. Letter from Ronald Caswell to the Ministry of Defence, April 29, 1964.

32 Lecture given by Charles Halt (USAF retired), Leeds, July 31, 1994.

33 Michael Roberts, *The Illustrated History of the United States Air Force* (Guild Publishing, London, 1989), pp. 193–194.

34 Letter to the author from Captain John E. Boyle, USAF, Chief, Public Affairs Office, RAF Bentwaters, Suffolk, September 30, 1988.

35 *Northern UFO News*, No. 152, December 1991.

36 *The Cerealogist*, No. 13, Winter 1994/5. *Salisbury Times*, August 23, 1994. *Sunday Telegraph*, December 18, 1994. *Air Force Monthly* magazine, November 1994.

37 *Worcester Evening News*, November 2, 1994. *Eversham Journal*, November 3, 1994.

CHAPTER 19 – AROUND THE WORLD

1 Two-page affidavit made available to the author by the FBI on July 13, 1988.

2 USAF Air Intelligence Information Report, March 18, 1958. Letter to the author from Richard W. Gronet, Director of Policy, National Security Agency, December 14, 1988. Letter to the author from Barbara Carmichael, Freedom of Information Manager, Department of the Air Force, February 13, 1988.

3 Ray Stanford, *Socorro Saucer* (William Collins Sons and Co. Ltd, Glasgow, 1978).
4 Undated Central Intelligence Agency report, circa April 1964.
5 Four-page Defense Intelligence Agency report, 1976.
6 *The MIJI Quarterly* (US Headquarters Electronic Security Command, 1978).
7 Defense Intelligence Agency report, 1986.

CHAPTER 20 – A COVERT AGENDA

1 The Mercury Theatre's 1938 production of H.G. Wells' *The War of the Worlds* (1898).
2 UFO Hypothesis and Survival Questions, National Security Agency, 1968.
3 New Mexico State Police report, December 15, 1976.
4 Memorandum from Lieutenant Colonel Charles Halt, USAF, January 13, 1981.
5 Statement released by John Lear, 1987.
6 Leonard Stringfield, *UFO Crash/Retrievals: The Inner Sanctum* (1991), pp. 50–52. Published privately.
7 Ralph Blum and Judy Blum, *Beyond Earth: Man's Contact with UFOs* (Bantam Books Inc, New York, 1978), pp. 109–118.
8 Gavin Gibbons, *The Coming of the Spaceships* (Neville Spearman Ltd, London, 1956).
9 February 3, 1959, Foreign Service Dispatch, made available to the author by H. Eugene Bovis, U.S. State Department, June 14, 1989.
10 Documentation made available to the author by Emil P. Moschella, Chief, Freedom of Information-Privacy Acts Section, Records Management Division, FBI, April 5, 1988.
11 Lou Zinsstag and Timothy Good, *George Adamski – The Untold Story* (Ceti Publications, Beckenham, 1983), p. 54.
12 Public Record Office file: AIR 2/16918. Crown copyright exists.
13 John Carpenter, 'Abduction Notes', *Mufon UFO Journal*, No. 329, September 1995. Copyright 1995 by the Mutual UFO Network.
14 John G. Fuller, *The Interrupted Journey* (Souvenir Press Ltd, London, 1980).
15 Budd Hopkins, *Missing Time* (Ballantine Books, Random House Inc, New York, 1989).
16 Budd Hopkins, *Intruders* (Sphere Books, Penguin Group, London, 1988).
17 Ibid.
18 Martin Kottmeyer, 'Why are the Grays Gray?', *Mufon UFO Journal*, No. 319, November 1994. Copyright 1994 by the Mutual UFO Network.

19 Keith Basterfield, 'Abduction Research in Australia', *Mufon UFO Journal*, No. 315, July 1994. Copyright 1994 by the Mutual UFO Network.

20 John Carpenter, 'Abduction Notes – "Phobias and Resolutions"', *Mufon UFO Journal*, No. 314, June 1994. Copyright 1994 by the Mutual UFO Network.

21 Interview with Nick Pope, Secretariat (Air Staff) 2a, Ministry of Defence, March 29, 1994.

USEFUL ADDRESSES

Those wishing to learn more about the UFO subject can do so by contacting the following magazines and organizations:

Phenomena
Mania Entertainment, LLC
220 Main Street, Suite C
Venice, CA 90291
www.phenomenamagazine.com

Fate
P.O. Box 460
Lakeville, MN 55044-0460
www.fatemag.com

UFO Magazine
5455 Centinela Avenue
Los Angeles, CA 90066
www.ufomag.com

The Mutual UFO Network
P.O. Box 369
Morrison, CO 80465-0369
www.mufon.com

Mysteries Magazine
1144 Rte. 12A
Surry, NH 03431
www.MysteriesMagazine.com

The J. Allen Hynek Center for UFO Studies
2457 W. Petersen
Chicago, IL 60659
www.cufos.org

The Center for Fortean Zoology
15 Holne Court
Exwick
Exeter
EX4 2NA
England

Fortean Times
Dennis Publishing
30 Cleveland Street
London
W1T 4JD
England
www.forteantimes.com

UFO Magazine (UK)
Quest Publications International Ltd.
Valley Farm Way
Wakefield Road
Stourton
Leeds
LS10 1SE
England

PICTURE CREDITS

INDEX

PARAVIEW

publishes quality works that focus on body, mind,
and spirit; the frontiers of science and culture;
and responsible business—areas related to
the transformation of society.

PARAVIEW PUBLISHING

offers books via four imprints.

PARAVIEW POCKET BOOKS
are traditionally published books co-published by Paraview
and Simon & Schuster's Pocket Books.

PARAVIEW PRESS, *PARAVIEW SPECIAL EDITIONS*, and
PARAVIEW CLASSICS use digital print-on-demand
technology to create original paperbacks for niche audiences,
as well as reprints of previously out-of-print titles.

For a complete list of **PARAVIEW** Publishing's books
and ordering information, please visit our website at
www.paraview.com, where you can also sign up
for our free monthly media guide.

TRANSFORMING THE WORLD
ONE BOOK AT A TIME

Related Books From
PARAVIEW PUBLISHING

The Phaselock Code: Through Time, Death, and Reality: The Metaphysical Adventures of the Man Who Fell Off Everest
ROGER HART

"Those with a thing for physics and an openness to Eastern philosophy will appreciate the vigor and the clarity of Hart's ideas about how we simulate reality, create time, and shape the world with our thoughts."—*Kirkus*

PARAVIEW POCKET BOOKS • ISBN: 0-7434-7725-1
Trade paperback, 368 pages, $14.00

Strange Secrets: Real Government Files on the Unknown
NICK REDFERN and ANDY ROBERTS

"The authors have uncovered such files from the U.S., British and former Soviet governments touching on alien visitations, the use of psychic spies and other strange subjects...This is a trove of entertaining stories for X-files fans and government skeptics."—*Publishers Weekly*

PARAVIEW POCKET BOOKS • ISBN: 0-743-46976-3
Trade paperback, 336 pages, $14.00

The Seventh Sense: The Secrets of Remote Viewing as Told by a "Psychic Spy" for the U.S. Military
LYN BUCHANAN, Foreword by Jim Marrs

"Buchanan's low-key tone, full of military jargon and acronyms, detailed protocols and much griping about army red tape, lends credibility to his account of life as a GI clairvoyant...[an] odd and interesting book."—*Publishers Weekly*

PARAVIEW POCKET BOOKS • ISBN: 0-743-46268-8
Trade paperback, 320 pages, $14.00

Looking for Orthon: The Story of George Adamski, the First Flying Saucer Contactee, and How He Changed the World
COLIN BENNETT, Foreword by John Michell

"One of the most brilliantly written UFO books I have ever come across."
—Jeff Rense, Paranet Radio

PARAVIEW PRESS • ISBN: 1931044-32-5
Trade paperback, 224 pages, $15.95

Swamp Gas Times: My Two Decades on the UFO Beat
PATRICK HUYGHE

"...one of the best journalists covering the UFO scene...fascinating, level-headed and filled with behind-the-scenes insights...highly recommended..."—Peter Robbins, UFOCity.com

PARAVIEW PRESS • ISBN: 1-931044-27-9
Trade paperback, 349 pages, $17.95

The Siren Call of Hungry Ghosts
JOE FISHER

"...a riveting detective story full of blind alleys, misplaced trust, deceit, and duplicity, all made doubly inspiring by the fact that none of the 'suspects' are of this world."
—Christopher Loudon, *Quill & Quire*

PARAVIEW PRESS • ISBN 1-931044-02-3
Trade paperback, 313 pages, $16.95

The Third Level of Reality: A Unified Theory of the Paranormal
PERCY SEYMOUR, Foreword by Colin Wilson

This is a reprint of a book originally titled *The Paranormal: Beyond Sensory Science*. "Seymour is one of the boldest and most exciting scientific thinkers of our time...I regard [this] as a masterpiece."—Colin Wilson

PARAVIEW SPECIAL EDITIONS • ISBN: 1-931044-47-3
Trade paperback, 188 pages, $12.95

Printed in the United Kingdom
by Lightning Source UK Ltd.
107109UKS00001B/186